W9-BXO-828

Praise for

DRIVING CHANGE
IN SPECIAL EDUCATION

WITHDRAWN

"*Driving Change in Special Education* is a significant book that is appearing at a crucial time. The book is the product of a significant special educator who has been an active participant among the 'engines of change' in special education for more than 50 years. His book provides the structure and much of the information needed for planning for the urgent future years. Many crucial issues emerge and are clarified in the cogent pages of this book. Indeed, Gallagher's book could serve as a mission statement for a generation of progress that has already begun!"

—**Richard L. Schiefelbusch, Ph.D.**
Distinguished University Professor Emeritus
Schiefelbusch Institute for Life Span Studies
University of Kansas

"This book, by our nation's premier thinker on special education, makes clear the genesis and state of special education's current public policies and resulting practices. Based on his broad experience in both academe and government, the author provides insightful analyses suggesting how policy and practice should evolve in the future to better serve children with special educational needs."

—**Edward Zigler, Ph.D.**
Sterling Professor of Psychology, Emeritus
Yale University

"Jim Gallagher's influence on the field of special education for nearly 50 years has been profound. Not surprisingly, he has made another remarkable contribution. This is a brilliant book by one of the brightest minds in our field. One will see and think about special education policy much differently after reading this book."

—Donald D. Deshler, Ph.D.
Professor and Director
Center for Research on Learning
University of Kansas

"This book breaks new ground in examining the policy decisions that lie behind current special education programs and services. It challenges all educators to examine key factors and criteria for making decisions in this area of education for the future. A wonderful contribution to the special education policy literature, it is a blueprint for educational decision-makers at all levels."

—Joyce Van Tassel-Baska, Ed.D.
Jody and Layton Smith Professor of Education
Executive Director, Center for Gifted Education
College of William and Mary
President, National Association for Gifted Children

"Gallagher's book is a must read for anyone trying to understand the forces creating the context for special education. He provides a framework for developing rational special education policy."

—Stanley L. Deno, Ph.D.
Professor of Educational Psychology/Special Education
University of Minnesota

"A truly insightful analysis of special education policy. The important influences on decision-making are examined across a number of vexing problems. The issues discussed are complex but Gallagher ably unravels the complexity and demonstrates how optimal solutions may be achieved. An invaluable resource for anyone interested in the dynamics of special education."

—**Kenneth A. Kavale, Ph.D.**
Distinguished Professor of Special Education
Regent University

"Gallagher's book should be read by anyone interested in why and how special education has become what it is and how we can influence its future. His case studies illustrate how seemingly abstract policy decisions are matters of great importance for the lives of children, parents, and educators. I really admire and enjoyed reading the book, and I hope it's a great success."

—**James M. Kauffman, Ed.D.**
Professor Emeritus of Education
University of Virginia

DRIVING
CHANGE
IN
SPECIAL EDUCATION

DRIVING CHANGE
IN
SPECIAL EDUCATION

TOURO COLLEGE LIBRARY
Kings Hwy

by

James J. Gallagher, Ph.D.
FPG Child Development Institute
University of North Carolina at Chapel Hill

WITHDRAWN

·P·A·U·L·H·
BROOKES
PUBLISHING CO.®

Baltimore • London • Sydney

KH

Paul H. Brookes Publishing Co.
Post Office Box 10624
Baltimore, Maryland 21285-0624

www.brookespublishing.com

Copyright © 2006 by Paul H. Brookes Publishing Co., Inc.
All rights reserved.

"Paul H. Brookes Publishing Co." is a registered trademark of
Paul H. Brookes Publishing Co., Inc.

Typeset by Integrated Publishing Solutions, Grand Rapids, Michigan.
Manufactured in the United States of America by
Versa Press, Inc., East Peoria, Illinois.

The case studies described in this book are composites based on the author's
actual experiences. Individuals' names have been changed, and identifying
details have been altered to protect confidentiality.

Library of Congress Cataloging-in-Publication Data
Gallagher, James John, 1926–
    Driving change in special education / by James J. Gallagher.
        p.   cm.
    Includes bibliographical references and index.
    ISBN-13: 978-1-55766-703-8 (pbk.)
    ISBN-10: 1-55766-703-9 (pbk.)
    1. Special education—Government policy—United States.
    2. Special education—United States.   I. Title.
    LC3981.G35   2006
    379.1'190973—dc22   2006001448

British Library Cataloguing in Publication data are available from the British Library.

8/16/06

Contents

About the Author

James J. Gallagher, Ph.D., William R. Kenan Professor Emeritus, School of Education, FPG Child Development Institute, University of North Carolina at Chapel Hill, 517 South Greensboro Street, Carrboro, North Carolina 27510

Dr. Gallagher received his doctorate in child and clinical psychology at The Pennsylvania State University. His early work was at the Dayton Hospital for Disturbed Children and in the Psychology Clinic at Michigan State University. He spent 13 years at the Institute for Research on Exceptional Children at the University of Illinois conducting research on children with brain injury and mental retardation and on the education of highly gifted children.

In 1967, Dr. Gallagher became the first director of the Bureau for the Education of the Handicapped (now the Office of Special Education Programs in the U.S. Department of Education), which was designed to carry out the new federal legislation on children with disabilities. He provided leadership for this program as the first major initiative for the federal government in special education.

In 1970, he became a Kenan Professor and Director of the Frank Porter Graham Center (now the FPG Child Development Institute) at the University of North Carolina at Chapel Hill. This multidisciplinary center conducted a wide variety of intervention research programs with young children. Dr. Gallagher also served from 1977 to 1986 as Director of the Bush Institute for Child and Family Policy, which introduced students to the analysis and development of policy for children.

Dr. Gallagher has written or edited more than 15 books and monographs and more than 150 articles on a broad range of topics in the field of exceptional children. He co-wrote the basic textbook *Educating Exceptional Children,* now in its 11th edition (Kirk, Gallagher, Anastasiow, & Coleman, 2006, Houghton Mifflin). Dr. Gallagher has been president of the Council for Exceptional Children, Vice President for Education of the American Association on Mental Retardation, President of the National Association for Gifted Children, and President of the World Council for Gifted and Talented Children.

In addition to receiving numerous awards, Dr. Gallagher was awarded the Gold Medal for Life Achievement in Psychology in the Public Interest from the American Psychological Association in 2005. *Driving Change in Special Education* reflects his continuing interest in public policy for children and families.

Preface

The preface of a book is supposed to be the place where the author tells the reader why he is writing the book and how it is organized. Unfortunately, many readers appear to believe it is a secret and intimate communication between author and spouse and do not wish to intrude or eavesdrop on such communication. Therefore, if you wish to hide something in plain sight, the best place to do it is in the preface.

Nevertheless, I am compelled anyway to follow the proposed format. For at least 5 decades, special education has been a meaningful, albeit a controversial, part of American education. The decision making that has taken place regarding children with special needs has often been chaotic and driven by many forces beyond the education system, so I wish to use my more than 5 decades of experience in this field to speculate on the future of these specialties.

Many individuals, organizations, and decision makers have their own agendas for students with special needs and must interact with one another to create meaningful and sensible public policy. All of these interactions are being made by fallible human beings and imperfect institutions so that any decision making has to keep these flaws in mind as well. It would be nice if decisions about children with special needs were made by individuals without reference to their own needs and desires, or if institutions would not put their own interests ahead of the interests of these children, but we all know that in the real world such things happen all of the time.

In this book, I have tried to construct three different futures that may lie ahead for special education. I have tried to use my experience in special education to construct the most likely of alternatives given what we now know and to spell out the advantages and disadvantages of each as best I can peer into the future.

This book is an attempt to discuss with you, the reader, the background of policy decision making and those rules and standards that shape the educational setting and practices for children with special needs. Although this book focuses on the future, much of what is written here deals with the past. I agree with the philosopher George Santayana, who once said, "Those who cannot remember the past are condemned to repeat it" (*The Life of Reason*, Vol. 1, 1905).

ORGANIZATION OF THE BOOK

The first three chapters of this book lay the groundwork of special education—the importance of establishing eligibility for special services and the various differentiated programming that has been included in the public schools. The next five chapters focus on the various elements of the important support systems that lie behind special education. These include personnel preparation and technical assistance, research and evaluation, finance and data systems, educational planning, and technology.

Although gifted children clearly are children with special needs, they differ so much from other exceptional children that Chapter 9 is devoted to their place in the educational enterprise. Chapter 10 deals with other forces impinging on special education, either from within education (e.g., accountability) or from outside education (e.g., competing priorities for funding).

With these 10 chapters as a base, I provide three alternative futures for special education in Chapter 11. In this last chapter, as is made clear in the other chapters, changes of the scope presented cannot be expected within a short time span, so the desired future must be a star guiding short-range decision making.

I have also stressed the four major instruments of change in our society—legislation, court decisions, administrative rule making, and professional initiatives. Each of these four mechanisms has played a huge part in special education's past and can be counted on to affect its future.

Finally, I have created five children with varying special needs to try to illustrate what various changes might mean to them and their parents. Included are Arnie, a child with autism; Bobby, a child with behavior and emotional problems; Cathy, a child with cerebral palsy; Gretchen, a gifted child; and Les, a child with learning disabilities. There could be 20 more students, obviously, but these five may help to focus attention on individual needs as well as on major social movements.

Acknowledgments

One of the major conceits that an author can have is to refer to himself as the *sole author* of a work. Instead, it should be clear that I am only a filter through which innumerable professionals have poured in their ideas, recently and over the years, and I am extremely grateful for all of their contributions.

I am particularly pleased to recognize the leadership of the FPG Child Development Institute at the University of North Carolina at Chapel Hill, who made this book possible by providing space and additional help and commentary. Don Bailey, the FPG Director has been particularly supportive in both his administrative and professional roles. Numerous other staff, such as Dick Clifford, Donna Bryant, Thelma Harms, Mary Ruth Coleman, Gloria Harbin, and others, have chipped in with thoughts and ideas that were valuable, particularly in the early childhood areas of the text.

I am deeply grateful to other colleagues who read sections of the text and commented on them. Drs. Rud and Ann Turnbull at the University of Kansas, Ron Haskins of the Brookings Institution, Professor Jim Paul of the University of South Florida, and Dr. Ed Martin, former Director of the U.S. Department of Education, Office of Special Education and Rehabilitative Services, gave wise counsel and advice. Naturally, there is only one person to be held responsible for errors in commission or omission in the text.

The editorial staff at Paul H. Brookes Publishing Co. were more than usually active in helping to produce the final version of this text. Melissa Behm, Vice President, took on important editorial commentary as extra duties beyond her major responsibilities. The book could not have been created without her commitment and intelligent leadership. Rebecca Lazo, Acquisitions Editor, also spent an inordinate amount of time editing and interacting with me. The help of Janet Betten, Book Production Editor, and Steve Peterson, Acquisitions Assistant, was also appreciated.

The preparation of the final manuscript is often an unappreciated task. Tanya Gscheidle and Michael Spencer played this role with intelligence and effort.

Finally, I would like to acknowledge with deep gratitude my wife of 57 years, Rani, who disproportionately took on the enormous task of successfully raising four active children while I was often about various professional issues. Rani also provided many incisive comments on the manuscript itself.

So much for the term *sole author.*

CHAPTER 1

Decision Making in Special Education

How Are Decisions Made?

The last half of the 20th century and the beginning of the 21st century have seen enormous changes in the care and education of children with special needs. This volume traces the course of interlocking decisions that have brought these changes about, identifies the forces that have influenced these decisions, and presents some alternative futures for the next generation of children with special needs. What decisions should policy makers reach about the future care of children who are different, who do not develop as other children their age do, or who have manifest disabilities or deformities? Past policy decisions are strikingly different from decisions made by current leaders, but they still affect educators' daily activities today. This volume shines a spotlight on these decisions as a first step toward improving policies and practices.

Policy decisions cast long shadows of influence on research, personnel preparation, and the delivery of services to children with disabilities and their families. For example, the policy of inclusion in the general classroom has stirred a large body of research and modified teacher preparation. Too often educators are unaware of the long-term impact of policy decisions and what can be done to initiate new policies or to change old policies that no longer seem to work. Examining past policy decisions and their repercussions can help guide the modification of current policies and the creation of new ones.

FROM PAST TO PRESENT

The treatment of children with special needs in the past has been a legacy of neglect (Safford & Safford, 1996). Among the early Greeks and Romans, decisions were often fatal to the children involved yet were supported even by the greatest thinkers of that age. Plato stated that "the offspring of the inferior, or of the better when they chance to be deformed, will be put away in some mysterious, unknown place as they should be" (quoted in Edman, 1928, p. 410). Aristotle was even more candid, stating that there should be "a law that no deformed child shall live" (quoted in Edman, 1928, p. 310).

Throughout history, the causes of disability have been attributed to an amazing collection of guesses, including "engaging in conjugal relations during menstruation or Lent or on Sundays which could result in lameness, leprosy, deformity, seizures, or infant death" (Boswell, 1988, p. 259). Children with disabilities, notably those who were blind or deaf, first received some consistent care in the 18th and 19th centuries (Safford & Safford, 1996). The Enlightenment and subsequent religious, humanistic, and rationalistic movements changed decision making regarding children with disabilities in the 19th century and beyond. Large institutions for care and education were established for children and adults who were blind, deaf, or mentally retarded (Scheerenberger, 1987). These institutions were often far away from family and community; implied was the precept that these individuals would always remain far distant from typical society.

The physician Itard's detailed description of his work with the Wild Boy of Aveyron in the 19th century—together with the detailed work of Seguin, one of his students—is one of the first documentations of a deliberate attempt to teach a child with mental retardation or emotional disturbance. Yet, systematic study of children with disabilities did not begin until well into the 20th century, when Werner, Strauss, Vygotsky, and others began to provide some ideas about how to aid the development of children with mental retardation (Matson & Mulick, 1991).

During the 19th century and most of the 20th century, the literature on exceptional children could mostly be found indexed under medical conditions. The label attached to the child was the name of the medical condition that the physician diagnosed (e.g., brain injury, Down syndrome). In medicine, discovery of a cause of a childhood disorder (e.g., epilepsy) often leads directly to treatment, so the diagnosis of a childhood disorder was seen as an integral part of the treatment program. But the same is not true in the education of exceptional children. Knowing that a child has a brain injury does not help to plan an educational treatment program for him or her. The medical classification of children with special needs is largely disconnected from the educational treatment program that these children receive.

The later part of the 20th century brought forth a new set of decisions that made children with special needs "a part of" not "apart from" the rest of the society (Kirk, Gallagher, & Anastasiow, 2003). How these dramatic changes came to be calls for explanation and raises questions about what decisions lie ahead for children with disabilities and their families.

In the 1960s and 1970s, special education was relatively free of criticism. Staff were praised for taking on a noble, if difficult, cause, and extensive resources (or so it seemed) were delivered to them. Critical voices began to emerge in the 1980s, calling into question just how well special education programs were working (Finn, Rotherham, & Hokanson, 2001). Multifaceted, this criticism focused on cost, accountability, the increasing number of eligibility categories, and the corresponding expansion of services, all of which demanded additional, already scarce resources. Kelman put the matter bluntly by asking,

> Would these resources be better spent on increasing per pupil spending in "regular" education? Are there groups of individuals other than the disabled (for example, children of color, children with low IQs who are not dubbed educable mentally retarded, and children facing harsh conditions at home) who might deserve these incremental resources as much or more than those now given priority by federal mandates in the Individuals with Disabilities Education Act (IDEA)? (2001, p. 78)

It is time to confront the contemporary issues troubling special education and consider new rounds of decisions about accountability, effectiveness, organization, and other equally critical topics. Decisions about changes in a complex society are rarely made in a vacuum. Ideally, decisions about children and education are made by individuals without reference to their own needs and desires or by institutions who do not put their own interests ahead of the needs of children. Yet, such decisions are made by fallible humans concerned with self-interest and imperfect institutions interested in survival, so any decision-making plan has to take those factors into consideration as well. No professional group or organization is powerful enough to realize its own agenda for children with special needs without paying attention to other organizations' interests or without taking heed of public policy makers who control the purse strings and create the rules. In this context of competing interests, how do educators and policy makers ensure that their actions yield positive decisions for the children they care for?

The diversity of social forces at work and the complexity of educational programming today make it necessary to search for organizational tools to use the mass of available information effectively. This volume is an attempt to discuss the background of decision making and the rules and standards that shape and determine the current educational setting and practices for children with special needs. Throughout, various models designed to enhance decision making and policy development are introduced. In the process, some of the needs, passions, and forces that have shaped past decisions—and will surely direct future decisions as well—are shared.

SOCIAL POLICY AND THE ENGINES OF CHANGE

Social policies are not initiated without deliberate and sustained effort. Someone or some authority deliberately decides to establish policies that are designed to achieve certain social or educational goals. For example, parents of a child with disabilities are at a major disadvantage when their views clash with the public school system. That is why legislators and judges set standards by which such conflicts can be resolved equitably. The parents are expected to take part in the design of an individualized education program (IEP) for their child, and they in turn expect to have their views considered. The federal Individuals with Disabilities Education Improvement Act of 2004 (PL 108-446), or IDEA 2004, contains a due process clause that allows parents to request hearings or examine their child's records in order to satisfy themselves that the procedures being followed are appropriate for their child. In this way, a social policy can level the playing field between parties whose conflicting interests might not have found a resolution independently.

Make no mistake about it—policy making is about power. Such power may be used for altruistic purposes, such as ensuring equitable treatment for children with disabilities, but without it, people become part of the chattering class: always discussing, never deciding. Power is merely a person's ability to achieve what he or she wants and to prevent others from doing what he or she opposes. In that sense, continued power struggles exist within families, between families and schools, between teachers and principals, and between schools and the larger society. The establishment of policy is the tool by which conflicts can be resolved in favor, one hopes, of the child with special needs.

So, what is social policy?

> Social policy creates the rules and standards by which scare resources are allocated to meet almost unlimited social needs. An effective social policy should answer the following questions:
> 1. Who shall receive the resources?
> 2. Who shall deliver the resources?
> 3. What are the resources to be delivered?
> 4. What are the conditions under which the resources are delivered? (Gallagher, 1994a, p. 337)

The allocation of "scarce resources to meet almost unlimited needs" means that not all desirable goals can be met and that there will be considerable competition for those resources that are available.

Let's apply this theoretical construct to an active example: public prekindergarten. If one considers a policy of providing prekindergarten services publicly, then the first question—"Who shall receive the resources?"—addresses the eligibility issue, and the policy needs to state whether participation is mandatory or voluntary. The second question in the definition—"Who shall deliver the resources?"—concerns the credentials of the adults who are playing a role in the program. Do teachers or staff need special preparation? Where does that preparation take place and who is going to pay for this special preparation? The third question—"What are the resources to be delivered?"—relates to program and differentiated curriculum and involves decisions about the degree of academic focus the program should have and the extent to which students with disabilities should receive services. The fourth question—"What are the conditions under which the resources are delivered?"—addresses the educational environment in which services are provided. For example, should children with disabilities be included in the general classroom?

Two puzzles regarding the creation and maintenance of policies have intrigued observers. The first is why some policies that have never proven themselves effective continue to remain in place. Policies, once made, remain in place unless they are changed, but why do people maintain practices (e.g., aversive conditioning) when they seem to be inappropriate or their effectiveness is doubtful? Why does administrative convenience seem to maintain one established age for starting school for all children in a district even when that policy is in direct contravention to what is known about developmental psychology and individual differences?

The second puzzle is why policies that seem to have merit are rarely considered. Various forms of resistance to change and other forces on decision making that go beyond the effectiveness of the intervention or program affect policy to a large degree. The rapid changes that have taken place in the special education field, and in society as a whole, have directed attention toward the process of change itself (Fullan, 1993). What are the forces that need to be present for change to take place, and above all, how can decision makers learn to create positive change? Four major engines shape and drive various observable changes. These engines of change are *legislation, court decisions, administrative rules,* and *professional initiatives*. This chapter considers examples of each of these change agents at work, and the change agents appear again in later chapters. All of these engines of change are vehicles for creating power.

Another device is a decision-making model (used in this volume) that displays the available options in response to a specific problem and matches these options against a variety of criteria through which one can make the most effective choice. The engines of change and the decision model are merely tools for making more comprehensible the extraordinarily complex phenomena that are continually interacting and shifting in their influence. One of the functions of social policy is to establish a framework for action that all can understand.

Legislation

One of the engines for formulating policy is legislation. The first identifiable legislation regarding the education of children with disabilities occurred after World War II when individual states, with their responsibility for designing education programs, attempted to provide additional funds to aid school districts in their quest for developing differentiated programs for these children. These first legislative efforts, however, did not include funds for building an infrastructure to support these programs. This turned out to be one of the significant roles of the federal government, which now provides funds specifically for research, personnel preparation, technical assistance (TA), demonstration, communications, and so forth (Gallagher, 1994a).

The federal government began a major series of legislative initiatives in the 1960s and 1970s. These initiatives addressed personnel preparation (Vocational Education Act of 1963, PL 88-210), established regional resource centers (Elementary and Secondary Education Act Amendments of 1967, PL 90-247), created programs for preschool children with disabilities (Handicapped Children's Early Education Act of 1968, PL 90-538), and took up a variety of disability-related issues (the Education for All Handicapped Children Act of 1975, PL 94-142; later renamed the Individuals with Disabilities Education Act [IDEA], PL 101-476). The omnibus Education for All Handicapped Children Act of 1975 and its subsequent amendments are among the most influential pieces of legislation focusing on the education and treatment of children with disabilities (Council for Exceptional Children [CEC], 2004; Etscheidt & Bartlett, 1999).

Education for All Handicapped
Children Act of 1975 (PL 94-142)

This comprehensive legislation incorporated a large set of legislative acts on specific topics such as personnel preparation, research, TA, and so forth. The six key principles at the heart of PL 94-142 have shaped special education and general education since the law was enacted in 1975.

1. *Zero reject:* All children with disabilities must be provided a free appropriate public education. This guaranteed educational service regardless of the problems or difficulties caused by individual students.

2. *Nondiscriminatory evaluation:* Each student must receive a full, individual examination before being placed in a special education program, with tests appropriate to the child's cultural and linguistic background. This provision was designed to ensure adequate assessment to children who might come from a different cultural background.

3. *Least restrictive environment (LRE):* As much as possible, children with disabilities must be educated with children without disabilities. This is the basis for the development of the inclusion principle, though it originally meant that a child should be placed in a setting most likely to benefit him or her.

4. *Due process:* Due process is a set of legal procedures to ensure the fairness of educational decisions and the accountability of both professionals and parents in making those decisions. If parents think a student's treatment is not intense enough, they have recourse through established procedures to have their voice heard.

5. *Parental participation:* Parents must be included in the development of the IEP, and they have the right to gain access to their child's educational records. Parents are perceived as partners in the planning process and not just service recipients.

6. *IEP:* The most complex of these six principles is ensuring an appropriate education for the child through the development of an IEP. Once parental permission has been received for the placement of a student in some form of special education services, there is an obligation to develop an IEP for meeting the student's needs. Few schools would do this without a mandate, but the later IDEA legislation clearly requires such IEPs. They have become a recognized part of special education services. The reason for mandating IEPs was to ensure that an individual plan would be made for a student with special needs rather than just removing the student from the regular education program.

The 1997 amendments to IDEA (PL 105-17) introduced important modifications to the original law. The 1975 law had unintended consequences that needed to be muted, and new circumstances arose that required change. For example, the initiation of charter schools required a separate amendment by which IDEA extended to charter schools the same duties that typical public schools have. In this way, legislators recognized that parents who enroll their children with disabilities in charter schools should not lose access to the benefits of IDEA as a consequence of that choice (Turnbull & Turnbull 2000). The most recent reauthorization of this omnibus legislation is IDEA 2004 (CEC, 2004).

Education of the Handicapped Act Amendments of 1986 (PL 99-457)

Another legislative milestone for children with disabilities was achieved when the 1986 amendments to the Education of the Handicapped Act (PL 99-457) were passed. This legislation was designed to encourage states to establish systems of care and stimulation for *infants and toddlers* with disabilities

> [t]o enhance the development of handicapped infants and toddlers and minimize their potential for developmental delay, to reduce the educational costs to our society. . . by minimizing the need for special education and related services after handicapped infants and toddlers reach school age . . . to enhance the capacity of families to meet the special needs of their infants and toddlers with handicaps. (Sec. 671a)

Although participation was optional, all states committed to planning, developing, and implementing statewide, coordinated, multidisciplinary, interagency programs of early intervention services. Many states accepted this role reluctantly because the states bore the major costs of this program rather than the federal government, which provided only planning and development money (Gallagher, Trohanis, & Clifford, 1989). This was one of many federal legislative demands on the states without the delivery of accompanying funds to carry out the requirements. This law was declared an *unfunded mandate,* regarding which states have been less and less willing to cooperate with the federal government.

PL 99-457 nevertheless broke new ground in a number of ways. It recognized that many different health, social, and educational agencies needed to work together to create a comprehensive system. It required the establishment of a state interagency coordinating council (ICC) appointed by the governor to advise and assist the lead agency in planning and operating the system. It also called for individualized family service plans (IFSPs), which are individual plans developed by a multidisciplinary team. Family members are part of the team, which has clear goals and stated outcomes, and IFSPs stress the role of the family in the design (Trohanis, 1989). PL 99-457 defined eligibility for services by a criterion of "developmental delay" instead of the presumed cause of the disability (e.g., mental retardation) and required that all children designated as having a disability be provided an IFSP.

These two pieces of legislation, PL 94-142 and PL 99-457, have transformed the service programs for school- and preschool-age children with disabilities in the United States and, in so doing, are true engines of change. They both represent the social philosophy of *vertical equity,* or the unequal treatment of unequals in order to make them more equal. Many other pieces of legislation have become significant in the programming and policies regarding exceptional children. Two of these are Section 504 of the Rehabilitation Act of 1973 (PL 93-112) and the Americans with Disabilities Act (ADA) of 1990 (PL 101-336). The Rehabilitation Act prohibits barriers to participation in activities or programs solely because of disability and was designed to provide equal access to services for children and adults with disabilities. The ADA extends to people with disabilities the civil rights already guaranteed to others without regard to race, color, national origin, gender, or religion. Such legislation extends beyond the school system and ensures rights in the community.

No Child Left Behind Act of 2001 (PL 107-110)

Sometimes legislation directed to all children or to general education has a significant impact on exceptional children, even if that impact was not expected and might even be coincidental to the original purposes. One such piece of legislation was named the No Child Left Behind Act of 2001 (PL 107-110) because of its emphasis on holding all children to some adequate standard of performance. Unfortunately, little initial attention was given to how this law would affect children with special needs. This has resulted in considerable confusion at the policy and implementation levels.

Accountability is emphasized in the No Child Left Behind legislation, and major stress was put on measuring the performance of schools and subgroups of children (e.g., children from poverty, English-language learners) in those schools in order to determine the adequacy of the educational programs and systems in each state. This purpose would be achieved by an extended use of tests and statewide assessments in grades 3–8. Each state determines its minimum performance for a school, and schools must demonstrate annual yearly progress (AYP) for the school or for subgroups of students; otherwise, sanctions are applied to individual schools and states.

As can be imagined, many exceptional children have difficulty with reaching levels of proficiency expected of the typical student. The development of alternative assessments to measure the objectives of programs for exceptional children has been encouraged, but schools continue to struggle with establishing standards of proficiency for all students when the student body includes children with significant impairments.

All schools are also expected to have *qualified personnel* in place by the school year 2006–2007, and what that requirement means for exceptional children remains to be fully interpreted. It should mean that teachers working directly with exceptional children must be certified in their area of specialty, but what, if any, waivers will be given if states fall short of that goal (as they surely will because of existing shortages) is yet to be determined. There is little quarrel with the goals of setting high standards and having highly qualified personnel. Just how this will be done for exceptional children will be a matter of continual concern.

Court Decisions

The courts represent another major change engine for establishing social policy. The large body of federal legislation for children with disabilities actually owes a great deal to the landmark *Brown v. Board of Education* decision (1954), which declared the "separate but equal" philosophy of segregation in educational settings was invalid and discriminatory on its face. As has been pointed out by many, if *students with disabilities* is substituted for *Negro* and *students without disabilities* is substituted for *white* in the *Brown v. Board of Education* ruling, the same issues would have played out in disability litigation.

But the *Brown* decision had even more impact than overturning the "separate but equal" concept. As Turnbull and Turnbull pointed out,

> *Brown* heralded the massive entry of the federal government into public education. Thus, it made significant inroads into an area that had been reserved almost wholly by state and local governments as their province. Over the long run, its effect has been to shift the balance of the federal system heavily toward the side of the federal government. (2000, p. 12)

During the last half of the 20th century, the courts played a significant role in protecting and verifying the educational opportunities for children with disabilities. Even when legislation affirmed the educational rights of children with disabilities, the laws were often stated in general terms that needed to be judicially interpreted before common educational practice could be established. Beginning with the *Brown v. Board of Education* decision, a series of court decisions central to the needs of children with disabilities and their families followed. Four of these decisions have been chosen for review in this chapter. These decisions have answered four major questions:

- Can children with disabilities have access to a free appropriate public education? (*Pennsylvania Association for Retarded Children {PARC} v. Commonwealth of Pennsylvania*, 1972)

- What does *appropriate* in the phrase "free appropriate public education" mean? (*Hendrick Hudson School District v. Rowley*, 1982)

- What does *least restrictive environment* mean? (*Roncker v. Walter*, 1983)

- How should children with disabilities be disciplined within the school system? (*Honig v. Doe*, 1988)

The individual parents involved in these cases were quite literally powerless in their arguments with the schools, which had the authority of the law and tradition on their side. One of the purposes of these court cases was to equalize the power and authority of ordinary citizens with that of the organizations and establishments of the schools. The decision that emerged in each of these cases provided further guidance to school systems as to how to make decisions about the education of children with disabilities.

Pennsylvania Association for Retarded Children (PARC) v. Commonwealth of Pennsylvania (1972)

The effect of this decision was to ensure every child with disabilities had access to a free appropriate public education. Prior to this case, the public schools in Pennsylvania had a rule that a child must have a mental age score of 5 years on an IQ test in order to attend public school. What this meant was that the schools had the right to refuse entrance to children with mental retardation because such children would be developmentally slower than the average 5-year-old. The schools might realistically keep children with developmental delays out of school until they were 8 or 10 years old using this legislative criterion. The PARC hired a young advocate and lawyer, Tom Gilhool, to make the case for them that the Pennsylvania law was manifestly unfair. Gilhool pointed out that the state constitution of Pennsylvania said that "all children in Pennsylvania were entitled to a free, public education" and he didn't see any exception after the statement that said "except children with mental retardation or poor speech or behavior problems" (*PARC v. Commonwealth of Pennsylvania,* 1972). So the issue was whether *all* really meant *all.*

The case was decided in favor of the parents. As a class action suit, the results of the case affected all children with mental retardation in Pennsylvania, not just the children of families who brought the suit; however, this was not the end of the dispute. People who had power and authority were loath to give it up. The court had to assign a *master,* whose task was to ensure that the court's decision was carried out. The master was employed for 3 years to ensure that the state and local schools implemented the decision.

Hendrick Hudson School District v. Rowley (1982)

This decision established the principle that children with disabilities deserve an appropriate education but that appropriate education does not necessarily mean the best possible education. Amy Rowley, a deaf student, had been placed in a general kindergarten class, and the school had gone to unusual lengths to prepare for Amy. Several staff members had taken a course in sign-language interpretation, a teletype machine had been installed in the principal's office to facilitate communication with Amy's deaf parents, and Amy had been provided with an FM hearing aid to amplify words spoken into a wireless receiver by teachers and fellow students (Turnbull & Turnbull, 2000).

An IEP meeting after kindergarten determined that Amy should attend the first grade in a general education classroom but would receive instruction from a tutor for the deaf for 1 hour per day in addition to speech therapy. The Rowley parents insisted that Amy be provided with a qualified sign-language interpreter in all of her academic classes; that seemed too much for the school, and it refused. The parents filed a suit claiming that the denial of the interpreter violated the "free appropriate public education" clause.

This case wound its way through District Court and the Court of Appeals before eventually coming before the Supreme Court. The issue at hand was whether the school system had the obligation to provide all possible assistance to the child with disabilities. The lower courts decided in favor of the parents. The Supreme Court decided, however, that it was not the school system's responsibility to *maximize* each child's potential. It was necessary to confer some educational benefit for Amy, and the Court concluded that this was being done sufficiently. Amy's performance in school was observed to be above average, and she was adjusting very well to that environment. The school system was not required to do everything that might be done to aid a particular child. As sometimes happens, the *Rowley* decision led to many other court cases. Because optimum provisions are no longer deemed necessary according to the *Rowley* decision, the issue in subsequent cases would be a question of how much help is enough.

Roncker v. Walter (1983)

This was a key decision supporting the inclusion of children with disabilities in the general education program. This case clarified how the schools should make decisions regarding the integration of children with disabilities into the general classroom. In this case, the parents of a child with moderate mental retardation wished for their son to attend school rather than be placed in a program for children with severe and profound disabilities. The court stressed the LRE clause in the legislation (PL 94-142) and asked the school to make the necessary adjustments so that the child in question could be educated in the general program. If special services were needed so that the child could make this adaptation, then the services should be brought to the general program.

The courts still recognized that some students with disabilities could be educated in segregated facilities because of their disruptive behavior or because the needed services could not be delivered in the general classroom. Nevertheless, the message to the schools was clear: the LRE clause must be taken seriously, and the environment of the general classroom and school should be modified to make it more responsive to children with disabilities.

Honig v. Doe (1988)

This decision was crucial in determining how schools are expected to discipline children with special needs. This case involved two students in San Francisco who were scheduled to be expelled for violent and disruptive behavior. Both teenage boys showed extensive disruptive behavior, and the schools initiated expulsion procedures. The lower courts decided that the schools were within their rights in taking that action, but their judgments were appealed. The Supreme Court decided that the behavior of these students was a manifestation of their disabilities, as the teenagers had been identified as having emotional disturbance. The Court therefore felt that the "zero reject" provision established in legislation (PL 94-142) would be violated. The schools could not expel a student who was covered under special education legislation. This fundamental decision has cast long shadows for the schools in terms of how they can discipline children with disabilities.

Summary

These four decisions, along with many other court decisions in the 1970s and 1980s, solidified the right to an appropriate education for children with disabilities. Litigation regarding provisions for exceptional children continues, but these cornerstone decisions laid the groundwork and precedence for the current batch of cases. For example, the *Rowley* case was upheld in a California case (*Fermin v. San Mateo-Foster City School District,* 2000) in which the parents claimed that their child was only making minimal progress on his IEP. The court decided that he was making meaningful progress toward his IEP goals and decided in favor of the school administration. In a similar case in Michigan (*Soraruf v. Pinckney Community Schools,* 2000), the court determined that the program proposed by the school for a child with autism was reasonably calculated to provide the student with educational benefits, even if some procedural violations in the student's placement had occurred. In a further case in Texas (*Houston Independent School District v. Bobby R.,* 2000), the court determined that it was unnecessary for the student to improve in every academic area in order to receive educational benefit from his IEP and pointed to increasing test scores as evidence for meaningful improvement.

The courts have decided that every child is entitled to a free appropriate public education and that education should demonstrate meaningful progress in the development of the child. Court disputes over details of the IDEA regulations, or other current issues, can be found in *Students with Disabilities and Special Education* (McEllistrom, Roth, D'Agnastino, & Brown, 2004), which assembles all available court actions in this field.

Administrative Rules

Basic educational legislation or court decisions for children with disabilities can call for the development of an IEP or an IFSP for infants and toddlers, but they cannot possibly answer all of the questions that such a requirement raises for state and local programs. For example, school systems that are anxious to carry out this provision in the appropriate way could ask, "Who convenes such a meeting? Who shall attend such a meeting? Should the IEP meetings be held periodically or just once for a child? What should be the expected output from such a meeting? What role should the parents be expected to play? How much time should elapse between the diagnosis, the identification of a child needing services, and the meeting itself?" The Office of Special Education Programs (OSEP) in the U.S. Department of Education crafted a set of regulations to answer these kinds of questions. Regulations are subject to written public comment, to which the executive branch is obliged to respond before the regulations become a part of the law. Once they have been established, the regulations actually have the force of law. In this way, the executive branch exerts its influence on the conduct of special education programs. Because it often manages the day-to-day operations of the legislated programs, these implementation regulations have an influence almost equal to that of the original legislation itself.

An example of how regulations can tilt legislation in one direction or another can be seen in the IDEA regulations regarding the LRE. Here the regulations interpret the law to favor inclusion of the child with disabilities in the general classroom:

> Least Restrictive Environment (LRE)
> (b) Each public agency shall ensure (1) that to the maximum extent appropriate, children with disabilities, including children in public and private institutions or other care facilities, are educated with children who are non-disabled; and (2) that special classes, separate schooling or other removal of children with disabilities from the regular education environment occurs only if the nature or severity of the disability is such that education in regular classes with the use of supplementary aids and services cannot be achieved satisfactorily. (§ 300. 550-556)

Regulations also shape the IEP by specifying, in detail, the membership of the IEP team:

(a) The public agency shall ensure that the IEP team for each child with disability includes (1) the parents of the child; (2) at least one regular education teacher of each child (if the child is in the regular education environment); (3) a representative of the local educational agency who is knowledgeable about the general curriculum. (Section 300.344)

Other sections of the regulations address additional details: the role of the general educator (Section 300.346), the content of the IEP itself (Section 300.347), and when the IEP must be in effect (Section 300.342). Such details can sharpen the law's requirements for educators. If there is a dispute about how these provisions are being implemented, then a series of hearings and meetings and even court decisions are required to settle the matter.

Professional Initiatives

The fourth engine of change involves the products of work and the judgments of the many professionals from diverse disciplines who work with children with special needs. When this professional effort has established sufficient experience or when clear patterns of research are identified, then the collective judgment of the professional community can be realized through changes in the administrative rules or even in subsequent legislation. In addition, professional testimony in court cases can influence court decisions.

Associations

One of the ways that professionals have made their voices heard in decision-making circles is by banding together in professional associations to advocate for change for children with special needs. Perhaps the oldest of these organizations is the American Association on Mental Retardation (AAMR; formerly the American Association of Mental Deficiency), which can trace its roots back to 1876.

In 1922, the Council for Exceptional Children (CEC) was established; in 2004, it had more than 60,000 members. Some of its divisions have been particularly active, including the Division on Developmental Disabilities, the Division for Learning Disabilities, the Division for Early Childhood, and the Council for Children with Behavioral Disorders. Each of these divisions has been especially effective on issues related to its clientele. The CEC has been intensely involved in proposing amendments and changes in legislation such as IDEA on the basis of the views and experiences of its members (Smith, 2001).

The American Speech-Language-Hearing Association (ASHA), established in 1935 and with more than 80,000 members in 2004, is another organization that has been influential in policy matters. There are many others—the American Occupational Therapy Association (AOTA), the National Association of Social Workers (NASW), and the American Physical Therapy Association (APTA), to name only a few.

In addition to professional organizations, parent associations organized to influence decision making have played an essential role as change agents. The Arc (formerly the National Association for Retarded Children) was an active influence in the 1960s and 1970s in the passage of legislation such as PL 94-142. Other disability-specific organizations of parents (e.g., American Society on Autism, the Learning Disabilities Association of America) have also played important roles in shaping decisions. Parents have been particularly effective in arguing for funding at both the state and federal level for programs for children with disabilities. Many legislators find it difficult to stand up to parents and tell them that there is no money to help their children in view of the often extravagant expenditure of funds for other, clearly discretionary, undertakings (Turnbull, Beegle, & Stowe, 2002).

Professional Standards

Professional associations may set up standards with regard to the credentials of personnel or to the conditions of educational treatment. Some that have done so are the CEC, the National Education Association (NEA), the National Association of School Psychologists (NASP), and the National Association for the Education of Young Children (NAEYC). Such standards are often honored in the development of administrative regulations so that these professional standards become the effective policy concerning young children and their families.

The CEC, the major professional organization in special education, has established standards for the preparation and licensure of special educators (CEC, 2000) that establish the requirements for teachers in all of the areas of exceptionality, plus early childhood, administration, and so forth. Examples of the knowledges and skills required by teachers of children with learning disabilities according to the CEC standards are the following:

Knowledges. The relationship between learning disabilities and reading instruction, including reading purpose, rate, accuracy, fluency and comprehension.

Alternatives for teaching skills and strategies to individuals with learning disabilities who differ in degree and kind of disability.

Skills. Use research-supported instructional strategies and practice for teaching children with learning disabilities. (2000)

The assurance that teachers possess such knowledges and skills increases the likelihood that children with disabilities will receive appropriate educational programs in public schools. The CEC (2003) has supplemented the extensive lists of knowledge and skills with performance-based standards that have been accepted by the National Council for Accreditation of Teacher Education (NCATE). These standards are divided into three sections: field experiences and clinical practice, assessment system standards, and special education content standards.

EARLY CHILDHOOD PRIORITY

This volume emphasizes early childhood special education for several reasons. Intervention in the early years can be effective, but it is the infrastructure, the support systems, that are being established in early childhood programs that can point the way to the future. Early childhood programs have fewer restraints imposed by systemic habits; consequently, policy makers can cope with issues afresh without being enveloped by past procedures or policies of traditional special education. For example, early childhood programs emphasize diagnosis less and try to develop an educational plan that addresses the developmental patterns that the child presents without wondering what to call it. Many disabilities and learning difficulties have medical and genetic etiology, but the treatment is often educational in nature. Consequently, what might be called an etiological point of view may not help too much in the design of educational programs.

Evidence available from research work with young children with disabilities has yielded the conclusion that it is very important to begin an intervention program with the child and family as early in the child's life as possible. In a masterful review of the major research conducted in this area, *The Effectiveness of Early Intervention,* Guralnick (1997) concluded that there is no longer any uncertainty about the answer to the most basic question, "Can intervention in the early life of young children with disabilities make a difference and improvement in that life?" Guralnick asserted that the answer is clearly "yes" and that researchers should now seek answers to the second-order questions: "What interventions are more effective than others?" and "What contextual factors influence the effective treatments for good or ill?"

An ambitious research program for early childhood proposed by Wolery and Bailey (2002) included building an infrastructure to enhance the translation of knowledge to practice. In many respects, research is the most revolutionary element in change because it is always revealing new information that necessitates modifications and adjustments in regulations and laws, if not entirely new legislation and rule making.

Sarason (1996) pointed out that "the verdicts of history are not all that kind to the experts of the past, as they will not be to most experts of the present.

History . . . is the cruelest of critics. It is also an instructive one" (p. vi). With additional knowledge and experience, the professional community can call for changes in existing policies and educational practice. All too often decisions reached by a policy maker are based on a limited understanding of the scope of the problem or the range of possible options that are available to address it. Once the policy maker has committed him- or herself to a particular solution, it is very difficult to introduce other options or possibilities. Some means must be found to inhibit a rush to judgment so as to consider the full scope of the issues involved and the benefits and costs of each potential solution. The crucial decision is how to choose between the various options proposed and what criteria to use to make the choice. A decision matrix is a tool to help in that process.

THE DECISION MATRIX

A decision matrix, such as the example shown in Figure 1.1, is one of the tools designed to simplify complex situations (Gallagher, 1994a). Decision makers often find themselves confronted with a variety of options and a similar variety of criteria on which to judge or weigh the options. The first step in constructing such a matrix is to identify on the vertical axis some possible options that could cope with the problems under consideration. The second step is to select criteria that have been used to weigh one option against the other and list these horizontally. The final step is to insert information or commentary at the intersection of the options and criteria in the matrix to aid in the choice between options.

Options

Figure 1.1 presents an array of options for educational programs for children with special needs. They represent some suggested actions in the field but certainly not all available options. For example, one option might be to make a payment to families sufficient to allow the mothers to remain at home rather than go to work. This option, however, seems to suffer from a heavy dose of unreality, given current socioeconomic circumstances, so it is not being listed in the presented array of options.

One of the options to be considered would be subsidies from either state or federal government for direct services for children with special needs; that is, financially supporting a program for children with disabilities, such as a preschool program for children with hearing impairments. The choice of how to use the subsidy could remain with local professionals. Direct subsidies for child care programs would be considered an option for young children with disabili-

	Criteria for choice						
Option	Cost	Personnel needs	Track record	Public acceptance	Administrative feasibility	Agency acceptance	Other
Subsidies for direct services for children with special needs							
Vouchers: Direct support to families							
Support to building infrastructure							
Subsidies for child care programs							
Direct payment for teacher preparation							
Tutorial services							
Status quo	0	−	−	−	+/−	+/−	

Figure 1.1. Decision matrix showing options for educational programs serving children with special needs.

ties in that it would present child care providers with personnel and financial resources with which they might include children with special needs in their programs. Direct payments for teacher preparation would be another option worthy of consideration because there has been a chronic shortage of personnel to educate children with special needs. Universities and other training institutions need encouragement to establish and maintain personnel preparation programs in this special field.

The voucher option would provide direct payments to parents who could then shop around for the most desirable services available for their child. For a child with disabilities, a voucher might be used to employ a speech-language pathologist to help with delayed speech or perhaps to pay for physical therapy. It is designed to give more choice and power to the family. Tutorial services are payments for direct one-to-one treatments, such as special speech and language therapies or physical therapies, often provided in a clinic or in the home of the child. The infrastructure option refers to building the organizational capacity of the services for children with special needs by creating such enterprises as TA centers or supporting research center studies on program effectiveness.

Although each of these options might be considered educationally desirable, the scarcity of resources makes it unlikely that the decision maker would be able to support them all. So, the purpose of the decision matrix is to try to analyze what is known in order to make decisions about which options ought to have the highest priorities in the annual budget of the state. Note that the status quo is included in the possible options to be considered if all other options cost too much or have other flaws that make them undesirable. Unless the status quo has sizable negatives, it might well be considered the most attractive of the available options. Subsequent chapters use the decision matrix to illustrate key policy issues.

Criteria for Choice

It is important in this decision matrix to display the various key criteria by which the decision maker can compare the options. The various criteria for choice shown in Figure 1.1 represent a typical array of factors taken into account in policy decisions. These criteria can be changed, somewhat, depending on the nature of the problem. For some issues, the attitude of certain subgroups in the general society might be important to consider and would be added to the matrix under criteria.

Cost is one criterion that is almost always present in the decision matrix. It is a significant factor for those in decision-making roles because it means the allocation of scarce resources that might otherwise be spent on some other goal. To some decision makers, cost is the key element that can trump any of the other criteria being considered. Obviously, some of the options will cost more than others, but cost is not the only criterion to be considered. Perhaps one of the options has an outstanding track record and that would make it a desirable choice even if it costs more.

Personnel needs as a criterion refer to the requirement for necessary special education personnel and an estimate of how many more would be added for each option. If there is a sizable shortage of qualified personnel, then certain long-range plans need to be considered that would fill that shortage. One also has to consider the capabilities or capacities of the institutions that will produce these new personnel.

Track record is a criterion that refers to evidence gathered from studies and research on effectiveness. What evidence is there that a particular strategy (e.g., vouchers) works? Literature reviews are a favorite strategy for academicians as it gives some indication of any positive results to expect from a given option.

Public acceptance as a criterion gives some indication of the degree to which the public, or some special public groups, are in support of the option. Few policies can survive if there are substantial public negative feelings about them. The presence of negative feelings does not necessarily militate against a particular option, but it does mean that some effort would need to be made to change that attitude before the option is seriously considered. Using a state-operated lottery to fund early education programs would be an example of an option that would face considerable public opposition.

Administrative feasibility refers to how easy a particular option would be to implement. If there are subsidies for programs for children with special needs, who decides how the subsidies are given and who should receive them? What kind of problems are there in administering a program? For example, the IEP has come under fire for the time consumed in reports, meetings, and other administrative work, and it might be considered a negative in this column (Gallagher & Desimone, 1995).

Agency acceptance is a criterion regarding the attitude of certain agencies to new policies that might affect their ongoing programs. For example, how will existing child care and Head Start programs feel about a new prekindergarten program? Their resistant attitude might not be critical to the decision, but implementation would be much easier if their feelings are taken into account in the planning.

The *Other* category in Figure 1.1 refers to criteria that would be added to consider specific problems. The matrix is not designed to yield a quantifiable result but to organize information for the decision maker. The same decision matrix data can be interpreted quite differently by a political figure who puts significant weight on the public acceptance of an option and by an administrator who is concerned with administrative feasibility.

Completing the Decision Matrix

One of the first steps in the decision process is to provide the decision matrix with information. How are the boxes of the matrix filled in? Different types of studies may be designed to provide information for specific dimensions of the matrix.

Finance Studies

One of the most needed bits of information is a determination of how much a given option or alternative will cost. Although cost is only one of many dimensions of decision making, it is usually quite important to legislators and others who must put up the money necessary to execute the policy. A finance study is one method of determining the cost of options. For example, the Cost, Quality, and Child Outcome Study (Helburn, 1995), which observed and rated 100 child care centers in each of four states, was able to provide useful information on what it costs to care for a young child under a variety of conditions (poor to excellent) of child care. Such a study can also indicate that high-quality programs cost more than low-quality programs. Finally, the discovery that many child care programs are of mediocre quality or less stirs up a further need for consideration of other options for young children.

Attitude Surveys (Polling)

What the public and key decision makers do related to public policy is clearly tied with how they perceive the situation, so attempts to determine those perceptions have an important role to play in identifying desirable options. This information could help fill in the column on public acceptance. For example, numerous studies have been done to determine the degree of public acceptance of parental vouchers for school selection as a strategy for giving more power to the parent. Some of the early studies revealed a strong antipathy to vouchers as an option because of a perception that they could pose a danger to public school support, but later the responses of randomly selected citizens became more evenly divided (National Council on Disabilities, 2003).

Legislative Analysis of Existing Policies

When federal or state legislation is proposed as an option for addressing a general public issue, the current rules, standards, and legislation should first be analyzed. In the case of new or universal prekindergarten programs, this analysis would include a review of policies related to Head Start, child care, young children with disabilities, and other relevant programs. For example, in the case of violence by a student in special education, there could be a review of what the current rules and regulations say. IDEA 2004 has indicated that the violence should be very serious before a student with disabilities is removed from school, particularly if the problem presented by the student is related to his or her disability. Decision makers have to take into account previous policies and events before they can develop new policies for handling the problem.

Literature Review

Typically, the first step of the academician is to conduct a comprehensive review of the existing literature in the relevant disciplines to see what has been said and done about the various options currently under consideration. In addition to traditional sources such as books and journals, the Internet has become a significant source. Such a review needs to cover the various facets of the policies under consideration. The information gathered through such a literature search can help fill the *Track record* column. For example, considerable work has already been completed on the efficacy of special education programs for young children (Guralnick, 1997), and a literature review should help develop realistic expectations about what a new program might do, together with confidence that meaningful gains can be made by a well-designed program.

Modeling After Others

In considering a future state law or regulation, the question may be raised as to whether some other state has done this before and what could be learned from that state's experience. An analysis of the factors that have helped or hindered one state in the development of a particular policy could assist another state in developing policy direction. If Georgia has already made progress with its prekindergarten programs, neighboring states such as Florida or Alabama are likely to study Georgia's laws and procedures to see what can be used in their own states. This is a sophisticated version of the age-old game Follow the Leader. For example, many states might not consider transportation a serious issue in prekindergarten programs, but previous work has indicated that transportation has indeed been a serious issue in a number of states, so the planning for a new state policy would need to take this issue into account (Gallagher, Clayton, & Heinemeier, 2001).

Policy Implementation

It is one thing to establish a policy through legislation or regulation and quite another to see that the policy is effectively carried out at the local level. For example, applied behavior analysis (ABA) is an instructional strategy in much use, but there needs to be certainty that it is being applied in an appropriate fashion. Also, the number of teachers currently qualified to use ABA techniques may be in doubt. Such doubts could reduce faith in an option or cause a major realignment in personnel preparation. Analyses designed to aid policy makers can generate a series of studies that yield useful information. It may be necessary to conduct several different policy studies so that a wide range of information is available on the options and on the criteria that will be used to choose an appropriate option. The next chapters look at other decision matrices that reflect decision making on particular issues in special education.

How this information may be used, however, depends on the individual value system of the users themselves. Which criterion has this highest priority? The policy analyst can determine accurate estimates of cost for an option but cannot decide how such information would be weighed by the decision maker. How would cost compare to the track record of a program under consideration? If the policy analyses directly contradict the assumption of some of the options, the proponents of these options must cope with the results of the analysis, whether they wish to or not. If the number of personnel needed to carry out a particular option exceeds any reasonable estimate of available graduates from personnel preparation programs, the advocates for that option have to explain how they expect to achieve their goal of a qualified professional for each child with disabilities. A wide variety of decisions have to be made concerning the identification of exceptional children, the educational placement of these students, the necessary curricular adaptations, and, of course, the evaluation of programs. All of these issues are taken up in subsequent chapters.

SOME CHILDREN WITH SPECIAL NEEDS

Decisions about public policy must of necessity take into account large groups of children, but its effects will be felt by individual children and their families. This volume illustrates those effects by using the case studies of five children with special needs and their families.

Arnie

Arnie is an attractive 7-year-old boy who has been diagnosed with autism. The family's friends and neighbors remark that he is a beautiful boy, and his parents feel the same way. When Arnie was 1 year old, his parents began to take note of some differences from the developmental norms that they had expected, and they decided it was time to express their concerns. Arnie was very slow in talking. He has always had difficulty in socializing and playing with others and in communicating with adults. Yet, he has been able to focus on equipment and inert objects and to spend time with them. His parents have taken him to a number of specialists, most of whom have confirmed the diagnosis of autism, which includes the series of behaviors that Arnie shows: the lack of socialization; the limited communication skills; and some of the repetitive motor movements, such as flapping his hands when under stress, support his diagnosis. Within the family, Arnie is able to establish relationships and express affection.

Arnie is not doing well in school and has been a difficult child for the kindergarten and first-grade teachers. Arnie's parents are hopeful that the educational system, which has become sensitized to the needs of children with autism, might provide them with the treatment and instruction that the parents have been told is necessary to help Arnie. School personnel and the parents have considerable discussions about the best approach to maximizing Arnie's development.

Les

Les is an 8-year-old boy, tall and slim for his age, who has been diagnosed with learning disabilities by the local school authorities and by psychologists who have seen him in individual diagnostic sessions. In contrast to Arnie, Les was not early considered a "problem child" and his development seemed reasonably typical until he reached school age. Les has been able to make friends with a small group of his peers, and he maintains those friendships. However, he has had some serious reading challenges. When Les's parents took him to a neurologist, the neurologist noted that he had a combination of developmental patterns that are often seen in children with learning disabilities, some visual perception impairments that cause him to reverse figures and letters, attention problems, and an inability to focus for a given period of time.

The local schools have agreed with Les's parents that he needs special assistance and have provided him, in addition to his third-grade teacher, with a special consultant on reading and learning disabilities who is providing lessons and tutorial exercises for Les and some suggestions for the teacher about how to help Les with his learning problems. Les's father had been particularly concerned because he had always believed that if a person tries hard enough, he or she will be successful in whatever it is he or she is learning. He's not totally convinced that Les is putting out a full effort on his lessons; otherwise, he figures, Les would be doing well because his intelligence seems to be at least average or above for his age group.

Bobby

Bobby is a big and energetic 9-year-old child who has been identified as having behavior and emotional problems. He has an older brother who also had been identified as a student with problem behavior in the middle school. Although ordinarily friendly and interesting to be around, Bobby sometimes frightens his peers and his teachers with uncontrolled outbursts of anger in which he threatens to hurt himself or others. Bobby lives with his mother and older brother. His mother has not been receptive to the school's identification of Bobby's difficulties. The school has assigned a specialist in children with behavior and emotional problems to Bobby and his teacher, and together they are trying to work out ways that he can gain self-control over his temper outbursts, which have caused other students to distance themselves from him.

Cathy

Cathy is a 10-year-old girl who has been diagnosed with cerebral palsy, a condition caused by damage to the motor control centers of the brain. Cathy was born with this condition, and it has influenced her motor skills development, speech development, cognitive development, and communication. One of the characteristics that her parents admire about her is her persistence in sticking with a task and her determination to complete it no matter how difficult it is for her. This 100% effort to the task she is given has also been noted by her teachers.

She is the second child in a three-child family and naturally has consumed a great deal of her parents' attention since she was born. Her mother has been concerned about her being physically hurt at school because she moves with the help of crutches and wheelchairs. The school staff has been concerned about her performance at school and has conducted a comprehensive evaluation, leading to an IEP for Cathy. The results of the evaluation of achievement, intelligence testing, and observation have led the school to believe she is a slow learner, and, although placed in the fifth grade, she is performing academically at the second- or third-grade level. Her parents get reports of her progress and believe she is brighter than the school gives her credit for and that her physical problems have interfered with a more effective performance.

Cathy has a few close friends in the classroom who help her out in getting from one place to another and who make sure that her special needs are met. Cathy herself is feeling frustrated at her inability to do as much in the classroom as she wants to. Recently, the school has attached some additional devices on a standard computer that allow Cathy to gain access to information available on-line, and she is currently experimenting with how best to use the computer for her own purposes.

Gretchen

Gretchen is an 11-year-old gifted child in the sixth grade. She has always been developmentally advanced, reading before 4 years of age. Her parents have reported her eagerness to learn about anything and everything around her. Gretchen has been a challenge for her teachers because her teachers need to find sufficient time to provide stimulation for her to continue to learn. She has mastered most of the material of the sixth grade already.

She has received excellent grades despite not seeming to be challenged or interested in her school work. Her parents are seeking some kind of special experience for her in the public schools to allow her to continue there, although they have already started to think about alternatives, such as private schools or homeschooling, if the public schools seem unable to provide the intellectual stimulation that she needs. She has two or three close friends in the middle school who are also excellent students.

Because of the diverse needs of each of these students, new and revised policies affect them and their families in different ways. The chapters follow these five children to see how the various decisions about programs and educational adaptations change their educational experiences and their lives.

CHAPTER 2

Finding Children with Special Needs

Eligibility

Whenever a decision is made to provide special resources to a sub-group of children rather than to all children, as happens when legislation is passed for children with disabilities, the issue of eligibility automatically becomes important. If a child is identified as having mental retardation, then the child and his or her teachers become eligible for additional resources that should allow the school to plan more effectively to meet the child's special needs. Educators are naturally concerned that only those children who fit the eligibility criteria of disability receive these scarce resources. The funds should not go to children who do not fit the criteria, even if the children have mild but educationally significant learning or social problems.

Thus, the criteria for various types of diagnoses are important because they determine how many children are eligible for special education services. In the mid-20th century, the number of eligible children with disabilities was relatively small. Blindness, deafness, mental retardation, orthopedic problems, and serious communication problems were generally all considered disabilities that would qualify students as part of the population of exceptional children. Since that time, a number of other categories have been added to the broad classification of disability, including learning disabilities; autism; traumatic brain injury; severe emotional disturbance; and other health impairments, including asthma, epilepsy, and rheumatic fever.

Why are different groups added to this omnibus disability classification? Sometimes the research community identifies a different group with common characteristics, such as children with traumatic brain injury, leading to a new classification, and it becomes important to focus on the particular needs of that group. Other times, parent organizations lobby for special attention for their group (e.g., attention-deficit/hyperactivity disorder, autism), hoping that the official recognition of their children's disability will make it more likely that the children will receive services.

The identification of children with special needs remains a dynamic process. As decision makers learn more about these conditions, they make finer and finer differentiations between categories, and views of the categories change and are modified. In the 1970s, Arnie would have likely been diagnosed as having mental retardation because of his obvious developmental delay. Now, his doctor knows enough to identify him as having autism, which distinguishes Arnie from other children with developmental delays. As the political landscape changes, emphasis and focus also change. At one time, *minimal brain injury* was an important term, and Les would likely have been labeled as such. Today, it has been replaced in the field by the term *learning disabilities.* Which children, and how many of them, are eligible for special services remains a key public policy issue.

DETERMINING ELIGIBILITY

The four engines of change have all played an important role in shaping the diagnostic criteria and identification procedures by which eligibility for special education services is determined. A major commitment to research from 1970 to the present resulted in new information that began to influence legislation, court decisions, administrative rules, and professional initiatives.

Legislation

When individual states such as Illinois and Michigan began special education programs for children with disabilities in the 1950s, the issue of definition became a matter of public policy (i.e., who is eligible for the services), as well as one of scholarly interest. When the Congress passed PL 94-142, the matter of definition became a federal policy issue as well. Subsequent amendments to this key legislation tended to expand the number of definitions and to require more precise indicators than an IQ score, which was a key indicator in much of the earlier diagnoses of mental retardation and learning disabilities.

When Congress passed the law providing services for infants and toddlers with disabilities, PL 99-457, a new approach to diagnosis and identification was adopted. Instead of seeking out the cause of the condition, the focus was on the degree of developmental delay. The amendments created the optional category "at risk" so that states could identify children who might be prone to disabilities at a later time in childhood unless action is taken. The infants and toddlers legislation has since been folded into the IDEA 2004, which contains the current definitions in use.

Court Decisions

The role of the courts in the discovery and identification of children with disabilities is to determine whether an individual child is being denied services or has been appropriately identified as having a disability that requires special services. Is the child eligible according to the legislation and rules, and are the appropriate services being delivered? Because IQ scores have been a key factor in the identification of some children with disabilities, courts have been asked about whether the use of IQ scores was appropriate, particularly for children from culturally different families (*Hobson v. Hansen,* 1967; *Larry P. v. Riles,* 1986). These children scored lower on IQ tests because of the tests' presumed cultural bias, and some children from culturally different families were being mistakenly identified as having mental retardation.

Another key use of the classification of disability was to prevent school systems from expelling students for violent or disruptive behavior, even if it could be shown that their misbehavior stemmed from their disability. The Supreme Court determined that, unless the student was a threat to injure himor herself or others, the student could only be suspended for 10 days; otherwise, the school's commitment to providing free appropriate public education was not being met (*Honig v. Doe,* 1988; *Prince William County School Board v. Willis,* 1989). IDEA 2004 allows the school to place students who violently attack other students or teachers in an alternative education setting for up to 45 school days, but the school must still provide these students with a free appropriate public education. The proper treatment for students with significant emotional difficulties remains a policy puzzle that will likely see more legislative action and court decisions as policy makers try to balance rights and responsibilities in such difficult cases.

Administrative Rules

No legislation could, or should, attempt to answer the multitude of questions that could be raised about the implementation of the law. It is the role of administrative rule making to answer issues or inquiries with regard to the details of the legislation. One rule stressed that the states were expected to take a proactive stance in the search for children with disabilities. Some form of Child Find was to be undertaken, with the details worked out by the state. The regulations for Child Find in the IDEA 2004 are as follows:

(a)   General requirement.
   (1)   The State must have in effect policies and procedures to ensure that—
      (i)   All children with disabilities residing in the State, including children with disabilities attending private schools, regardless of the severity of their disability, and who are in need of special education and related services, are identified, located and evaluated; and
      (ii)   A practical method is developed and implemented to determine which children are currently receiving needed special education and related services. (§ 300.125 [a] [1])

Once students have been screened, the schools must undertake a comprehensive evaluation of those students who did not pass the screening standards. The identification procedures for children younger than age 5 are not as complete as they could be. In their review, Wolery and Bailey pointed out the disparity in prevalence across states: "For example, at the infant-toddler level, Alabama, Louisiana, and Iowa serve less than 1% of the population whereas Hawaii, Massachusetts, and West Virginia serve more than 3% of their populations" (2002, p. 90). Each state is responsible for its own definitions, and such disparities may result from differences in the definitions being used in the states, or in a less-than-enthusiastic effort at Child Find, or perhaps both. Once a child is identified, he or she *must* be provided with special services. States, under heavy financial pressures, may be less than enthusiastic in seeking all eligible children.

IDEA 2004 requires all states to have a "comprehensive Child Find system" to ensure that all children who are in need of early intervention or special education services are located, identified, and referred. The lead agency for Part C of the IDEA Early Intervention Program and for Part B/619 (serving preschoolers with special educational needs) in each state is responsible for planning and implementing a comprehensive Child Find system. In some states, the lead agency for the two programs is one and the same, whereas in others different agencies oversee the two programs (U.S. Department of Education, 2004).

Professional Initiatives

The professional community, through research and experience in programs for children with special needs, has forced rule changes and a broadening of eligibility criteria. A generation of scientists have wondered about the malleability of the human condition and have conducted a variety of intervention studies designed to see what children who are at risk for developing disabilities could do if provided with maximum opportunities (Campbell & Ramey, 1994; Guralnick & Neville, 1997; Weikart & Schweinhart, 1997). The answer appears to be that intervention pays off in reduced referrals to special education, decreased retention rates, and more positive attitudes of the students.

Another question that has been raised is whether children with mild disabilities that are apparent only when the child is challenged by school requirements can be found earlier in the child's life. In one study of 1,700 students enrolled in special education programs, only 16% of them had been identified by age 3, and only 29% by age 5 (Palfry, Singer, Walker, & Butler, 1987), so it is clear that early identification is lagging for many of these children. It should also be clear that children with mild learning disabilities or communication problems are difficult to identify before they enter public schools.

A large sample of children drawn from the National Institute of Child Health and Human Development (NICHD) study of early child care was examined to determine if it is possible to identify children with developmental delays in the preschool age range (LaParo, Olsen, & Pianta, 2002). A group of children who consistently scored 1.5 standard deviations below the mean on standard measures of mental development were categorized as "assessment identified." These children and their families were compared with a randomly selected sample of children of similar ages from the larger NICHD sample. It turns out that several factors are associated with children who are assessment identified, with the most prominent being negative scores on the home observation scales, maternal sensitivity, and low income. Other measures such as maternal depression and child temperament did not show up as strongly. The authors believed that the study showed the importance of early psychosocial factors and underscored the need for home-based community outreach programs for early screening and intervention. With many children in child care at an early age, the possibilities of screening children with developmental delays are increased, and policy makers can consider starting intervention earlier, when such treatment can be more effective, rather than waiting until school failure reveals the problem again.

STRATEGIES IN EDUCATIONAL ASSESSMENT

McLoughlin and Lewis (2001) presented four steps in a modern educational assessment: identification and referral, determination of eligibility, program planning, and program implementation and evaluation (see Table 2.1). Note the emphasis on prereferral intervention in identification and referral strategies prior to the determination of eligibility. Instead of students being referred directly to special education because of their poor school performance, an intermediate step, which was established through additional administrative rules, recognizes the potential role of the environment in the condition of the child (Chalfant, 1989). A child study team made up of a master teacher, psychologist, and principal would meet with the classroom teacher and discuss possible strategies to help the student prior to any referral to special education.

As pointed out by Hickson, Blackman, and Reis, the prereferral process

> Reframes the question from what is wrong with the child to what is wrong with the educational connection between a child with problems and a classroom environment that seems, based on the child's continuing pattern of failure, to be unresponsive to the child's learning deficits and instructional needs. (1995, p. 286)

If the prereferral process does not yield educational improvement, then, as McLoughlin and Lewis demonstrated, there follows a requirement for the full assessment of the student to determine his or her eligibility for special services. If the student is found eligible, then the next step is the design of an IEP and, fi-

Table 2.1. Steps in educational assessment

1. Identification and referral
Screening and teacher identification of students with school problems
Prereferral intervention strategies
Referral and notification of parents

2. Determination of eligibility
Design of the individual assessment plan
Parental permission for assessment
Administration, scoring, and interpretation of assessment procedures
Report of results
Decisions about eligibility

3. Program planning
Design of the individualized education program (IEP)
Parental agreement to the IEP

4. Program implementation and evaluation
Implementation of the IEP
Ongoing monitoring of student progress
Annual review of the IEP
Periodic reevaluation of eligibility

From McLoughlin, J., & Lewis, R. (2001). *Assessing students with special needs* (5th ed.). Upper Saddle River, NJ: Prentice Hall; adapted by permission.

nally, the implementation of the program and a plan for evaluation of its effectiveness. The IDEA 2004 specifically noted that students from culturally diverse families, who are often overreferred, should receive prereferral attention.

Fuchs, Fuchs, and Speece (2002) identified a similar four-phase process in which the first phase is an attempt to allow the school to sort out those who do not belong in special education by providing some institutional support to the classroom teacher to see if that support results in tangible gains for the student. A failure to respond to a modified environment or adaptive lessons may then signal the need for serious consideration of special education services.

PROCESSES OF DISCOVERY

Each of the children who were introduced in Chapter 1—Arnie, Les, Bobby, Cathy, and Gretchen—had been observed to respond in an undesirable way to the standard demands of the education program. Gretchen's response was to perform 3 years above her grade level, and this outstanding performance created problems for the teacher. The other children performed below a satisfactory level. These five children had to be identified as eligible in order to receive the additional services they needed. How were they discovered? What kind of identification and assessment did they receive? How did the condition or label that has been attached to them evolve from earlier times? How early in their development were they noticed? How did they become eligible for special services? Their stories can help to answer these questions and review the roles played by the four engines of change: legislation, court decisions, administrative rules, and professional initiatives.

The field of special education is constantly influenced by larger social trends (see Chapter 10). Even definitions and identification procedures are subject to these forces. During the 1960s and 1970s, the field was influenced by a wave of optimism regarding the development of children and the malleability of the human condition (Gallagher & Ramey, 1987). This optimism about the effects of appropriate educational intervention continues to fuel the special education programs today.

The core "problem" (e.g., deafness, mental retardation) of a child with disabilities was once seen as inborn. Educators and policy makers now realize the key role that environment can play in child and family outcomes. They understand how unfavorable social environments can have a serious negative effect on child outcomes and how positive social environments can reduce, but not necessarily eliminate, genetic anomalies and the effects of the disability. The processes of discovery are evident in relation to the five children in this volume.

Arnie and Autism

The diagnosis of autism for Arnie is not in much dispute. He was diagnosed around the time of his second birthday, and the school was well aware of his condition when he entered. But where did the diagnosis of autism come from, and how has it changed from its original meaning? The major engines of change in the identification of autism were discoveries from professional research and clinical practice that were then reflected in changes in legislation, as well as in a variety of court decisions.

Professional Initiatives

Current knowledge about autism owes much to the perceptive observations of earlier professionals. Autism was formally identified by psychiatrist Leo Kanner (1973), who found a combination of symptoms that seemed to represent a specific clinical entity. Others confirmed this syndrome despite also discovering a wide variation in ability and other skills among this population (Volkman, Cohen, & Paul, 1986). Kanner's core set of symptoms included delayed communication skills, very poor social skills, and a variety of behavior mannerisms that call attention to themselves (e.g., head banging, repetitive motor motions [rocking]).

Kanner described a particular case that contained several of the qualities that distinguish children with this condition.

> He could, since the age of $2\frac{1}{2}$ years, tell the names of all the presidents and vice-presidents, recite the letters of the alphabet forwards and backwards, and flawlessly, with good enunciation, rattle off the Twenty-Third Psalm. Yet, he was unable to carry on an ordinary conversation. He was out of contact with people, while he could handle objects skillfully. His memory was phenomenal. The few times when he addressed someone—largely to satisfy his wants—he referred to himself as *You* and to the person as *I*. (1973, p. 93)

Kanner and other observers noted that a distant and cold mother was an accompanying factor and felt there was a causal linkage between the mother's behavior and the resultant child syndrome (Bettelheim, 1967). Further data and research (Lord, 2001) made it clear, however, that autism spectrum disorders cannot be attributed to a poor parent–child bond or to parental misconduct, which, if seen, might well be the result of parental frustration with the child's behavior.

Legislation

PL 94-142 included children with autism under the category "Other Health Impaired." Revised definitions in subsequent legislation included autism as one of the major categories of disabilities. The current definition in the IDEA 2004 is as follows:

> (1) "Autism" means a developmental disability significantly affecting verbal and nonverbal communication and social interaction, generally evident before age 3, that adversely affects a child's educational performance. Other characteristics often associated with autism are engagement in repetitive activities and stereotyped movements, resistance to environmental change or change in daily routines, and unusual responses to sensory experiences. The term does not apply if a child's educational performance is adversely affected primarily because the child has a serious emotional disturbance, as defined in paragraph (b) (9) of this section. (§ 300.7 [b] [1])

In addition, the Children's Health Act of 2000 (PL 106-310) expands the activities of the National Institutes of Health with respect to autism. Research grants and regional centers of excellence in autism were established through the Centers for Disease Control and Prevention.

Court Decisions

Parents of children with autism have brought a number of cases claiming that the schools were not responding to the professional call for intensity of treatment. Through greater clinical experience, intensity of treatment has emerged as one of the important variables of successful management. The National Academy of Sciences report recommended 25 hours per week as a base for effective treatment (Lord, 2001); however, many schools with scarce resources have tried to find other options for children with autism. The *Union School District v. Smith* (1994) case began with a school placing a child with autism in a "communicatively handicapped class," supplemented by behavior modification counseling. The child's parents objected and, after finding private placement, requested reimbursement. The court determined that the school program was indeed inappropriate, as it did not address the student's need for a more restrictive and less stimulating environment (Turnbull & Turnbull, 2000).

Some solution has to be found between the schools' lack of resources and the need for intensive treatment of a child with autism, or the courts will see many more of these cases. The National Academy of Sciences report suggested that the state develop an emergency fund, perhaps supplemented by Medicaid, which could be provided to local schools that are unable to meet the requirements of the expensive treatment for children with autism (Lord, 2001). Of course, the ultimate solution would be to find, through research and investigation, other modes of effective treatment that are not as expensive. The major challenge for those planning for Arnie is to have an IEP that incorporates all of his deviations from behavioral and social norms in a comprehensive treatment program designed for improvement of communication and social skills, along with a reduction of tantrums.

Administrative Rules

The IDEA and its subsequent regulations clearly intend that, whatever the circumstances, a child is entitled to, and should receive, a free appropriate public education. If Arnie's parents think that a newly established charter school might have a better chance of serving him, he is still entitled to all of the services his public school provides.

> The LEA [Local Education Agency] must have on file with the SEA [State Education Agency] information to demonstrate that in carrying out this part with respect to charter schools that are public schools of the LEA, the LEA will—
> (a) Serve children with disabilities attending those schools in the same manner as it serves children with disabilities in its other schools.
> (b) Provide funds under part B of the Act to those schools with the same manner as it provides those funds to other schools. (§ 300.241)

Les and Learning Disabilities

Les has been identified as a child with learning disabilities, which makes him a member of the largest group in special education (about half of the total number of all students identified with disabilities). Surprisingly, it is a term of relatively recent origin, first introduced by Samuel Kirk in 1963, although the condition itself was well known under different terminology before that date (Strauss & Kephart, 1955). Two of the more popular of these terms in the mid-20th century that are no longer used are *minimal brain injury* and *brain dysfunction* (Keogh, 1994).

One of the reasons for implying neurological dysfunction, even without a positive neurological diagnosis, was that the child revealed patterns of behavior that could not be accounted for by any other explanation (e.g., a child who performed at a 10-year-old's level in auditory learning and at a 5-year-old's level in visual learning). No set of environmental conditions or interpersonal relationships could account for such an intraindividual result. The Illinois Test of Psycholinguistic Abilities (ITPA) was once designed to identify such discrepancies (Kirk, McCarthy, & Kirk, 1968). Also, the patterns of behavior seemed to resemble those individuals with clearly identifiable brain injury. The extensive research on this topic had much to do with shaping subsequent legislation and rules.

Legislation

The category of *learning disabilities* was included in the Education of the Handicapped Act Amendments of 1968 (PL 89-750) as one of the array of conditions of disability that would be eligible for the various provisions under that act. Ever since then, it has become a recognized category of eligible children in such subsequent legislation as PL 94-142 and the IDEA amendments.

The IDEA 2004 definition is as follows:

> (10) "Learning disability" means a disorder in one or more of the basic psychological processes involved in understanding or in using language, spoken or written, that may manifest itself in an imperfect ability to listen, think, speak, read, write, spell, or to do mathematical calculations. The term includes such conditions as perceptual disabilities, brain injury, minimal brain dysfunction, dyslexia, and developmental aphasia. The term does not apply to children who have learning problems that are primarily the result of visual, hearing, or motor disabilities, or mental retardation, of emotional disturbance, or of environmental, cultural, or economic disadvantage. (§ 300.7 [c] [10])

Professional Initiatives

The breadth of the definition of learning disabilities is impressive, as is the number of professions who can claim a contribution to the development of the term. Neuropsychology, psychiatry, education, psychology, speech and language pathology, optometry, and occupational therapy all have some element of learning disabilities within their purview. This is one instance in which the determined work of a variety of professional fields, together with the work of an active advocacy group (Learning Disability Association of America [LDA], formerly the Association for Children with Learning Disabilities [ACLD]), has become incorporated into legislation and court cases.

The prevalence of the condition has been estimated as anywhere from 1% to 5% of the school population, depending on which professional definition is accepted; however, the U.S. Department of Education (2000) estimated the prevalence as being between 4% and 5%. The rapid growth of the prevalence figure to about 5% of the school population would seem to be enhanced by a logical fallacy engaged in by many professionals eager to find resources to cope with children with learning problems. This fallacy is that if all children who have learning disabilities have problems in school, then all children with learning problems in school have learning disabilities. In actuality, of course, children have learning problems in school for a wide variety of reasons, many of them environmental or due to other disabilities. If all of those children having problems in school are included in the definition of learning disabilities, then the category will balloon to even greater numbers (Kavale & Forness, 1998).

Administrative Rules

The original concept of learning disabilities (Bateman, 1965) included *intra-individual differences,* meaning diverse patterns of development within the same child. This concept has been replaced in current legislation and regulations by discrepancies between measured ability and achievement. The discrepancy concept has become one cause of the rapid growth of the number of children identified with learning disabilities.

MacMillan and Speece observed that the search for an intelligence–achievement discrepancy for the diagnosis of learning disabilities has enormous costs. Furthermore, they even questioned whether such use of standard tests is justified until professionals have a better handle on just what the category of learning disabilities stands for:

> To continue to engage in eligibility testing as currently construed strikes us as an enormous waste of time and talent. In the debate over IQ, defenders of the test pointed to the utility for purposes of classification but conceded that IQ scores had little, if any, utility for prescribing treatment given the omnibus nature of the tests. (1999, p. 126)

The dissatisfaction with the discrepancy between IQ score and achievement in identifying students with learning disabilities has become so great that alternative ways of finding children with special learning problems, such as Les, have been sought. The state of the discrepancy term has been summarized by

Vaughn and Fuchs (2003): "Fundamentally the assumption underlying the IQ–Achievement discrepancy model have not been supported" (p. 138). It does not reveal intensity of disorder, inform instruction, or reveal reliable information.

Given these findings, another alternative that has been proposed is that learning disabilities may be defined as "inadequate response to instruction" (Speece, Case, & Molloy, 2003). Such a definition makes no statement about the origin of the problem but identifies children who are behind their classmates in level and rate of performance. One concern about a definition based on response to instruction is that it might mistakenly identify students who are responding poorly to inadequate instruction. If high-quality instruction is being provided and the student is responding unsuccessfully, there can be assurance that the child has a learning disability needing attention.

Fuchs, Mock, Morgan, and Young proposed a two-level version of how to implement services based on responsiveness to instruction:

> The first of the two levels would be a mainstreamed classroom in which the teacher has been supported by the district to implement research validated instruction. At the second level, small groups of three to six nonresponsive students would participate in a demonstrably effective standard-treatment protocol. (2003, p. 168)

The relative lack of research evidence to support this alternative criterion of responsiveness to instruction suggests that it will not be codified very soon, but as a professional initiative, it represents an attempt to go beyond a definition that has been flawed. Some waivers could be provided to districts wishing to try out this new approach without committing the entire country to an as yet unproven construct and set of procedures.

Court Decisions

Children with learning disabilities have profited from a variety of court cases that have referred in general to children with disabilities. Relatively few court cases have been brought forth through this category (Turnbull & Turnbull, 2000). The largest number of cases involves the failure of school districts to identify correctly a child with learning disabilities, resulting in academic or physical harm to the student (e.g., *Ali v. Wayne-Westland School District*, 1992).

Cathy and Orthopedic Disabilities with Mental Retardation

Cathy has been diagnosed as having cerebral palsy, with some accompanying borderline mental retardation. Cerebral palsy is a condition characterized by paralysis, weakness, incoordination, and/or motor dysfunction and can have other cognitive or emotional problems associated with it. Although Cathy may not meet all of the diagnostic criteria for mental retardation, she still is able to qualify for special services under the label of orthopedic impairment.

Legislation

As described in the IDEA 2004, the term *orthopedic impairment* means

> A severe orthopedic impairment that adversely affects a child's educational performance. The term includes impairments caused by congenital anomaly (e.g., clubfoot, absence of some member, etc.), impairments caused by disease (e.g., poliomyelitis, bone tuberculosis, etc.), and impairments caused by disease (e.g., cerebral palsy, amputations and fractures). (§ 300.7 [c] [8])

As is true with a number of children with disabilities, Cathy has more than one condition that classifies as a disability and that complicates educational planning for her. The orthopedic disability of cerebral palsy creates problems of mobility and use of her arms in writing or in using the computer. These can be coped with by wheelchairs or crutches to aid her mobility and with some special equipment, which allows her to communicate via the computer.

In addition, Cathy also appears to have mild mental retardation, and this requires some additional adaptations of the standard curriculum in order to maximize her academic capabilities. It is not inevitable that a child with cerebral palsy would also have mental retardation. Many children with cerebral palsy have average and above average levels of intelligence, but there is a somewhat higher likelihood that the neurological condition that creates cerebral palsy may also influence negatively the intellectual growth of the child, and so it was with Cathy.

The IDEA 2004 reveals a shift in the mental retardation definition, including adaptive behavior as well as cognitive functioning: *Mental retardation* means "significantly subaverage general intellectual functioning existing concurrently with deficits in adaptive behavior and manifested during the developmental period that adversely affects a child's educational performance." *Adaptive functioning* means having the skills to adapt to one's living environment (e.g., communication, self-help, social skills). It was added to the definition when it was noted that some students with low IQ scores but strong adaptive skills were still performing well in society.

Court Decisions

A wide variety of court decisions can affect Cathy and her right to a free appropriate public education. One of these decisions is *PARC v. Commonwealth of Pennsylvania* (1972) in which the state of Pennsylvania had a rule requiring children to have a mental age of 5 before being allowed to enter public school. Because Cathy experienced some developmental delays, this rule could have kept her from entering school at the age of 5 as her age mates were doing. The federal district court decided that because the Pennsylvania constitution said that *all* children were entitled to a free appropriate public education, this rule, in effect, canceled out a child's right to that education by delaying it until some future time when he or she could get a qualifying score in an IQ test. The court struck down that age-related provision.

Administrative Rules

PL 101-336 stipulated that schools and other public institutions must build ramps and any other accommodations so that children with mobility difficulties have access to learning environments necessary to an appropriate education. Because Cathy's condition of cerebral palsy interfered with her ability to be mobile and, for example, climb stairs, her school had to make sure that it complied with the ADA's requirements in order to ensure Cathy's access to a free appropriate public education.

Professional Initiatives

The major changes in the definition of mental retardation seem to be driven by professional initiatives as well as major social changes. A series of research studies were conducted to show that children diagnosed as having mental retardation could respond positively to a stimulating environment (Campbell & Ramey, 1995; Garber, 1988; Kirk, 1958; Weikart & Schwinehart, 1997) and cast doubt on the predictability of early diagnoses when special intervention was employed (Guralnick, 1997).

The evidence that a disproportionate number of minority students were being diagnosed as having mental retardation and were being placed in special education fed a growing reluctance to identify children as having mental retardation. The President's Committee on Mental Retardation (1970) pointed out that many children were classified as having mental retardation while in school but not before the school day began or after it was over. This report also questioned the reliability of mild mental retardation diagnoses. A seminal article by Dunn (1968) called into question the educational utility of the terms "educably retarded"' and "mild mental retardation." A reduction in the percentage of children labeled with mental retardation (Kirk, Gallagher, & Anastasiow, 2003) was a consequence of these various professional initiatives.

The prereferral consultation was followed with Cathy. The team felt that perhaps her disability was hiding more talent than was apparent in her current performance. They suggested some testing accommodations, such as taking off time limits on her work and the addition of special lessons on a computer adapted for her disability that would allow her to respond on the keyboard without writing, which was a special problem for her.

In many instances, prereferral teams' suggestions have had the effect of diminishing or removing the problem seen by classroom teachers and making a referral to special education unnecessary. In Cathy's case, however, these suggestions did not work. She continued to perform at a very slow and inaccurate pace and so was referred for special education placement. The IEP for Cathy will no doubt include the need to upgrade her achievement levels and learning skills and make adaptations for her motor and mobility problems.

Bobby and Emotional Disturbance

Bobby has a label that has been used for many decades: child with emotional disturbance. However, the attitudes about and diagnoses of emotional disturbance particularly in children, have varied remarkably over time. Kirk, Gallagher, and Anastasiow summarized the unhappy history of those now called *emotionally disturbed*:

> Two centuries ago children with behavior problems were believed to be possessed by the devil or insane, or mentally deficient. When attention was paid to them at all, they were shut away in large institutions with very little attention directed to their education. (2003, p. 256)

Professionals working with such children have become much more optimistic about outcomes of treatment (Rutherford, Quinn, & Mathur, 2004).

Legislation

The definition of the label *serious emotional disturbance* in PL 105-17 is:

(i) The term means a condition exhibiting one or more of the following characteristics over a long period of time and a marked degree that adversely affects a child's education performance—
   (A) An inability to learn what cannot be explained by intellectual, sensory, or health factors;
   (B) An inability to build or maintain satisfactory interpersonal relationships with peers and teachers;
   (C) Inappropriate types of behavior or feelings under normal circumstances;
   (D) A general pervasive mood of unhappiness or depressions; or
   (E) A tendency to develop physical symptoms or fears associated with personal or school problems.

(ii)   The term includes schizophrenia. The term does not apply to children who
       are socially maladjusted, unless it is determined that they do not have se-
       rious emotional disturbance. (§ 300.7 [c] [4])

One of the legislative issues not yet settled is whether to include children who
are socially maladjusted in this definition. These are children who cannot con-
form to commonly accepted social norms. Is Bobby "seriously emotionally disturbed" because he shows "inappropriate types of behavior or feelings under
normal circumstances"? The distinction between serious and prolonged internal disturbance (emotional disturbance) and the acting out of such feelings (behavior disturbance) has not impressed many clinicians or teachers, who feel most
of the children they encounter have a mixture of both.

A full supply of terms is designed to describe Bobby's behavior and the
behavior of students like him. These terms include *emotionally handicapped, socially maladjusted, behaviorally disturbed,* and *having social and emotional problems.*
All of these terms refer to four common features:

- Behavior that goes to an extreme—that is not just slightly different from
  the usual

- Problem that is chronic—that does not quickly disappear

- Behavior that is unacceptable because of social or cultural expectations

- Appearance of being chronically unhappy and dissatisfied with oneself and
  the environment (see Rutherford et al., 2004)

In addition, once a term is included in legislation or court decisions, it tends
to take on a life of its own and is difficult to replace. The term *seriously emotionally disturbed* was used in federal legislation and became a part of special education. In PL 99-457, the word *seriously* was removed.

Although the U.S. Department of Education has suggested 2% of school
children as a modest prevalence figure, other experts suggest that 3%–6% or
even higher would be an appropriate figure (Kauffman, 1994). These differences
in prevalence are due to the lack of a consensus about the definition of emotional disturbance. The conceptual difference appears to be that *social maladjust-
ment* implies that the causes of the condition may be in the environment rather
than the child, whereas the causes of *serious emotional disturbance* seem more internal to the child or, at least, to the family.

Court Decisions

One of the interesting aspects of this category is the question of what happens
to children and young adults who commit offenses and are subsequently in-
carcerated. The courts have ruled that such children remain under the protec-

tions of the IDEA; that is, they are still entitled to a free appropriate public education while in a juvenile detention facility or prison. A gray area appears once the child reaches the age of 18 and is no longer considered a child under the IDEA.

Professional Initiatives

A massive amount of research has been conducted regarding the causes of emotional disturbance (Kazdin, 2003; Plomin & McGuffin, 2003), and its diagnosis has changed the way that courts and legislation have looked at the condition. They see it as treatable given the proper amount of resources and commitment (Rutherford et al., 2004).

The use of punishment in changing behavior in a positive direction has been shown to be ineffective by decades of research evidence. The current trend in controlling unacceptable behavior is to conduct a *functional behavior assessment*. This means a careful assessment of the nonfunctional behavior that a student like Bobby would engage in and then the creation of situations in which his nonfunctional behavior no longer serves a purpose (known as positive behavior supports). *Positive behavior supports* create environments and patterns of support around the child to help him or her look on the problem behaviors as a waste of time and energy. Positive behavior supports do require time for some assessment to determine the purpose for the negative behavior in the first place.

Bobby has been involved in numerous pushing and shoving incidents at lunchtime with the boys in his class. Careful observation suggests that Bobby feels his status as a tough kid is being threatened by these boys, and he is reacting to that threat. Instead of disciplining him for fighting, the teacher may send Bobby as a daily messenger to the principal's office, thus changing the lunchtime environment so that Bobby is away from the threat to his self-image that might have been taking place. Bobby can even be praised for his good job as a messenger. Bobby's IEP will contain positive expectations for progress and other functional behavior assessments designed to improve his behavior and build in positive social skills.

A continuing controversy exists on the "stay put" requirement that keeps the child with disabilities in his or her regular classroom while disputes about his or her placement and his or her behavior are ongoing. This is particularly sensitive in the case of a child with disabilities who has become physically abusive to classmates and teachers. A conflict of rights exists: the right of the child with disabilities to a free appropriate public education is at odds with the rights of the other students and the teacher to personal safety and established classroom order. As noted earlier, IDEA 2004 now gives the school the authority to place children like Bobby, who threaten the well-being of other children or teachers, in an alternative educational setting for up to 45 days.

Gretchen and Gifted and Talented

The public decision making regarding children such as Gretchen, who seems to be considerably ahead of her age group in cognitive development, is quite different from decision making regarding children with disabilities. The importance of a definition in the case of children with disabilities lies in establishing federal eligibility for special services. In the case of Gretchen and her gifted classmates, no federal monies are provided for direct services, and therefore there is little motivation to haggle over fine points of definition; however, a general definition has been agreed on, and most of the states that have programs for gifted students follow this definition rather closely.

> Children and youth with outstanding talent perform, or show the potential for performing, at remarkably high levels of accomplishment when compared with others of their age, experience, or environment. These children and youth exhibit high-performance capabilities in intellectual, creative, and artistic areas; possess an unusual leadership capacity; or excel in specific academic fields. They require services or activities not ordinarily provided by the schools. Outstanding talents are present in children and youth from all cultural groups across all economic strata and in all areas of human endeavor. (Ross, 1993)

Legislation

The one piece of identifiable legislation at the federal level for the education of gifted students was the Jacob K. Javits Gifted and Talented Students Education Act of 1988 (PL 100-297), or Javits Act, which provided small sums of money for research and programs and established a National Research Center on the Gifted and Talented, based at the University of Connecticut. The influence of even such a small piece of legislation (funded by only $11.25 million) is shown by the priorities that the law set encouraging work on gifted students from economically disadvantaged and culturally diverse families. The number of articles and research projects focusing on that priority immediately increased. This law is now subpart 6 of No Child Left Behind.

Court Decisions

A number of court actions relate to the education of gifted and talented students, but most of them have been focused at the state level and have consequently not had a major impact on the national scene (Karnes & Marquardt, 2000). A number of legal procedures through the Office of Civil Rights have been brought against school systems because of the general lack of cultural diversity among students in school programs for gifted students. When local school systems are able to demonstrate good faith effort in seeking out students from a mix of cultures, no legal action is generally taken. The Office of Civil Rights cases have caught the interest of school systems, many of which have redoubled their efforts in seeking gifted and talented students from low-income neighborhoods and diverse cultural backgrounds.

Administrative Rules

Most of the rule making is found at the state level, where most of the legislative initiatives for gifted and talented students have taken place. An example of such a rule would be denying admittance to kindergarten programs for children until they reach a certain age (5 years generally). This means that students like Gretchen who are developmentally advanced cannot enter kindergarten early, even though their social and cognitive development is easily the equal of the other students in the kindergarten program. Some states (e.g., North Carolina) have passed legislation allowing early admittance to kindergarten once a student meets certain conditions.

Professional Initiatives

Professional associations such as the National Association for Gifted Children (NAGC) and The Association for the Gifted (TAG) in the CEC have developed a set of professional standards for programs and personnel who work directly with such students. For example, the NAGC (1991) standards state, "NAGC maintains that gifted students, like other children with special needs, require a full continuum of educational serves to aid in the development of the students' unique strengths and talents." This policy encourages special honors classes and advanced placement programs as part of a total program for gifted students at the local level.

Many professionals are frustrated that that the federal government recognizes the special needs of children with disabilities but not those of students like Gretchen, whose potential may have future consequences for the larger society. In this regard, equity has assumed a higher priority than excellence in educational support.

Infant and Toddler Eligibility

There is probably no clearer differentiation between professional knowledge and public action than the concern about infants and toddlers. For decades, the professional fields have known about the critical period of birth to 3 (infants and toddlers) for children with developmental disorders. In those years, a child with disabilities either is identified and has a treatment plan begun or is ignored until school age or until symptoms become so severe that they call attention to themselves.

Yet this is the last age group to benefit from public policy concerns about welfare. The lack of educational institutions at this age probably accounts for this difference. It is much easier to provide funds to public schools or even prekindergartens to aid a child in his or her adjustment than it is to provide support to individual families (Neuman, 2003).

Of the five children we have been following, Arnie was found in the infant and toddler stage because of his parents' concerns and his clear set of symptoms. Cathy was identified at birth by the medical staff but did not automatically receive educational intervention at that age. Les, Bobby, and Gretchen received later identification of their special needs because of their lack of clear symptomatology and the absence of systematic review of their development.

Legislation

The emergence of legislation and subsequent regulations for infants and toddlers with special needs resulted in a very different approach to definition and eligibility for services. There was no longer any emphasis on traditional diagnostic categories such as *emotional disturbance* or *mental retardation.* It was harder to make such a diagnosis for children so young, and diagnoses were not useful with children younger than 3 (PL 99-457). The eligibility criteria became as follows:

(a) As used in this part, *infants and toddlers with disabilities* means individuals from birth through age two who need early intervention services because they—
  (1) Are experiencing developmental delays, as measured by appropriate diagnostic instruments and procedures, in one of more of the following areas:
    (i) Cognitive development
    (ii) Physical development, including vision and hearing
    (iii) Communication development
    (iv) Social or emotional development
    (v) Adaptive development; or
  (2) Have a diagnosed physical or mental condition that has a high probability of resulting in developmental delay.
(b) The term may also include, at a state's discretion, children from birth through age two who are at risk of having substantial developmental delays if early intervention services are not provided. (§ 303.16 [a-b])

Note the focus on developmental delay rather than the proposed cause of the developmental delay. The cause may not lead to treatment, but the delays and strengths do. The pattern of delays and strengths form the hallmark of the individualized family service plan (IFSP), mandated for children with disabilities and their families from birth to age 5. A more extended discussion of the IFSP may be seen in Chapter 3.

Section (b) also includes children who are at risk of having developmental delays. This section accepts the proposition that professionals can intervene in the early years of a child with special needs or with a risk of developing special needs and can perhaps prevent developmental delay from occurring in its full form. For the first time, special educators, in working with preschool children, have been placed in a preventive role in working with children who are at risk, instead of a remedial role.

Once the developmental delay concept has been put into effect in the definition and eligibility standards for young children, such a change also calls into question the viability of the standard diagnostic categories for school-age children. If it is unclear whether the child should have a diagnosis of learning disabilities or mental retardation, what difference would each diagnosis make in the IEP? Many people believe that the IEP would look substantially the same because the child is still coping with developmental delays, and the IEP team members are still attempting to strengthen the child's abilities and cope with his or her limitations, regardless of diagnosis.

Court Decisions

One of the roles that courts have played is to address the protestations of the schools or other service providers in the face of legislative mandates. For example, PL 99-457, the act providing services for the infants and toddlers with disabilities, mandates that every young child who is identified in a state shall be provided special services as needed. A number of states protested that the federal government was forcing an unfunded mandate on the states and that they did not have the funds to comply. The lack of funds has been an argument for not providing services used in a number of cases (e.g., *Missouri v. Jenkins,* 1995; *Rainey v. Tennessee,* 1976), and it has failed in every case. The courts merely directed the schools to find the necessary money from the state legislature or from other available funds and to plan to have these funds in future budgets.

Administrative Rules

The rules in providing services for young children with disabilities focus on the role of the parents. The law establishes a state interagency coordinating council and requires that 20% of the council's members be parents of infants or toddlers with disabilities. Parents have the right of access to their child's educational records, and parents have the right to object to the release of personal information that might be embarrassing to the family. As Turnbull and Turnbull pointed out about the IDEA and the ADA, "The two laws (and their rules) indisputably can confer great benefits for families . . . individual families face the future with optimism and more arrows in their quivers than ever before" (2000, p. 315).

THE IMPACT OF RACE ON DIAGNOSIS AND CLASSIFICATION

The identification of children who are eligible for special education services has led the field of special education into a major social issue. As educators examined each child and referred him or her to special education, they found different proportions of children representing different ethnic and racial backgrounds (Donovan & Cross, 2002). Figure 2.1 shows the percentage of children placed in special education by race/ethnicity. Although 15% of students in the current resident U.S. school population are African American, they make up 20% of those who are in special education. The proportions of Hispanic and white students in special education basically correspond with their percentages in the resident population, while Asian American students appear in special education only one half as frequently as their proportion in the general population

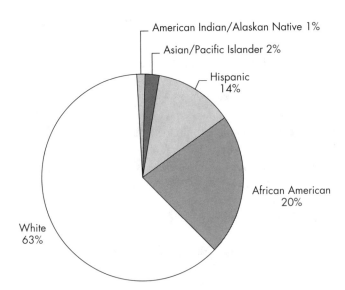

Figure 2.1. Percentage of students ages 6–21 in special education by race/ethnicity, 1998–1999. Reprinted from the U.S. Department of Education, Office of Special Education Programs. (2000). *Twenty-second annual report to Congress on the implementation of the Individuals with Disabilities Education Act.* (Table AA3). Washington, DC: U.S. Government Printing Office.

(U.S. Bureau of Census, 2000). Why is there an overrepresentation of African American students? Even more striking is the high percentage of African American students in programs for mental retardation (33%) and emotional disturbance (26%) (U.S. Department of Education, 2000). Schools have been subject to criticism about diverting African American students from educational opportunities by putting them in special education categories (Harry, 1994).

The disproportion issue is of large concern to special educators. Despite the suggestion that such statistics say more about the socioeconomic conditions in which African American students are raised (Kirk, Gallagher, & Anastasiow, 2003), many believe that these prevalence figures indicate that race may play a part in special education assignments. The U.S. Congress received many inquiries about possible civil rights violations related to special education placements and asked the National Research Council of the National Academy of Sciences in 2001 to assemble a group of experts to determine whether any disproportion existed, and if it did, what the causes of these differences between cultural subgroups could be. The Office of Civil Rights asked the National Research Council to look at the proportion of various cultural groups in programs for gifted students as well.

Figure 2.2 shows the risk index for each ethnic group in the three major diagnostic categories. The risk index is calculated by dividing the number of students in a given racial or ethnic category served in a given disability category (e.g., learning disabilities) by the total enrollment for that racial or ethnic group in the whole population. In the diagnosis of mental retardation, African American students are identified twice as often as white students and four times as often as Asian American students (Donovan & Cross, 2002). Although the figures for identification of students with learning disabilities in Figure 2.2 seem reasonably equal among African American, white, and Hispanic groups, each of them is identified at a rate of almost 3 to 1 over Asian American students.

For the label of serious emotional disturbance, the spread in student race/ethnicity is conspicuous. African American students are identified at a rate of 1.5 to 1 over white students, 3.0 to 1 over the rate of Hispanic students and 7 to 1 over the rate of Asian American students. Clearly, forces outside and inside the educational establishment are affecting these numbers to make them so unbalanced. The National Academy of Sciences panel proposed to search for the answers to four major questions by examining the available literature and by interviewing specialists (Donovan & Cross, 2002).

1. Is there reason to believe that there is currently a higher incidence of special needs or giftedness among some racial/ethnic groups? Specifically, are there biological and social or contextual contributors to early development that differ by race or ethnicity?

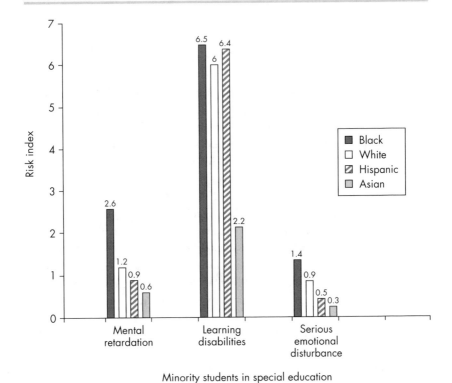

Figure 2.2. Risk indicators by race. (From Donovan, S., & Cross, C. [Eds.]. [2002]. *Minority students in special and gifted education.* Washington, DC: National Academies Press; adapted by permission.)

The panel concluded that the answer to this question was clearly "yes." Different rates of mild disabilities in ethnic and racial groups seem attributable to the effects of poverty. Poverty is unequally distributed among racial and ethnic groups and is closely associated with low birth weight and higher rates of exposure to harmful toxins. It also seems to result in a less supportive home environment.

2. Does school independently contribute to the incidence of special needs or giftedness among students in different racial/ethnic groups through the opportunities that it provides?

The panel also answered "yes" to this question. Furthermore, the panel noted that high-quality education is related to financial status, with the more experienced and better teachers providing the faculty for schools in high-income areas. It would take a higher financial commitment to schools in poor neighborhoods to equalize the advantages of high-quality education, and there is little evidence that this is being done.

3. Does the current referral and assessment process reliably identify students with special needs and giftedness? In particular, is there reason to believe that the current process is biased in terms of race or ethnicity?

The panel is not certain of the answer to this question. When teachers identify more children from low-income neighborhoods than from higher-income neighborhoods, are they revealing their own biases or are they merely correctly identifying the children who are in trouble, a disproportionate number of such children coming from minority families? Perhaps some racial bias exists in the assessment procedure, but the panel is sure that many students who need and can benefit from those programs are not being found.

4. Is placement in special education a benefit or a risk? Does the outcome differ by race or ethnic group?

Do special education services pay off for children or does the placement of students in special education merely relegate the students to low expectations and limited teaching? The panel points out that parent advocacy and teacher quality, both of which correlate with higher-quality interventions, are less likely in low-income school districts where minority children are concentrated. The panel is quite clear, however, on one point: "There is substantial evidence with regard to both behavior and achievement that early identification and intervention is more effective than later identification and intervention" (Donovan & Cross, 2002, p. 6). The panel noted that the usual process of identification for special education has been based on a "wait-to-fail" principle, and they recommended much earlier identification and intervention at a developmental time when it is easier to diminish and remediate developmental delays.

DECISIONS AHEAD

Major questions remain to be answered before educators and policy makers can move confidently into a brighter future for special education and for the children whom they wish to help. This and each subsequent chapter close with a few of the significant questions that require attention.

Purpose: Diagnoses

Should professionals diagnose for cause of the condition or for educational intervention? As discussed earlier, the linkage between medical diagnoses and educational intervention can be weak. Unlike clinical medicine, in which the correct diagnosis generally leads to the proper treatment, a diagnosis such as Down syndrome or fragile X syndrome rarely leads to a definitive educational plan without much further multidisciplinary analysis. The cause of the condition might enable medical doctors to provide neurological or genetic treatments (e.g., gene replacement) that could result in improvement or cure, but professionals working with children with disabilities must be aware of the question they wish diagnoses to answer. If they are seeking eligibility for educational services, then they are interested in a pattern of developmental delays that they must plan for and intervene in appropriately.

Systemization of the Prereferral System

Although many school systems follow a prereferral process in which the classroom teacher attempts to intervene with the child prior to full referral for special education services, such practices are unevenly followed across the country. In many respects, the procedure of prereferral consultation is similar to the medical practice of prescribing the lowest dosage of a medicine and then observing the results. If the patient does not improve, a higher dose or stronger medicines may be prescribed with a greater risk of other complications. Prereferral consultations in education are the least potent educational treatment that can be tried before moving on to stronger measures in special education. Because there seems to be some benefit to this procedure, should this process be formalized in legislative regulations so that everyone uses this process as a prerequisite to referral for special education services? Legislation is periodically reauthorized, which gives the opportunity for legislative language to be added for the prereferral process (Chalfant, 1989).

Creation of Measurement
Instruments for New Definitions

Professionals sometimes fail to realize that measurement instruments arrive to meet perceived needs and not before! The intelligence test by Alfred Binet was created because he wished to have an instrument that could separate children with cognitive limitations from those who are just doing poorly in school. When people look for a measure of social development of 3-year-old children and fail to find it, it is because no one has realized the importance of studying this characteristic at this age (Shonkoff & Phillips, 2000).

Even when measurements such as those that might provide the careful delineation of learning difficulties are clearly needed, they may be missing or inadequate because no one has yet realized how much time, effort, and resources must be invested to create a valid and reliable instrument. A minimum of 5 years would be necessary to complete the cycle of initial construction, trial run, revision, full field test, distribution, and so forth. If science flies on the wings of its measuring instruments, then researchers need some more planning for instrument development before they will be able to take flight. Nor should tests be the only measuring instruments to be constructed. Structured parental interviews or description of learning environments (Harms & Clifford, 1990) or classroom observation protocols can provide useful information as well.

In the search for children who need help, educators and policy makers need to be clear as to what questions they are trying to answer. Do they wish to determine the origin or cause of the child's disability or do they wish to discover developmental patterns that will aid in planning an IEP for him or her? The answer to these questions will determine the future search for information about the child.

CHAPTER 3

Differentiated Programs for Children with Disabilities

C hapters 1 and 2 outline how decisions are made in establishing special education, determining eligibility criteria for receiving services, and identifying children who need special education services. This chapter covers the decision making involved in answering the following questions: "What will educators and policy makers design for these students with special needs that is special?" and "How should the standard education program be changed to meet individual needs more adequately?" The design of a program for school-age children with disabilities often starts from the general education program or curriculum. If the goal of the school is to produce students who can read and comprehend much of the world around them, then this can be a starting place for determining how many of the requirements each child with disabilities should meet and how these requirements should be changed.

The question is "How do educators help students who are several grade levels behind in academic performance meet the general education standards?" If children such as Arnie, Les, Bobby, Cathy, and Gretchen differ from the other children so much that they are labeled exceptional, then major changes in content and teaching style are needed in order to make the general education program appropriate for them. This is why there is a call for differentiated programs for such children (Graham & Harris, 2003).

DETERMINING REQUIREMENTS FOR DIFFERENTIATION

Chapters 1 and 2 address engines of change—legislation, court decisions, administrative rules, and professional initiatives—and their roles in decision making. These four forces have been present in the decisions as to what the programs should be for exceptional children, if the programs for children with typical development do not work or are not appropriate for children with special needs.

Legislation

PL 94-142, the Education for All Handicapped Children Act of 1975, initially called for the development of an IEP for each child with special needs, and all subsequent amendments include this requirement. The most complex of the six principles established by this law, the IEP has been a constant source of controversy since its first appearance.

The IEP is the foundation for differentiated programs for individual children. Typically, it has goals for academic, social, and self-control behavior. The IEP is designed to note specifically the ways in which a program should be differentiated for an individual student and includes appropriate methods of assessment and required accommodations and services. The IEP team is required to ensure that the student is in the LRE and has access to a free appropriate public education. However, legislation cannot possibly address all of the necessary details involved in the process of IEP construction (e.g., who should attend the IEP meetings, how parents should be involved). A large part of the controversy over the principle of the IEP lies in the difficulty with implementing it.

The usual strategy used to deal with problems that have arisen with experience, or were ignored in the first place, is to amend the existing legislation rather than to create new legislation. IDEA has been the successor to PL 94-142 and has seen numerous amendments to the earlier provisions. The latest version, IDEA 2004, makes it clear that students with disabilities should have access to the general education curriculum.

For example, IDEA 2004 takes out the provision that planning for transition from school to work should begin at age 14 and now states that such planning must begin by age 16 (CEC, 2004). This change is apparently resulting from a legislative desire to give exceptional children as much contact with the general education curriculum as possible before moving into career planning.

Court Decisions

The courts are a powerful tool that has been used to ensure equity for children with special needs. Regarding differentiated programming, the courts reinforce the inclusion principles and ensure a free appropriate public education. Because the concepts of inclusion and LRE are rather general, courts often must specify just what is appropriate in individual cases. A legal device for shaping behavior developed by the courts has been the establishment of presumptions (Stowe & Turnbull, 2001). The most familiar legal presumption is that a person is presumed innocent until proven guilty. The comparable presumption in disability law is that a student will be included in general school environments to the maximum extent appropriate for benefit to the student. Just as in a trial where the prosecution bears the burden of proof of guilt beyond a reasonable doubt, the educator is under pressure to demonstrate that, even after providing supplemental aids and services, the child with disabilities cannot be educated in an inclusive setting.

In *Board of Education, Sacramento Unified School District v. Holland,* (1994), the courts went to considerable extent to explain what was meant by the presumption favoring inclusion:

> The Act's presumption in favor of mainstreaming (inclusion) requires that a handicapped child be educated in a regular classroom if the child can receive a satisfactory education there, even if it is not the best academic setting for that child. (1994, p. 1403)

In other words, benefits beyond the academic program justify inclusion, such as interaction with peers without disabilities and development of social skills. The court was not impressed with the possible negative effects of including the child with disabilities in the general classroom yet recognized the need to minimize the demands on the classroom teacher.

When an appropriate array of supplementary aids and services are present, the courts often respond positively to the school plan for inclusion. In *Jonathon G. v. Lower Merion School District* (1997), parents who opposed inclusion were rebuffed by the court because of supplementary services that were present, including a "learning support teacher," a speech-language pathologist, a reading specialist, and a counselor to minimize the child's anxiety. Etscheidt and Bartlett (1999) reported many favorable court decisions when the school testified to the presence of a variety of supplementary aids and services. They concluded, "The key to efforts to educate children with disabilities in regular education settings is good faith, meaningful considerations of the provision of supplementary aids and services" (p. 173).

Arnie's IEP points out that he becomes agitated and upset in unstructured and noisy situations and needs periods of calm and one-to-one instruction. Thus, periodic removal of Arnie from the general setting is necessary in order to ensure that he responds well to the education setting. But such arguments for removing Arnie for a period of time must be made in writing, and the school must be ready to provide evidence to counter the presumption that the child would be better off in the general education setting. The schools of Cathy, Les, and Bobby would have a more difficult time justifying departure from the general education program because the presumption is that the general classroom is the best setting for them. Such a presumption always assumes that the resources necessary to their special education will be present.

Fewer court cases address early childhood services because the number of children is much fewer and there has not been an established public-school bureaucracy with which to conflict. When a dispute arises, it often involves the proposed method of treatment. In *Still v. DeBuono* (1996), parents had a dispute with the Department of Health, which was providing some treatment for an autistic child. The parents wanted applied behavior analysis (ABA) therapy, but the state agency did not agree. The department did not provide this therapy because it did not deliver such therapy for children younger than 3. The court decided in favor of the parents because the agency was providing the available treatment instead of a treatment based on the needs of the child. This is an all-too-prevalent occurrence. A child often gets what the local agency has available rather than what he or she needs (Lewis, Lewis-Palmer, Newcomer, & Sticher, 2004).

Administrative Rules

When major changes in educational procedures are proposed by legislation, often a multitude of details must be addressed. The courts are often not sufficiently knowledgeable about the details of the educational programming to provide the answers to questions regarding inclusion, such as how to determine when a child should be removed from the classroom for special therapies or instruction. Therefore, the responsibility for specifying the requirements for differentiated programming falls to the responsible state or federal agency, which must write detailed regulations to try to give guidance to educators attempting to carry out the policies mandated by legislators. Two policies in which the administrative rules have mushroomed over the past years have been the IEP and inclusion. These rules often have a major impact on the policies themselves.

The law guarantees that an IEP should be adopted, but administrative rules determine how the IEP is implemented. It is in the implementation that substantial conflict has developed. For example, a special educator wishing to carry out the policies correctly would want to know who should attend the IEP meetings, what the role of the parents should be, what happens if the parents don't wish to participate, what actual dimensions should be included, and so forth. Administrative rule making must state explicitly the answers to these questions.

An example of a regulation directing the plan for students with disabilities is the requirement for transition services to be part of the IEP. This requirement, in turn, came from the professional insight that students often reached the end of their school experience with little or no planning for what comes next. The IDEA 1997 regulation 300.347 aims to ensure that some thought is given to the differentiated programming in the next phase of the student's life:

Transition services. The IEP must include—
(1) For each student with a disability beginning at age 14 (or younger, if determined appropriate by the IEP team), and updated annually, a statement of the transition service needs of the student under the applicable compo-

nents of the student's IEP that focuses on the student's courses of study (such as participation in advanced-placement courses or a vocational education program); and

(2) For each student beginning at age 16 (or younger, if determined appropriate by the IEP team), a statement of needed transition services for the student, including, if appropriate, a statement of the interagency responsibilities of any needed linkages. (§ 300.347 [b])

One of the other clear presumptions of the legislation and accompanying regulations is that parents should play a key role in the IEP development for a child with disabilities. This presumption is made clear in the IDEA 1997 regulations (300.345), which place the burden of proof on the schools if the parent is not present at the IEP meeting. The school must make an extended effort to enlist the parent's cooperation, and it must document that effort.

(d) Conducting an IEP meeting without a parent in attendance. A meeting may be conducted without a parent in attendance if the public agency is unable to convince the parents that they should attend. In this case the public agency must have a record of its attempts to arrange a mutually agreed on time and place, such as—

(1) Detailed records of telephone calls made or attempted and the results of those calls;

(2) Copies of correspondence sent to the parents and any responses received; and

(3) Detailed records of visits made to the parent's home or place of employment and the results of those visits. (§ 300.345 [d])

The administrative rules cover a multitude of issues and questions. A sample of a few rules addressing professional–parent relationships are

• If parents refuse to use mediation, they may be required to meet with a disinterested third party to learn about the benefits of mediation before proceeding to a due-process hearing, though they cannot be required to participate in mediation proceedings.

• Any party aggrieved by an administrative decision on a complaint under Part C has the right to bring a civil action in state or federal district court. The court must receive the records of the administrative proceedings, hear any additional evidence (at a party's request), and grant appropriate relief based upon a preponderance of the evidence (20 U.S.C. § 1439 [a] [1]).

• Any parents involved in administrative proceedings have the right to be accompanied and advised by counsel or other people with special knowledge or training in early intervention; to present evidence and confront,

cross-examine, and compel the attendance of witnesses; to prohibit the use
of evidence not disclosed to them at least 5 days before the proceeding; to
obtain a written or electronic verbatim transcript; and to obtain written
findings of facts and decisions (34 C.F.R. § 303.422).

See Turnbull and Turnbull (2000) for an extended discussion of these regulations and their implementation.

Professional Initiatives

The professional community has contributed to the differentiation of programming for children with special needs in many major ways. When legislators or
court decisions call for a *universal design for learning* (UDL) to allow children
with disabilities to have alternative avenues to master key concepts, it is the responsibility of the professional community to create such alternative avenues.
Another professional responsibility is the establishment of content standards
on which the standard curriculum is based. Because many children with special needs are not able to meet high content standards in the sciences or language arts, this has put pressure on educators to design alternative plans for
such children as Arnie, Les, Bobby, and Cathy. Another major professional contribution involves many intervention projects that have been carried out over
the past few decades. These required the design of intervention content, which,
in turn, could become part of the special education curriculum, especially in
the early years when little guidance or standards were available from the mainstream community.

STANDARDS MOVEMENT AND SPECIAL EDUCATION

Any major initiative in general education has the potential to influence children
with special needs. One example of this impact can be seen in the standards
movement. Many Americans have been concerned about a lack of rigor in the
general education curriculum. In an attempt to repair that problem, major efforts
have been made to establish high standards in content fields such as science,
mathematics, and social studies and to develop tests that measure students'
mastery of these high standards (McDonnell, McLaughlin, & Morrison, 1997).
Such tests almost always determine the curriculum because teachers are anxious
for their students to do well, and they teach to the content of the tests. As is
usual in general education initiatives, special education professionals were not
consulted:

> It appears that special education has not played a major role in the development
> of either state content standards or specific curriculum frameworks in most states.

Rather, special education's involvement has generally been limited to a review of standards and curriculum documents prepared by other educators, if then. (McDonnell et al., 1997, p. 35)

The legislators who composed Goals 2000: Educate America Act of 1994, which mandated content standards, made it clear that when they said, "All children should reach these standards," they included children with disabilities. States have likewise expected that students with disabilities should participate in statewide, end-of-year examinations. The requirement that children with disabilities take the tests was done in the spirit of including students with disabilities in opportunities to experience high content standards. Now there are concerns about whether these are reasonable expectations for some students with disabilities. The National Academy of Sciences established a panel of educators and social scientists for the explicit purpose of trying to blend the needs of children with disabilities with the goals of the standards movement (McDonnell et al., 1997). This panel pointed out that although the standards have been established mainly in the content fields, many of the special educational goals for students with disabilities, which are spelled out in their IEPs, involve outcomes in vocational, workplace skills, and other areas of learning.

Should Arnie be expected, at the secondary level, to master standards in mathematics or science when his IEP will likely include his learning some useful vocational skills, transitions from school to work, and so forth? The assumption that it is important and necessary for *all* students to master complex content information in formal course areas overlooks the entire area of vocational education and career education.

EARLY EDUCATION PROGRAMS

Professional initiatives to develop early education programs have been numerous. These include early intervention programs, curriculum development, and extensive work with families (Guralnick, 1997; Kendziora, 2004; Turnbull & Turnbull, 2000). One of the earliest professional initiatives was an early intervention research project conducted by Kirk (1958). In a carefully designed study, he compared groups of young children with mental retardation who had early intervention with comparable groups of children with mental retardation who did not receive services. The two groups of children with mental retardation (community and institutional) who had early stimulation based on their developmental needs improved substantially over their comparison groups, with some of the children no longer being considered mentally retarded. Yet little notice was made of this study. Apparently, the other social forces needed to stir public action (e.g., political acceptance, professional interest, financial viability) were not present at that time. If the study had been done 10 years later, it would likely have played an important part in the move toward early intervention.

Research often must await the right social climate to catch the public's eye. In a review of early intervention programs, Guralnick (1997) confirmed the earlier results that differentiated programming based on individual needs did result in a one half to three quarters standard deviation gain on achievement and intelligence tests (8–12 IQ points). This provided the rationale for investing resources in this age group.

Two other events substantially influenced the public attitude and interest toward early childhood. The first was the establishment of the Head Start program in 1965 (through the Economic Opportunity Act of 1964, PL 88-452), which was designed to help students from lower socioeconomic backgrounds to get ready for school. The second event was the development of *Sesame Street,* the long-running public television program designed to help children learn basic information that would help them in school.

If it had not been for Head Start, which focused attention on the development of young children from lower socioeconomic backgrounds (serving 4-year-old children at first, then some 3-year-olds), it might have taken a good deal longer to focus public decision makers on the needs of young children with disabilities (Zigler & Styfco, 1994). *Sesame Street* was staffed by a mixture of child development specialists and entertainers, which resulted in an unusual combination of entertainment and preschool developmental lessons. Several generations of children and their parents have enjoyed this popular program, which focuses public attention on the importance of the preschool years in preparing children for entrance to school (Wilcox & Kunkel, 1996). Although the program did not achieve the strong positive results with children from lower socioeconomic levels as was hoped, it became a part of the American scene and remains so until this day.

INDIVIDUALIZED EDUCATION PROGRAM (IEP)

One of the major tools for program differentiation is the IEP. This allows the IEP team to plan for alternative programming to meet curriculum goals and also to ensure that the student has the skills and attitudes to be ready for learning. Although highly individualized, IEPs contain some common information. One of the key elements in the IEP is some statement of the student's present status. The present status is the place from which the individual program will develop. In order to obtain a status statement, school records and the administration of some appropriate measures must be incorporated. Another section of the IEP lists the annual goals, which reveal what is expected for the student if his or her individual program goes well. Next, the objectives section includes a quantifiable measure of growth designed to meet the general goals statement. Also included is a list of the special education services that would counteract the difficulties the student is experiencing, according to his or her present status. Another key element in the IEP is a section that outlines how the student's progress will be assessed. An annual review of the IEP is expected to satisfy the staff that progress is being made and to suggest some additions or changes if progress is not sufficient.

Members of the Individualized Education Program Team

The IEP team includes the parents of the student and any personnel who work with the student to provide services. Curriculum adaptations for children with special needs require well-trained personnel from many disciplines. Certainly, the professional initiatives for such personnel preparation need to be observed and monitored. Personnel preparation programs for young children with disabilities are just being developed in many instances and may need help from the various engines of change. Who makes the important decisions about a program for a young child with disabilities? One of the ways in which decisions are made regarding such innovations as multidisciplinary programming is to designate, by law, what disciplines can work with infants and children with disabilities. Part C of the IDEA does that, and a list of specialists can be seen in Table 3.1.

This does not mean, of course, that professionals from all of the disciplines listed are expected to deal with each child, but there is an expectation that professionals in those disciplines relevant to a particular child should be included in the development of an IEP, an IFSP, or the long-term plans for the child and family. For example, Cathy should be seen by her physician, occupational therapist, and physical therapist to plan a regimen of physical activities to help her increase mobility. Children with physical handicaps often have a problem in getting access to education because of mobility problems, and these problems should be dealt with as a part of a comprehensive IEP. For her communication problems and her learning difficulties, Cathy should also receive help from the speech-language pathologist and special educator.

Bobby and other children with behavior problems would probably interact with a psychologist and a social worker in addition to the special educator. The psychologist should have some ideas on how to cope with the behavioral outbursts, and the social worker would have the difficult job of working with a family hostile to the school in the hopes of interpreting the school's goals and procedures.

Arnie would have a wide array of specialists forming a multidisciplinary team to help him. The physical therapist should help with his motor incoor-

Table 3.1. The role of multidisciplinary staff

Specialist	Function
Audiologist	Determines if hearing losses are present
Ophthalmologist	Determines if vision losses are present
Early childhood special educator	Plans and administers a program for mediation of impairments and coordinates special therapies
Physician	Determines if a biological or health deficit exists and plans treatment
Nurse	Provides a plan for adequate health care
Occupational therapist	Promotes individual development of self, self-help skills, play, and autonomy
Physical therapist	Enhances motor development and suggests prostheses and positioning strategies; provides needed therapies
Psychologist	Provides a comprehensive document of the child's strengths and weaknesses and helps the family cope with the stress of having a child with disabilities
Social worker	Assists the family in implementing appropriate child-rearing strategies and helps families locate services as needed
Speech-language pathologist	Provides the necessary assessment plan for needed therapies and delivers services in appropriate cases

From Kirk, S.A., Gallagher, J.J., & Anastasiow, N. (2003). *Educating exceptional children* (10th ed. p. 93). Boston: Houghton Mifflin; reprinted by permission.

dination, the speech-language pathologist would try to increase Arnie's spoken language, and the psychologist and special educator would surely be working on his current developmental status and how lessons need to be modified to fit his particular behavior patterns.

It is easy enough to call for multidisciplinary planning and implementation of programs, but it is difficult if the specialists are not geographically in the same place. We can hope that educators will become used to these adaptations of current practice so that the skills of each specialty become used to the maximum for children who have many needs to be satisfied.

Of course, Gretchen will need some additional personnel to help her with her highly advanced thinking and achievement, which causes planning problems for the general education teacher because Gretchen has already mastered the majority of her curriculum for her grade level before the first day of school. Gretchen could use the psychologist to properly assess her advanced skills and then perhaps some content specialists to provide her and the general education teacher with some challenging curriculum projects in those content fields where she has been especially productive (Van Tassel-Baska, 2003). All students require well-qualified professionals for an appropriate education. If educators and policy makers cut corners on this, they will never know the full potential of children with special needs.

Role of the Individualized Education Program Team

The IEP team is responsible for creating an IEP that all members agree on. The team must address many questions: Should the student have access to a calculator or word processor? Should alternative tests be considered? Should cooperative learning or reciprocal teaching be considered? Is assistive technology required? Does the student require a paraprofessional to assist him or her? Should the general education teacher and the special education teacher consider coteaching? Should the general education teacher be provided time for additional training on issues such as behavior management? The questions that each IEP team must answer will change depending on the student's needs.

One of the shortcomings of IEP team planning is a potential lack of access to new knowledge about treatment on the part of the team members. Such teams are often asked to plan for students like Bobby, whose tendency to physical and verbal violence is disturbing the teacher. Yet, if the team members are not aware of the current research on *positive behavior supports*, they cannot include some positive features to the plan.

POLICY IMPLEMENTATION AND ITS PROBLEMS

Although all of the engines of change have been instrumental in creating the differentiation of programs for children with special needs, there remains the problem of policy implementation. Each of the changes described here conflicted with the status quo and often with well-established procedures and values. Such policies as inclusion, content standards, and special discipline, while solving some problems, create some others. The IEP and IFSP, a plan for young children with special needs, are outstanding examples of implementation problems. They were designed to ensure the individualization of programming for students but have been met with many concerns and some outright resistance.

When the IEP appears to be working effectively, it is given credit for establishing better relationships between the teacher and the family or helping the family to be more effective in grasping what the goals of the school are with regard to their child. The IEP can also shape the goals and program directions for individual children so that all of the educators involved with a child understand what the purposes of the special programming are and what the IEP team is attempting to accomplish. Also, when the IEP appears to be working, it provides a consistent instrument for checking on the progress that individual children are making. Teams have a chance to determine whether the child is profiting from their efforts.

Table 3.2. Individualized education program (IEP) benefits and drawbacks

Benefits	Drawbacks
Better relationship between the teacher and the family	Perception of IEP as paperwork with no real meaning
Better understanding of special education program for family	Heavy time demands on teacher
Clarification of goals and program directions	Lack of support or involvement by other staff
Production of information on academic progress	Possible result of a narrow and rigid curriculum
	Lack of consistent parent involvement

From Gallagher, J., & Desimone, L. (1995). Lessons learned from implementation of the IEP: Application to the IFSP. *Topics in Early Childhood Special Education, 15,* 353–378; adapted by permission.

But there are many perceived negatives, as well, as Table 3.2 shows. In many instances, the IEP is seen as mere paperwork, with more forms to fill out, and it certainly requires a lot of time on the part of the teacher and other personnel involved. One of the unintended consequences of the IEP may be that the program for the child is limited to the stated goals in the document itself, and there are no perceived reasons to go further with this child beyond the IEP goals. Despite the major effort to use the IEP as one of the tools to get parents involved with their child and the school, widespread lack of consistent parental involvement in the program has been reported.

Parents themselves sometimes say that when they signed on to an IEP program, they did not really understand it or its consequences. Parents also report that they are intimidated by the situation of an IEP meeting when they walk into a room with seven or eight specialists who all have ideas about what they think the child should be doing. Parents generally have little background or preparation for such a meeting (Gallagher & Desimone, 1995).

As mentioned in Chapter 1, policy is about power. In this instance, legislative efforts have been made to provide power to the parents involved in the life of their own child. In selected instances, school personnel may resent the power given to parents. From their standpoint, the power is being taken away from the educators, who know what to do, and given to the parent, who has not had the training of the professionals. Consequently, administrators may follow the letter of the regulations but not the spirit of the parent involvement.

Certainly, many steps could be taken to improve the IEP conference and the subsequent family–school relationships. One simple step might be a videotape of a successful IEP conference that could be shown to the parents prior to their own IEP conference so they could obtain some notion as to how this process works. It would be helpful if more special educators faced up to the possible power struggle and understood the psychodynamics of the complex interactions in the IEP conference itself.

INDIVIDUALIZED FAMILY SERVICE PLAN (IFSP)

IFSPs have some of the same problems as their cousins, IEPs. Gallagher and Desimone (1995) made several suggestions for the improvement of the IFSP process:

1. Prepare parents and professionals.

Many parents come to the IFSP sessions ill prepared to play the role expected of them. Professionals have acknowledged that parents need to be better educated about their role prior to the IFSP meeting. This is not surprising given that participation is a novel experience for many parents and that it is somewhat unnerving to be surrounded by a group of professionals asking them what they want for their child. An orientation meeting for the parents about the IFSP, perhaps supplemented by videotapes of a good IFSP session, could help ease the concerns of many parents.

Professionals, too, may find these IFSP sessions to be quite novel and may need some preparation as well. They can learn more about helping the parents feel comfortable in the session and encouraging them to express their views. Some short-term workshops should be sufficient for this purpose.

2. Take enough time.

Crafting an effective IFSP takes time, and time is often something that professionals have in very short supply. They find themselves hurrying through their paperwork so they can get to their hands-on contact with parents and child. Bailey (1991) pointed out that organizations need to realize that time is the most important resource they can provide for their staff that would allow them to develop high-quality interpersonal relationships, service planning, and delivery.

Any one professional should have to participate in a finite number of meetings and IFSPs. This might mean that not every professional should meet with the committee as long as the substantive areas are covered by someone at the meeting. And there should be a limit to how many IFSPs any staff member should be responsible for developing and writing.

3. Schedule a mandatory review and update.

The only way to make the IFSP a living document is to pull it out every 2 or 3 months and adjust it to meet the current circumstances as well as see to what extent the original goals were met or were even appropriate, given the benefit of hindsight. This recommendation would seem to be odd given that the law requires a 6-month review, but such a review is easily overlooked under the pressure of other tasks. It is clear that the establishment of policy, while important, requires appropriate implementation if it is to succeed in its purposes.

In elementary school, students are expected to be respectful of other students and of the teachers, to avoid physical confrontations, and to share and cooperate in the various tasks that are a part of the school program. The degree to which educators should tolerate departure from those social standards and what can they do about such departures also makes up a part of the individual planning for the students. The decisions regarding the programming for young children as appears in the IFSP are quite different from the IEP because there is no guidance from the regular school curriculum in terms of planning. Also, the greater importance of the family brings them more into the active planning to improve the developmental progress of these young children.

INDIVIDUALIZED EDUCATION
PROGRAMS AS PROGRAM DIFFERENTIATION

Program differentiation can be seen through the lens of the IEP, which addresses the specific ways in which program differentiation will work for an individual student. The following two subsections show selections from Les's and Bobby's IEPs. Note the differences and similarities.

Les

Table 3.3 presents some of the highlights from the IEP for Les, the boy with a specific learning disability. Les has been determined to have the ability to succeed in school, but he has not been achieving as expected. So, the main question is "Why is Les having trouble with grade-level reading comprehension skills?

According to his IEP, Les is expected to gain at least a grade level in reading comprehension as measured by standardized tests. It has also been noted that Les is down on himself because of his inferior performance in school, and so another goal is for Les to gain more confidence in his abilities. Children with learning disabilities also have been reported as having many social difficulties in addition to their academic difficulties, so educators have been sensitive to the social domain (Kavale & Forness, 1996).

A key element in any IEP is the special education services that will counteract the current trends seen in Les's school performance. In this instance, a specialist in learning disabilities and dyslexia will provide Les with some remedial reading lessons. Exercises in phonics, using his intact auditory sense, may help him unscramble the visual cues he must learn in reading. The remedial expert will present Les with periodic oral reading tests to check his progress. If Les's

Table 3.3. Individualized education program highlights for Les

Present status

Les is a boy of average or above average abilities, but he has been having severe problems with reading. This problem has caused him to lose confidence in his own abilities. He refers to himself as "dumb."

Annual goals

Les is expected to improve his reading comprehension scores by one grade level by the end of the school year. He is also expected to have a higher opinion of himself by that time.

Objectives

Les will improve one grade level on the Iowa Test of Basic Skills during the school year.

Les will gain 20 percentile points on the Coopersmith Self-Concept scale.

Special education services

Les will be given 30-minute tutorial sessions 3 days per week from a specialist in learning disabilities who will use auditory stimuli to help Les with his visual perception problems.

Les's parents will be given some additional remedial exercises that can be applied at home to supplement Les's tutorial work. Positive reinforcement will be given to improve Les's self-image.

How to measure progress

A portfolio of writing assignments will be kept to indicate the progress Les is making in language usage and development.

The Coopersmith Self-Concept scale will be readministered.

use of written language is an issue, then a portfolio of his written assignments, when arranged chronologically, can display his growth.

Finally, Les will be given a self-concept test at the beginning of his program and again near the end of the school year to indicate whether his self-image has improved over time. There is some concern that a 30-minute tutoring session three times per week with the specialist just might not be enough to turn his situation around, and so more intense and longer treatment periods might be called for. The IEP team will look carefully at his progress at the annual review to determine what changes should be made. None of these changes would be likely to happen without the legislation and rules requiring it.

Bobby

Table 3.4 provides the IEP highlights for Bobby, the student with emotional and behavior problems. Because these plans are truly individual, Bobby's program does not resemble Les's program very much. In terms of present status,

Table 3.4. Individualized education program (IEP) highlights for Bobby

Present status

Bobby is a pleasant-looking boy of average ability who is decidedly behind in school achievement for his grade level. He has had a long history of temper outbursts that have frightened other children and interfered with his social acceptance. Bobby's mother blames the school's incompetence for his misbehavior.

Annual goals

Bobby will reduce his classroom outbursts, improve his academic status, and form some friendships during the school year.

Objectives

Bobby will reduce by 25% his weekly outbursts by June 1.

Bobby will improve by .75 grade levels on the Stanford Achievement Test for reading and math.

Bobby will form one or two friendships evident to the teacher by June 1.

Special education services

Bobby's IEP recommends a functional assessment of his behavior in order to identify the causes or triggers of his temper outburst. A team of people has been identified to conduct such an assessment and report to the general education teacher with the results. A special consultant on behavioral problems will work with Bobby's teacher to develop special strategies to cope with Bobby's outbursts.

How to measure progress

A chart of the number of outbursts over time will be kept by Bobby's teacher.

The Stanford Achievement Test will be administered.

---

more attention is paid to Bobby's behavioral outbursts, which always catch the attention of the teacher and those around him. He is clearly not ready to learn. But attention should also be paid to the fact that Bobby's achievement has suffered. Even though he has average ability, he performs quite below the grade level average in academic subjects, not an uncommon experience for children with emotional or behavioral problems.

The annual goals for Bobby are for him to reduce his behavioral outbursts, so the program differentiation focuses on discipline and proactive behavior. A comprehensive set of special education services includes some attention to his academic problems as well and to the social problems brought on by his temper outbursts.

The services for Bobby require a multidisciplinary team whose first task is to determine just what precedes and follows these outbursts. What sort of environmental conditions trigger the outbursts, and what hidden rewards may Bobby be receiving for them? This investigation is called a *functional behavior assessment*. *Functional behavior assessment* has been defined as "a systematic process for developing statements about the factors that contribute to the occurrence and maintenance of problem behavior, and, more importantly, serve as the basis for developing proactive and comprehensive behavior support plans" (Sugai, Lewis-Palmer, & Hogan-Burke, 1999). Bobby will be interviewed by the consultant about how successful his attempts at self-control have been. When the team finds what throws Bobby over the edge with his temper or what hidden benefits he is deriving from his tantrums (perhaps attention or status with his peers), then the same consultant will work with Bobby on methods of self-control to help him become aware of his feelings and substitute more appropriate actions before an outburst takes place (e.g., asking to leave the room, going to a seat next to the teacher's desk).

Unlike Les's parents, who are eager to help, Bobby's mother seems less receptive to participating as part of the IEP team. She wonders if Bobby's race (African American) has something to do with the way he is treated and whether other boys receive the same disapproval for their behavior. A secondary goal for the IEP team is to help Bobby's mother to support the program as something positive for Bobby's development through home visits with a counselor when possible.

One of the benefits found in the examination of Bobby is that he seems to be eager to reach some level of self-control and that he is occasionally embarrassed by his own behavior. The therapist will work with Bobby to help him become aware of what triggers an outburst (e.g., he feels he has been insulted by some other boys) and how he can handle his feelings in some alternative way, perhaps by writing a story or rehearsing to himself his need to inhibit his reactions.

The evaluations of Bobby's IEP seem straightforward. Bobby will have the number of his outbursts charted, and he can even keep a chart on himself on the number of times he has slipped. In this way, he can have a visible graph of his improvement over time. Some gains in achievement may occur merely from a more tranquil atmosphere in the classroom, less distracting than previous discordant emotions that pulled Bobby's attention away from learning.

ADAPTATIONS IN PRESENTATION AND METHOD

The research evidence supporting individual intervention, although sparse, does report gains in early literacy skills, computational skills, and spelling. Such interventions may improve social and behavior problems as well (Lane, 2004). Two major adaptations are expected to take place in programs for children with disabilities: 1) changes in the presentation of material and 2) changes in methods to prepare students for the learning experience. A few examples of presentation modification and readiness for learning are provided to give the reader some concrete differentiation.

Presentation Modification

Even though instructional goals are the same for children with disabilities as for their classmates, the manner of presentation must sometimes be changed in specific ways to encourage effective student performance. If a student with disabilities is having trouble mastering the content that is delivered in the traditional manner, then an alternative presentation may make conceptual mastery more likely. The UDL, which applies the architectural principles of universal design developed by Ron Mace to education, proposes that alternative methods of presenting curriculum materials be considered in order to better fit the needs of the student. In mathematics, that may mean that instead of the traditional presentation of problems, math concepts could be illustrated in a visual or spatial way, which would be easier for Les or Bobby to master.

Arnie, Les, Bobby, and Cathy are substantially behind their classmates in academic mastery, which is one of the reasons they have come to the attention of special education. To improve their achievement, the team providing instruction needs to focus on remediation skills. The special education teachers have an array of such skills available to help general education teachers adapt their manner of presentation.

Social Studies

One of the difficulties in determining the effectiveness of differentiated instruction is the measurement issue itself. Standard achievement tests, often used in statewide assessment programs, do not provide a clean distinction between various methods of instruction. For example, it is unclear how to tell whether content-driven models emphasizing breadth over depth are superior to constructivist and child-centered models of instruction.

Scruggs and Mastropieri reviewed a body of research and conducted their own investigations comparing the performance of samples of students with learning disabilities on content-driven models and coached elaboration with a series of prompts such as the following:

EXPERIMENTER: Anteaters have long claws on their front feet. Why does it make sense that anteaters have claws on their front feet?
STUDENT: I don't know.
EXPERIMENTER: Well, let's think. What do we know about anteaters? For example, what do they eat?

STUDENT : Anteaters eat ants.
EXPERIMENTER: Good! And, where do ants live?
STUDEN : In holes in the ground.
EXPERIMENTER: So why does it make sense that anteaters have long front claws?
STUDENT: So they can dig for ants. (2003, p. 371)

These investigators found that samples of students with learning disabilities performed significantly better using coached elaboration than direct instruction, even though such an approach might take more instructional time.

Another useful strategy is *curriculum-based measurement*, which uses weekly examinations on curriculum materials and learning styles to measure gains in students with learning disabilities under a variety of different types of instructional approaches. Fuchs, Fuchs, McMaster, and Al Otaiba (2003) reported that under special education programming, children with learning disabilities performed significantly better than students with low achievement in the regular classroom. When the students with learning disabilities were returned to the regular classroom, their progress suffered, which calls into question the quality of instruction being given to students with learning disabilities in the general classroom.

Mathematics

The area of mathematics has the clearest set of standards established by the National Council of Teachers of Mathematics (NCTM), which intends that all students have equivalent opportunities and all students attain high levels of performance (NCTM, 2003). But how close do educators come to meeting those aspirations? Cawley, Paramar, Foley, Salmon, and Roy (2001) provided a comprehensive mathematics examination for a national sample of 937 general education students (grade levels 3–8) together with 197 students with mild disabilities. They found that the performance of students with mild disabilities was considerably and substantively lower than that of students in general education across computation, even when 15%–20% of the students in general education did not meet the standards. Problem solving was even more of a difficulty for the students with disabilities. Students are easily misled by cue words. Given the problem, "A boy has three times as many apples as the girl. The boy has 6. How many does the girl have?" many students answer "18" instead of the correct answer, "2," because they saw the word "times." Yet the differentiation of instruction that clearly seems called for is not often visible. Paige (1999) reviewed 126 course syllabi in elementary mathematics and found only one providing instructional differentiation that had references or course components to help children with disabilities.

Cawley and colleagues pointed out that

> Significant numbers of general education students in Grade 8 failed to demonstrate mastery of the basic computational processes. Yet, these same students are expected to go on to secondary school and participate in highly advanced and complex programs of mathematics. (2001)

Teacher preparation should be taking these results into account and preparing for students whose mastery of mathematical processes is less than optimal. It is not sufficient to tell students to try harder.

Science

Cawley, Hayden, Cade, and Baker-Kroczynski (2002) reported an attempt to modify the junior high science program to include students with disabilities. In these classrooms, a hands-on approach to the design and implementation of science projects included children with learning disabilities and children with emotional disturbance. Science teachers worked with special education teachers to present the material using problem-based, small-group instruction. The same assignments were given to all of the students, and both the performance and behavior of the children with disabilities justified the adapted presentation. These authors concluded, however, "In the main, neither special education nor science education has developed and validated comprehensive programs of science education to meet the needs of students with severe ED [emotional disturbance] or LD [learning disabilities] in the GE [general education] classroom" (p. 425).

Reading

For other content areas such as language arts and social studies, the key to effective performance is the ability to read. The failure to read efficiently was at the heart of much of the difficulty of children with mild disabilities, such as Les, Bobby, and Cathy, and that difficulty increased over time. Fuchs and colleagues (2002) explored some additional cues to decoding for children with disabilities in kindergarten. Thirty-three teachers were randomly assigned to three groups: PA, phonological analysis conducted by teacher; PA + PALS, Peer Assisted Learning Strategies for Kindergarteners (Fuchs et al., 2001); and a control group. By focusing on phonological analysis, the performance of young children with disabilities meaningfully improved on word attack and word identification as a group. However, some children with disabilities showed little or no improvement, convincing the authors that much more work was needed to find the key to helping such students learn to read.

What they did discover was similar to the findings in mathematics and science: By changing the style and method of instruction, educators can improve the performance of children with mild disabilities without changing the goals of the content area. This is the real meaning of "gaining access to the general education curriculum." The differentiation in this case was not in the content goals but in the manner of presenting those goals in multiple ways beyond the excessively verbal and abstract presentation of many general educators.

Readiness for Learning

There has often been an unwarranted assumption that students are ready and even eager to learn. This might be true of students like Gretchen, who have been rewarded for their school performances. Certainly this is not true of many students whose past academic experience is littered with bad experiences and whose own personal and family histories have not led them to view school positively. One of the problems with many students with disabilities is that they have behavior habits that interfere with their readiness for learning. Cathy and Les have a deficit in necessary attention skills to maintain focus on the lessons. The goal here is to provide reluctant students with some skills and strategies that will increase their confidence and place them in greater readiness for learning.

Bobby and Arnie experience hyperactivity, which prevents them from focusing on the material at hand. Specific attention can be paid to improving the students' self-control. Learning self-control turns out to be a very complex set of processes (Polsgrove & Smith, 2004), which include

1. Accurately observing one's own behavior

2. Recognizing current behavior as inadequate

3. Identifying the behavior that is inadequate or inappropriate

4. Recognizing behavior that is required in a given situation

5. Selecting and implementing a set of strategies to regulate this behavior

6. Objectively evaluating performance and altering it accordingly

A relatively recent effort to aid learning readiness involves specific instruction in social skills (Kavale, Mathur, & Mostert, 2004). These skills are important not only for efficient work in the classroom but are central to later vocational success. Part of the definition of disability in Cathy's case has been the inability to be socially adaptable, in addition to her cognitive delays. Caldarella and Merrell (1997) developed a taxonomy of five broad dimensions: social skills, peer relation skills (e.g., controlling temper, handling conflicts), academic skills (e.g., listening to directions, working independently), compliance skills (e.g., following rules, using free time productively), and assertion skills (e.g., initiating conversations, inviting peers to play). Such a taxonomy is useful for targeting particular areas of social skills to attack through direct or indirect instruction.

Although the goal of *social skills training* (SST) appears to be included more and more in IEPs, the evidence of SST's effectiveness is limited. Despite expanding programs in SST, the research evidence has so far shown these methods to be only modestly effective in modifying the behavior patterns of children with emotional and behavioral problems. It is likely that patterns of behaviors built over years will be resistant to attempts to modify them. Gresham (1998) and others consider these methods of instruction in improving social skills as experimental in nature, and they need to continue to be modified on the basis of research evidence.

Gresham, Sugai, and Horner (2001) reviewed the outcomes of SST and found modest results. Gresham (1998) noted the four objectives of SST: 1) promoting skill acquisition, 2) enhancing skill performance, 3) removing competing problem behaviors, and 4) facilitating generalization and maintenance. The interventions for SST were most often modeling, coaching, behavioral rehearsal, and performance feedback. Gresham, Sugai, and Horner (2001) suggested that improvement in SST depends on more frequent and intense treatment than has been done in most reported programs. The treatment must be directly linked to the individual's social skill deficits and cannot disregard the types of social skills deficits that the individual is displaying.

Discipline

There has been a punitive disciplinary mood abroad in the schools called *zero tolerance*, in part due to various waves of violence that have erupted in schools. There is less tolerance for finding out why Bobby is behaving the way he is and more of a tendency to get tough as a way to inhibit further violent misbehavior. Rutter (2003) presented a summary of what is currently known and what remains to be found through research about student violence. He pointed out that educators and researchers have made significant progress in establishing relationships and linkages, but the causal mechanisms that create these linkages remain a mystery. For example, there is the clear linkage between low IQ scores and student violence, but how one of the factors causes or influences the other remains to be discovered. In addition, Rutter pointed out that the vast majority of researchers have had little or no background in genetics and biological processes. The result is that such factors are often ignored by investigators who focus on the environmental impact of such variables as the child's fearlessness and maternal depression, both of which may have genetic underpinnings (Plomin, 2003).

A number of distinguished panels established by the U.S. Department of Education and Congress (e.g., Gottfredson, 1997) suggested a proactive approach to behavior problems, whether through better preparation for coping by teachers or the establishment of preventive programs beginning early in the school career of students seen as behavior problems or threats. The use of *functional behavior assessment* to identify those triggers to aggressive behavior for a particular child is another method suggested (Nelson, Mathur, & Rutherford, 1999). The teacher tries to find out what is causing Bobby to misbehave and then attempts to introduce changes in his environment that would result in his not needing to act in this way. No one has yet documented informal evaluation studies that the IEPs designed for such children have the desired effect or that the functional behavior assessments improve the situation for the student and the school, but the informal judgments are positive (Smith, 2001).

Whole School Intervention

Much of the interesting recent research has dealt with interventions that involve the entire classroom or school rather than just the individual. Schoolwide positive behavior support attempts to adopt universal support structures for an entire school and rely on the general changes to support children with disabilities as well (Turnbull et al., 2002). Universal support is taught directly to all students in a wide range of school settings (e.g., classrooms, hallways, playground, cafeteria, library). The goal of universal support is to reduce significantly or eliminate as many problem behaviors as possible for as many students in the school as possible. Functional behavior assessments can then be conducted for individuals with special adaptation problems. Such an approach has been documented to result in fewer discipline referrals and less use of time-outs and inschool suspensions. The specific training of teachers and administrators is, of course, a key element in the success of universal support strategies (Liaupsin, Jolivette, & Scott, 2004).

A series of recent studies report positive effects. For example, the Good Behavior Game works by altering the social environment of the classroom. It uses classroom behavior management and student teams who reward students for prosocial behavior (Kellam & Anthony, 1998). Another example is a program called Peace Builders (Flannery et al., 2003). This program's goal is to change the characteristics of the setting that triggers aggressive and hostile behavior and to increase the daily frequency and salience of both live and symbolic prosocial models. The five basic rules of that program are 1) praise people, 2) avoid insults, 3) seek wise people as advisors and friends, 4) notice and correct hurts that have been made, and 5) right wrongs.

DECISIONS AHEAD

Several following chapters present the case for a support system to undergird special and general education teachers. The unsolved problems presented here are often indicators of missing support system elements that are necessary for confronting the unresolved issues or decisions about differentiated programming.

Solidification of the Inclusion Model

There is clearly a trend by political decision makers and many professionals to opt for inclusion as the major venue for providing special services for children with disabilities. This is seen in legislative amendments to IDEA and in the regulations that require a written notice if the school staff plans to do anything other than inclusion in the IEP. The courts have also reinforced this position by supporting inclusion with recent decisions.

But the policy of inclusion assumes the availability of resources to support the classroom teacher, such as special education consultants or TA systems. These resources are not present in many school systems or present only in some symbolic fashion. Decision makers also lack solid research-based evidence on the short-term and long-term outcomes of inclusion for children with disabilities, when the inclusion process has been done properly (Turnbull & Turnbull, 2000).

Research and intervention projects need to be designed carefully to identify the most effective way of carrying out the inclusion model and to determine for whom these strategies work and for whom other models seem desirable. For example, is inclusion the best strategy for children who are deaf and in need of special communication skills not easily available in the usual classroom? How about students like Les? Will they get sufficient remediation to meet learning disabilities such as dyslexia? The answers to numerous questions like these will sharpen the understanding of the best ways to implement the policy of inclusion.

Creation of Differentiated Curricula

There is little debate that children with disabilities need alternatives to the presentation of the standard curriculum in general education and sometimes to the curriculum content itself. But where are the organized or systematized lessons that teachers can use for such differentiation? Are decision makers to leave to each general education or special education teacher the responsibility for producing these alternative lessons, or are more elaborate efforts called for, such as an organized curricular development to aid teachers in their efforts? A sixth-grade teacher is not expected to create the sixth-grade curriculum, only to present it with skill and sensitivity. Special educators should not be expected to create alternative curricula from scratch. An audience admires the concert pianist who plays the compositions of others with style and grace. Listeners do not expect him or her to compose the music. The same should be true for teachers.

Special efforts have been made to identify and produce high interest–low difficulty readers for students who are behind in reading. These books present age-appropriate themes and stories, but the language in the stories is simplified so that students with reading problems can still understand them. Educators and researchers may need a major effort to generate some standard ways to differentiate programs in math, reading, language arts, and other content areas and to recognize that few teachers have the time or energy to produce such products.

Improvement of Individual Planning Efforts

Despite the manifest benefits that accrue from the use of IEPs that help team members focus on the needs of each child, complaints about the blizzard of paperwork, the high number of meetings, and so forth should prompt efforts to modify the existing procedures. IDEA 2004 provides some pilot efforts on this direction. Should the full-scale IEP be used only for those with more serious needs and abbreviated goal setting and treatment plans used for those with milder problems? Should there be attempts to develop a group IEP for small groups of students with similar support needs who can be given a common plan for the group instead of one for each student? The stories of schools producing IEPs on a photocopier may be false, but they make the point that many students have common academic problems (e.g., decoding reading passages) or difficulties in making friends, which could yield a common strategy. Not every problem is so unique that it deserves a special tutorial or individual work.

This chapter addresses the decisions about what to teach (content) and how to teach (changes in instructional environment and style for children with special needs). What is particularly evident from the discussions is that a single professional, even one with special training, is unlikely to be able to do the entire job necessary for these children. The special educator may have special approaches to learning but may lack the in-depth science or social studies knowledge to create a meaningful program. General education teachers may be excellent at organizing and presenting knowledge while lacking the psychological insight to understand a student with disabilities or the techniques to cope with him or her. In early childhood education, it is even more evident how much educators and decision makers should rely on other disciplines, each of which brings some special knowledge to the IEP or IFSP. Educators need others around them to become a part of the education team if they are to provide Arnie, Les, Bobby, Cathy, and Gretchen with a free appropriate public education.

Special educators have hardly settled some of the most difficult program implementation issues that they face, and now is the time for a major coordinated effort to develop strategies and materials that are transferable from one district to another. Robert Frost was not thinking of special educators when he wrote about having promises to keep and miles to go before sleeping, yet this concept seems quite appropriate to the current situation.

CHAPTER 4

Personnel Preparation and Technical Assistance

This chapter is the first in a series of five chapters, each of which represents a major component of a special education support system. The search for policies to enhance the quality of programs for exceptional children begins with personnel preparation. Personnel preparation programs cannot, however, provide all of the support that teachers of children with disabilities need. Technical assistance (TA), another kind of support in special education, describes a variety of efforts to provide new information, special instructional strategies, and classroom management on a targeted short-term basis.

It takes more than sheer dedication to teach children like Arnie, Bobby, Cathy, Gretchen, and Les. Both special educators and general educators need a background in child development and instructional content and strategies to adapt the regular curriculum to meet students' special needs. As is true of the other support elements noted in this volume, careful and deliberate planning and decision making are necessary for an effective personnel preparation program. Each support system component requires multiple decisions to be made, at all levels of government. The current practices in personnel preparation for children with special needs has been the result of many past decisions that have been made in the process of responding to major questions in the past. Some of these questions are

- How does one organize a personnel preparation program that generates a continuous and predictable flow of teachers and administrators who are knowledgeable and skillful in educating children with special needs?

- How does one fund such an effort and at what level of government or the private sector should financial support be sought?

- How does one help teachers who are already on the job to improve their skills in working with children with special needs?

The emphasis on inclusion has raised an additional issue. Now the special educator is expected to play the role of consultant to the general educator, and this role change has important implications for personnel preparation.

The rapid development of early childhood programs in the United States has placed a special burden on personnel preparation programs and the need for qualified early childhood teachers, in addition to those specializing in working with children with special needs. Early and Winton (2001) surveyed 438 directors of early childhood personnel preparation programs in both 2-year and 4-year higher education institutions to find out how large the problem is and what special issues are raised by these program directors. Although they estimated that there are more than 1,200 personnel preparation programs in the United States (testifying to the level of interest in this topic area), the survey identified a series of consistent problems:

- Personnel preparation programs are experiencing a major shortage of faculty.

- A limited number of faculty have backgrounds in diversity.

- More than half of the program directors of early childhood programs do not have bachelor's degrees.

- Many programs do not have coursework focusing on such exceptional groups as children with disabilities, children from different cultural backgrounds, or children with limited English proficiency.

Early and Winton (2001) suggested that resources be earmarked to support early childhood teacher education programs and also to address the lack of diversity in early childhood faculty. Finally, they argued for the improvement of working conditions in the early childhood workforce. The problem is much larger, including the general education programs as well as programs for children with special needs.

BACKGROUND OF PERSONNEL PREPARATION DESIGN

Support systems for the educational programs of children with disabilities, such as personnel preparation and TA, do not magically appear. They must be planned for and supported through legislative or administrative policies. The quality of such programs then has to be enhanced by the development of professional standards. Of the four major engines that shape decision making, legislation and professional initiatives have had a particularly significant impact on personnel preparation. The courts have not often been involved with personnel preparation except to endorse the presence of well-prepared personnel for children with disabilities.

Although state programs for children with disabilities necessitated the development of special education teacher training programs in state universities, these were largely only master's degree programs until the mid-1960s. Certainly no leadership training programs were available on a systematic basis. As late as 1965, only four programs in the United States offered doctoral degrees in the field of special education: Teachers College at Columbia University, Peabody College in Nashville, the University of Illinois at Urbana-Champaign, and Wayne State University in Detroit. This shortage of leadership programs was not so much due to a lack of interest in children with disabilities as to the economics of higher education. The personnel preparation programs in special areas such as mental retardation and learning disabilities were too small to be economically feasible for higher education. The relatively small number of students in such programs, together with the need for experienced faculty, made the costs prohibitive for most colleges and universities. Clearly some form of subsidy was needed as an incentive for higher education institutions to become involved in figuring out how to organize and maintain personnel preparation programs. Similarly, professional associations such as AAMR, CEC, and ASHA had to become involved in setting professional standards in the special fields that provided the structure for personnel preparation programs.

Federal Legislation

The federal investment in personnel preparation is the most extensive support program linked to special education. The first effort began in 1958 with the Education of Mentally Retarded Children Act (PL 85-926), which provided resources to train teachers to educate children with mental retardation. This was followed by the Teachers of the Deaf Act of 1961 (PL 87-276), which required training instructional personnel for children who were deaf or hard of hearing. From that beginning, there has been an enormous expansion of programs to educate special education personnel working with all manner of children with special needs, with the exception of gifted students.

The U.S. Congress and the Bureau of Education for the Handicapped (now OSEP) in the U.S. Office of Education instituted support grants for higher education institutions that would pay for fellowships for students and additional stipends for faculty in this special field. Given this additional incentive to higher education, leadership training programs multiplied, producing a generation of special education administrators, teacher trainers, and university faculty members needed to staff these rapidly growing programs. The current OSEP appropriation of more than $80 million for personnel preparation is testimony to its usefulness as a key support feature for programs in special education (Kirk et al., 2003).

One of the requirements of IDEA 2004 is that each state should develop a comprehensive system of personnel development (CSPD), designed to ensure an adequate supply of qualified special education teachers. A CSPD would include the following:

- A systemwide process for coordinating preservice and in-service training programs

- A systemwide method of identifying personnel needs

- An accountability tool for allocating and using resources

- A procedure for disseminating promising materials and practices derived from educational research and demonstration projects

Another use of legislation to upgrade programs can be seen in No Child Left Behind, which requires that all teachers who are participating in Title I programs must be highly qualified. In this case, "highly qualified" means, "Public elementary and secondary teachers must be fully licensed or certified by the state and must not have had any certification or licensure requirements waived on an emergency, temporary, or provisional basis" (Title I, Part A, Subpart 1, Sec. 1119). Although the law does not mention special educators, as such, the implication is clear. Any special education teacher also should be highly qualified in the same fashion. If school districts fail to live up to this standard and performance standards for all students, then punitive steps could be taken, with the state department of education providing TA to help the local district to come up to standard. If the annual yearly progress (AYP) standard is not met for 2 years, parents may have the option of placing their child in another school.

Needs for Personnel Preparation

Once the federal government made a commitment in the special education field, it had to determine how many resources should be allocated and what direction such personnel preparation should take. One of the most difficult tasks for decision makers is to get reliable information on such issues as teacher shortages, effectiveness of training, and reasons for attrition. Congressional and state legislators want this information, too, as a guide for updating legislation and funding priorities. For example, in 2000, Congress mandated the Study of Personnel Needs in Special Education (SPeNSE) to find out if teachers were adequately prepared to teach children with disabilities and to document variations in personnel preparation. More than 8,000 local administrators, preschool teachers, general and special education teachers, speech-language pathologists, and paraprofessionals were interviewed over the telephone. These personnel formed a nationally representative sample of districts and agencies (Carlson, Schroll, & Klein, 2001). The general impression of shortages in special education was confirmed by the SPeNSE data, which reported that more than 12,000 teaching positions were left vacant because no suitable candidates were found and that another 33,000 special education teachers were not fully certified for their main teaching assignment. Eighty-four percent of administrators reported a great to moderate shortage of qualified applicants for teaching students with emotional disturbance, and 45% of administrators reported hiring teachers who were less than fully qualified.

When special education teachers were asked whether they planned to stay in the profession, the teachers seemed to have a moderately more pessimistic view than general education teachers. Of those special education teachers who plan to leave as soon as possible (6% of the workforce), 17% said that their workload was not manageable, and 76% said that paperwork (e.g., required record-keeping for children with special needs) interfered with their teaching responsibilities. These were higher percentages than those obtained from teachers who planned to stay.

Table 4.1 presents a summary of those skills that special educators in the SPeNSE are most and least comfortable with (Carlson et al., 2001). Special educators reported that they feel most comfortable with planning effective lessons and monitoring students' progress and adjusting instruction. They are confident in their ability to use appropriate instructional techniques. These results suggest that they feel they have been well prepared to handle the academic side of the instructional process.

They also reported that they are skillful in working with parents and managing behavior, which is puzzling. The idea that students with aggressive outbursts are skillfully handled does not seem to be supported by observers. One of the most often heard complaints is the problem of managing behavior in the classroom, and there hasn't been much evidence for close relationships with parents either. Where does such confidence stem from?

Concerning their weakest skills, special educators noted problems in accommodating students from culturally and linguistically diverse backgrounds. This highlights the distance between the teachers and the families of the children they are serving. The demographics of special education and general education teachers confirmed that an overwhelming number of the special educators were

Table 4.1. Special educators' view of mastery of skills

Most skillful	Least skillful
Planning effective lessons	Accommodating the learning needs of students with diverse cultural and ethnic backgrounds
Monitoring students' progress and adjusting instruction	
Working with parents	Using literature to address problems
Using appropriate instructional techniques	Using technology in instruction
Managing behavior	

From Carlson, E., Schroll, K., & Klein, S. (2001). *OSEP briefing on study of personnel needs in special education.* Washington, DC: WESTAT; adapted by permission.

both female and white. The demographics of the teaching staff often do not re-flect the demographics of the student body. In 1999–2000, 16%–17% of newly hired teachers in the mid-South and South regions were African Ameri-cans, with smaller percentages in other regions. In the West, 14% of new hires were Asian. Obviously, a redoubled effort needs to be made to recruit more teach-ers from minority backgrounds and to find out why this profession is not more attractive to them (Early & Winton, 2001).

Despite a recent push in the use of technology in special education, many teachers reported a low comfort level in their skills in the use of technology. They feel they need more TA to build their skills and confidence. These results are a major cause for concern.

Although the data coming from the SPeNSE study will be analyzed more extensively, they clearly indicate that special education teachers are frustrated by some aspects of their jobs and welcome help by people who can strengthen the skills they gained in preservice training. The shortages described in the study also need to be put into the context of high attrition and retirement rates, which means that the field is always lagging somewhat behind the iden-tified needs. Data from SPeNSE (2002) confirmed that it takes more than pass-ing a law to meet the teacher shortages in special education.

Professional Initiatives

Although the other three policy engines address the parameters of special edu-cation and determining who should be served and where they should be served, the rules for the actual conduct of special education has been left mainly to pro-fessional groups and professional initiatives. One of the more successful of the professional groups in promulgating roles of special education has been the CEC. Established in 1922, the CEC aims to set professional standards. Since 1976, the CEC has had a partnership with NCATE. Under this partnership, NCATE is responsible for accreditation of the overall higher education teacher education unit, whereas the CEC is responsible for reviewing special education prepara-tion programs within the higher education unit. In 2000, the CEC published *What Every Special Educator Must Know,* the guide for individual special educa-tors and, in particular, for those who aspire to prepare special educators.

When an institution of higher education is interested in becoming accred-ited (and practically all colleges and universities are interested in meeting these standards), they apply and receive the NCATE Curriculum Guidelines. These guidelines include the CEC guidelines for initial and advanced programs in special education. After a self-study, the higher education institution prepares a folio describing its program and resources for personnel preparation, and the CEC evaluates the special education section of the application. Detailed stan-dards are available to flesh out the following areas (CEC, 2000):

- Maintenance of procedures for continued interaction with graduates, school systems, teachers, and organizations, on the part of the special education program

- Integration of multicultural issues throughout the program

- Development of a curriculum for the preparation of special education personnel that includes procedures for the study of the recommendations of national professional organizations

- Practicum standards

- Resources available to support an effective special education professional preparation program

- Maintenance of an effective special education faculty

- Student recruitment, selection, and support

- Relationship to the community and local schools

One of the professional standards regarding certification and qualification follows: "Professionals ensure that only persons deemed qualified by having met state/provincial minimum standards are employed as teachers, administrators, and related service providers for individuals with exceptionalities" (CEC, 2000, p. 3). This standard is an admirable goal, but the chronic shortages of fully qualified personnel in most of the special education fields continue despite best efforts (Hebbeler, 1994). A great deal more money must be invested in personnel preparation, or alternatively, a different way of delivering services to these children must be found in order to come close to meeting the standards.

When teachers have completed their certification process, they are recognized as professionally competent. In 1987, the National Board for Professional Teaching Standards, an independent, nonpartisan, nonprofit organization devoted to the recognition of excellence in teaching, was established, partly in response to the *A Nation at Risk* report (Gardner, 1983). Teachers with 3 years of experience and a certificate in their area of teaching may volunteer for the process, knowing that National Board Certification is a symbol of professional teaching excellence. Teachers can earn a certificate for special education, but none yet exists for teachers of the gifted. Teachers who volunteer for this examination go through a series of performance assessments that include student work samples, videotapes, and rigorous analysis of their classroom teaching and student learning. They also must show a depth of subject knowledge and understanding of how to teach each of the subjects to their students. This would coincide with the general portrait of what makes a master teacher. More than 16,000 teachers have received National Board Certification, including many teachers of children with special needs.

The five core propositions followed by the National Board for Professional Teaching Standards are as follows:

1. Teachers are committed to students and their learning.

2. Teachers know the subject they teach and how to teach that subject to students.

3. Teachers are responsible for managing and monitoring student learning.

4. Teachers think systematically about their practice and learn from experience.

5. Teachers are members of learning communities.

This advanced certification program is another effort demonstrating the necessity to plan and develop special organizations to achieve particular education goals.

SIGNIFICANT ISSUES IN PERSONNEL PREPARATION

The rapidly changing field of special education has caused some problems with the existing personnel preparation and TA programs. Two of the most important are

1. How can new responsibilities for special educators be incorporated into existing personnel preparation programs?

Many special educators were trained to deliver instruction and other services directly to children with disabilities and received little preparation on collaboration and consultation. A new model of service delivery of special education services has put the special educator in the role of consultant or advisor to general education teachers rather than the deliverer of direct services. With inclusion becoming the main service delivery model for children with disabilities, mastering this consultant role is now required. How should the existing personnel preparation programs be modified to take this new role into account and how can programs help in-service specialists who are now asked to play a very different part?

2. How can multidisciplinary experience be provided to specialists when the established programs have been determinedly single discipline?

Personnel preparation programs must take a multidisciplinary approach in order to bring to bear the knowledge and skills of neurologists, psychologists, social workers, physical therapists, speech-language pathologists, and others to complex planning and program implementation. This is particularly true in programs for specialists working with young children with disabilities, for whom health, social services, family counseling, and other special services all play significant roles in service delivery.

OSEP at one time provided money to support the development of 10 multidisciplinary personnel preparation programs in institutions of higher education, which required the collaboration of departments across standard university departmental lines. The multidisciplinary programs reported some very positive results. Yet, when the grant money ran out after 5 years, only one of the 10 university programs maintained a multidisciplinary program (Rooney, 1994). Apparently, the innovation was too much for the universities to adapt to permanently. Professionals are still looking for some way to institutionalize within higher education the concept of multidisciplinary preparation. One of the barriers to such change is the departmental structure of the university itself, each department with its own rules and requirements, which often makes collaboration across departments difficult.

With early childhood programs being clearly organized around multidisciplinary concerns, personnel preparation becomes even more of a mix of training from a variety of disciplines and settings (Winton, 2000). Special educators focus on the needs of a particular child and family, but specialists in infant and early childhood services try to influence a system of caregiving around each child. The concept of the child embedded in surrounding circles of family, community, and agency can be a helpful preparation for the educator in early childhood (Bronfenbrenner, 1989). A special educator may be prepared to work with Arnie and his autistic symptoms, but he or she has probably learned little about how to interact with other agencies that also play a role in the total treatment program for Arnie. An interdisciplinary core of courses taken by majors from different departments is one way to provide a base for collaborating professionals (Bailey, Farel, O'Donnell, Simeonsson, & Miller, 1986). A blend of special education and maternal and child health courses can prepare specialists to work more collaboratively with other disciplines, institutions, and agencies.

Blended Personnel Preparation Programs

Programs in early childhood education may well point the way to greater collaboration among disciplines in special and general education at all grade levels. There has been a genuine effort to develop blended teacher preparation programs, mixing the requirements of early childhood education from NAEYC and the requirements from early childhood programs for children with disabilities (Miller, Fader, & Vincent, 2001).

For example, the state of North Carolina currently has seven state- and NCATE-approved blended early childhood education/early childhood special education teacher preparation programs. Five of the programs are housed in departments of child development and family studies, and two are in departments of elementary education. In order to gain state approval, each program had to be developed and implemented through interdisciplinary teaching by faculty from early childhood education, early childhood special education, child development, and other related disciplines on that campus.

North Carolina also established a Birth to Kindergarten (B-K) Higher Education Consortium composed of faculty from various institutions and disciplines. This consortium established policy and practices within this new system of blended education. The development of the new institutional arrangements seems to be critical to the effective operation of such blended programs because it creates a multidisciplinary structure and represents a substantial departure from existing higher education personnel preparation programs that are limited to a particular department.

The rapid development of early childhood intervention programs for children with disabilities has created a major problem in personnel preparation. Higher education institutions often do not have courses on how to help infants and toddlers and their families and also do not have faculty members with the necessary expertise to teach in this special field.

One example of decision making to meet that problem was the development of a faculty-training program designed to help faculty members expand their skills and understanding so that they could include knowledge of infants and toddlers in their coursework or even begin to design courses for presentation in early childhood special education curricula. Bruder, Lippman, and Bologna (1994) created a series of 5-day institutes for volunteer faculty members in New York. These institutes included topics such as the history and legal basis of services to this population, family-centered service delivery models, early intervention service parameters, personnel competencies across and within disciplines, and the IFSP. After these institutes, each of the participants (38 faculty members from 15 higher education institutions) developed a follow-up training contract that might include a redesign of practicum facilities, the creation of a new course, and other improvements. This strategy has resulted in an expanded role of higher education in the early intervention field and represents an effective way of rapidly expanding the training facilities to prepare for a fresh new area.

Preparing General Educators for Teaching Children with Special Needs

All of this discussion about the preparation of special education personnel needs to be viewed in terms of the training for general education teachers who, if the movement toward inclusion is successful, will have substantial responsibility for the education of children with special needs. Darling-Hammond and Mc-

Laughlin (1999) proposed the use of standards-based strategies as an organizing concept around which personnel preparation can be developed. In other words, if clear goals are specified for the individual child or for the classroom, then the other mechanisms of schooling—curriculum, teaching, organization and other resources—can be brought together to attain these goals.

Standards-based policies that set expectations for student learning and teacher performance can produce a more focused effort, particularly with rewards and sanctions for students and teachers that follow on the performance of the students. Reaching an agreement on just what instructional goals will be sought, however, is no simple task. Advocates of inquiry strategy approaches (i.e., helping students discover concepts) and of direct instruction approaches (i.e., presenting the necessary ideas directly by the teacher) both have their arguments for why their way is the right way to prepare teachers, and both are probably correct, given the set of assumptions that each group begins with.

The manner of instructing preservice teachers can be quite different depending on the value placed on inquiry strategies or direct mastery of knowledge. Hawley and Valli (1999) proposed school-based professional development involving all of the staff so that there is mutual support and transfer of training. This would include special educators on the teacher teams to provide aid in efforts of inclusion.

These days, general education teachers are being trained to make adaptations for teaching students from lower socioeconomic backgrounds. It is puzzling that children with disabilities rarely are found as a central part of preparing general education teachers. This omission can hardly be seen as accidental because major publicity, attention, and resources have been provided to programs for children with disabilities since the 1960s. Many general education teachers struggle with teaching children with special needs in the general classroom, and this supports a strong argument for special attention to be paid to issues regarding children with disabilities in teacher preparation.

TECHNICAL ASSISTANCE FOR TEACHING EXCEPTIONAL CHILDREN

The formal personnel preparation program in higher education is one major source of support for program quality for children with disabilities. In-service teachers and educational programs also benefit from TA services, a variety of efforts to provide new information, special instructional strategies, and classroom management on a targeted short-term basis.

In 1984, Yin and White studied general TA efforts and found that TA consists of two main perspectives: 1) a means of using knowledge to adopt and implement a practice or procedure and 2) a means of incorporating an intensive, two-way communication process that uses a variety of strategies to promote change, innovation, and improvement. Furthermore, they observed that these two building block perspectives intersected with six ingredients for a TA organization:

1. The access to a knowledge base

2. The availability of competent TA providers

3. The use of various communication channels

4. An understanding of the characteristics of the users of TA

5. A workable TA structure

6. The availability of operational resources

These principles hold good today, and many institutions of higher education and OSEP regional resource centers have arranged to provide these services.

Technical Assistance Beginnings at the Federal Level

Various TA programs have emerged with a growing recognition of the enormous range of information and skills needed to provide high-quality services for children with disabilities and the specialists' recognition of their own limitations in knowledge and skills as single providers. When the demonstration program titled the Handicapped Children's Early Education Program (HCEEP) was established in the late 1960s, its goal was to demonstrate exemplary practices for young children with disabilities (Gallagher, 2000a). Although each of the original 20 demonstration centers funded by HCEEP had exhibited areas of excellence, the staff clearly needed additional assistance so that all of the elements of the demonstration program were of high quality. The staff of the demonstration program was quite ready to admit that although they were good at some program elements, their skills were sorely lacking in other elements. The range of elements—including health, psychiatry, nutrition, cultural differences, and special education—could intimidate the most professional staff.

In one instance, service providers at a high-quality preschool program for children with mild disabilities might suddenly face a child with autism, like Arnie, having never worked with a child with autism before, or they may face a child in a wheelchair, like Cathy, without having any experience in physical therapy or mobility training. Where could they go to get help? Local universities did not seem to have such assistance available in the time frame that the special educators wanted.

In addition to working with children who had problems that they had not encountered before, leaders in the HCEEP demonstration centers experienced a number of other problems. How could they develop plans for evaluation or accountability? Were there architectural advances that could help them set up a good physical environment? How could they develop a yearly budget or help their staff get additional training? The Bureau of Education for the Handicapped (now called OSEP) recognized the problem in the early 1970s and, after a national competition, established a TA system at the University of North Carolina that was designed to provide rapid response to the needs of the demonstration centers. The Technical Assistance Development System (TADS) established communication with the various demonstration centers and worked with each of them to develop a TA plan.

First, each center would do a needs assessment of its most pressing needs at the current time. Then, it would develop a plan with clear goals and objectives for providing help for meeting such needs. If the goal was getting more staff training, the TA center might provide staff on a short-term basis for specialized training or alert the director of the center in their region where such training could be obtained. Sometimes, only a telephone call was needed to have material sent from the TA program to the center to meet a particular problem.

There was also the problem of keeping up with current developments. The field of early childhood special education was rapidly expanding, and the HCEEP service centers often had only a vague idea about new developments that were occurring in the field. The TA center, through its dissemination and organizing regional conferences, met much of the need for advanced information. The mere presence of TA was a source of security for teaching staff, who recognized that someone out there was devoted to the task of helping them. At times, all service providers empathized very well with the slogan of the Children's Defense Program: "Dear Lord, be good to me. The sea is so wide and my boat is so small." The presence of TA helped the self-confidence of the service deliverers for the programs that were being served.

Using his 30 years of experience in the TA field, Trohanis (2001) listed the major principles of TA followed by the National Early Childhood Technical Assistance System (NEC*TAS), formerly TADS:

- Client centeredness, friendliness, and responsiveness to needs, priorities, strengths, and readiness

- Goals and results focused so as to make a difference

- Access to knowledge from research and proven models, practice, and policy

- Recognition of the value of diversity in ideas and people

- Availability of different strategies, resources, and technologies

- Commitment to building trust and an ongoing personal relationship with the client through active two-way communications

- Dedication to the provision of high quality and timely TA services that may vary in amount, duration, and intensity

Trohanis elaborated on the psychological dimensions of the TA process:

- We offer individualized TA, including consultations, research and information services, review and critique services, electronic mail services, and resource referrals.

- We offer TA services in a group context, including training workshops, topical conferences, meetings for state teams, teleconferences, satellite video conferences, Internet listservs, print and audio product, web-based information dissemination, and other means.

OSEP has been a leader in the building of TA systems, but many other agencies have also taken the responsibility for TA help for their clients.

Technical Assistance for Early Intervention

The field of early intervention is one that has experienced field-based training due to the lack of university-based training programs in early childhood and the suddenly accelerated need for competent teachers in this specialty. McCollum and Yates (1994) described four separate types of field training that came from statewide collaboration from a partnership of the University of Illinois, the Illinois State Board of Education, and the University Affiliated Program at the University of Illinois at Chicago.

Each of these field-based training options earns the participant credit in the credentialing process. The four options include participation in demonstration training sites, staff mentoring, field validation, and tuition reimbursement:

1. *Demonstration training sites*—Early intervention personnel visit one of eight sites that were chosen as models. A daylong training session is conducted at the site, and an individual training action plan is completed by the demonstration site coordinator and the trainee at the end of the session.

2. *Staff mentoring*—Individual guidance is presented to personnel in areas of special need (e.g., teaming, collaboration, assessment) by mentors who have previously been identified by the Partnerships Project. Each mentor–trainee partnership must document 8 hours of contact time, after which the trainee is presented with a certificate of completion that adds to his or her credentials.

3. *Field validation*—Students are asked to complete a performance task that provides a field-based alternative for personnel who cannot attend university courses. (Such tasks cover areas such as assessment, teaming, and fami-

lies.) Each task has at least three separate subtasks and requires about 15 hours to complete. They are then evaluated for accuracy.

4. *Reimbursement of tuition*—This provides support for tuition for a trainee to attend appropriate college courses without the financial difficulty of paying for the coursework.

Development of university capability in early childhood was recognized as necessary to meet long-range personnel needs. This is a combined approach, using both university- and field-based facilities, that could provide a model for upgrading other personnel as well as early interventionists. Many of the innovations in personnel preparation have been noted initially at the preschool level, probably because the need is so great and resistance by status quo practitioners is not so manifest. This also illustrates the importance of extensive planning for the organization of TA at the elementary and secondary levels.

It should be clear that just scheduling in-service training opportunities might not be sufficient. The experience must be meaningful to the participants, or it will not result in improved service delivery. A study of 242 early childhood service providers who had experienced in-service training rated their reaction to the experience (Sexton et al., 1996). They rated passive didactic training techniques, such as lectures, handouts, and lists of resources, as much less likely to result in actual practice changes than dynamic strategies that included observations of teacher modeling, small-group discussions, and opportunities to practice targeted skills. Just as professionals have a goal of high-quality service delivery to children with disabilities and their parents, they need to have high-quality training opportunities as well.

OSEP has directed one of the most extensive efforts at TA. They established six regional resource centers that collectively provide TA in programs for children with disabilities in all 50 states. Their major tasks are to assist state education agencies in systemic reform, which involves help through regional conferences, product development, TA, and help with the development of their comprehensive personnel preparation plan. These six regional centers, together with the Federal Resource Center, form a network for information sharing and problem solving to help the states meet their responsibilities in programs with children with disabilities. This network is a recognition of the need for developing system components to provide high-quality services.

Other Technical Assistance Efforts

Many special education service delivery programs have existed as lonely castles without easy access to professional support or assistance. Consequently, they have only the skills and knowledge of the onsite staff to guide them in their decisions regarding high-quality child care. The establishment of various TA programs, perhaps as regional centers within a state, would allow local providers to have access to a wide variety of consultation and support personnel that seems necessary for high-quality programs.

One source of TA is the network of Resource and Referral Centers (http://www.naccrra.org/), funded by a combination of state and local sources with additional help from the Child Care Bureau (http://www.acf.dhhs.gov/programs/ccb/index.html) in the U.S. Department of Health and Human Services. These centers have been established to aid parents in finding proper child care resources for their children, but they also provide some short-term training and assistance to early childhood programs, depending on the staffing and commitment of the individual centers (Kagan & Cohen, 1997).

One of the important aspects of high-quality service in programs and personnel preparation is the development of a support infrastructure. Kagan and Cohen discussed this need related to child care services:

> As public investments in early care and education increase, a larger percentage of government funding—we estimate at least 10%—needs to be invested directly into building and maintaining the infrastructure, including support for resource and referral agencies, parent information and engagement; data collection, planning, governance, and evaluation; practitioner professional development and licensing; faculty licensing, enforcement, and improvement; program accreditation; and other quality improvement activities. (1997, p. 36)

Each of these major federal agencies identified the need for TA, more or less independently of each other. Many state departments of education have also become aware of the need for TA but are currently struggling with limited personnel. In addition, there is the problem that the same individual who monitors programs also is expected to provide TA for them—two incompatible roles. One of the important aspects of TA is to allow the client to express concerns about what is going on in the program and to admit important needs so that help for the program can be provided through TA. But if the same person who is giving TA is also monitoring the program for quality, then it is less likely that the person will admit the limitations of the program. Also the person playing these dual roles of technical assistant and monitor often gets confused as to which role he or she is playing at any particular time. The vast majority of programs for young children have little or no TA available to them.

State Needs For Technical Assistance

Although TA is often thought of in terms of helping professionals to provide more effective services for children with disabilities, states and communities can utilize it as well. Harbin (1988) pointed out some universal needs for TA for states that are trying to implement programs for young children with disabilities:

1. *Strategies for influencing key decision makers*—TA can facilitate the identification of key decision makers and develop strategies for gaining their support.

2. *Child find activities*—Often such efforts are fragmented or negligible. TA can help with the coordination of child find activities.

3. *Eligibility criteria*—The development of noncategorical eligibility criteria for young children with disabilities that does not open the flood gates can be a TA outcome.

4. *IFSPs and IEPs*—The development of procedures that meet the diverse needs of families and yet are not intrusive into the family's life would be a goal of TA to state agencies.

5. *Case management*—Should the case manager come from the most relevant discipline or should he or she be trained specifically in case management? States may require TA in setting up the rules for this provision.

6. *Transition models*—A troublesome area is the requirement for transitions from one agency to another for children age 3 and later transitions when children move into elementary school. The development of transition models can be one goal of TA.

7. *Funding*—Lead agencies need to locate and know how to utilize funds from sources such as Medicaid, Early Periodic Screening Diagnosis and Treatment, and private insurance. TA can be helpful on this point.

8. *Interagency coordination*—Many states may require TA to improve the functioning of their interagency council, local interagency groups, and coordinated policy development.

9. *Qualified personnel*—TA can provide information about high-quality pre-service and in-service training models across disciplines.

10. *Health/education interface*—Special TA may be needed to set up rules for working with children who are medically fragile or who depend on technology.

Although agencies may have the expertise to cope with some of these administrative problems, it would be rare that they can handle them all, and that is where TA to agencies can be useful. How should the limited TA dollar be spent between the two very different strategies now in use? One of the existing TA strategies has been to provide support for professionals who are providing di-

TOURO COLLEGE LIBRARY

rect services to children with disabilities and their families. This means that TA specialists are acquainted with the newest instructional adaptations in special education and can provide needed information and support for the teacher or specialist who works directly with the child in question.

A second TA approach has been to provide help and assistance to support agencies in their planning activities, their responsibilities for accountability, and other tasks. Here, the TA specialist needs to know a good deal more about the special education infrastructure and special designs for statewide planning and resource allocation. Both of these approaches obviously have merit, but how should the available resources be divided and which one should be emphasized, given scarce dollars and a multitude of program goals? At the present time, both strategies seem to be in use for these purposes.

DECISIONS AHEAD

More key decisions need to be made in the field of personnel preparation in special education than for any of the other support features. Not only do ways to produce high-quality personnel need to be found but also methods of organizing a system for continuing the flow of such high-quality personnel into the system and, hopefully, keeping them there. Some additional issues that also need attention follow.

Cultural Differences

The rapid influx of children and families who come from different cultural backgrounds in special education programs has put a premium on greater understanding and cultural awareness on the part of special education personnel. No one has yet answered convincingly the question of why so few people from culturally diverse backgrounds see this profession as attractive. It is too easy to suggest that the students from these backgrounds who are academically qualified have many other career options available to them. Some may detect a societal bias that puts a disproportionate number of students from culturally diverse backgrounds into special education (Donovan & Cross, 2002) and may not want to associate themselves, as teachers, with discriminatory actions and programs. It is important that special education professionals find the answer to this puzzle so that they can have a better balance of instructional staff.

Limited Training for General Education Teachers

The general public would be surprised to discover the limited degree of knowledge and skills general education teachers have regarding children with special needs. In too many instances, these teachers have not attended even one

TOURO COLLEGE LIBRARY

class on the topic of children with special needs despite the fact that it is precisely these students, like Arnie, Les, Bobby, Cathy, and Gretchen, who are most likely to cause them difficulty. Although special educators may provide some help and counsel on these students, it is important for general education teachers to have some knowledge of students with special needs and their instructional adjustments so that they can use the special education advice most effectively.

Need for University Reform

The goal of blending multiple disciplines into an overall personnel preparation program in special education runs into a variety of bureaucratic barriers within institutions of higher education. Each teacher education program (e.g., elementary education, science education, remedial education, special education, mathematics education) has its own faculty to protect, its own courses to teach, and its own students to gather under its curriculum blanket. Rational arguments and pleas for collaboration have yielded little in action or reform. From the standpoint of the program directors of each of these self-contained programs, there is much more to lose in these collaborative adventures than to gain. If special education professionals wish change to occur, they must think of the structural and reward changes that encourage reform.

The creation of a new structure in the school of education, such as the Center for Teacher Preparation or the Institute for Personnel Preparation, would create an expectation that personnel preparation programs should involve the collaboration of programs incorporating knowledge and skills from various disciplines. Withholding funds is another way of influencing change. When funds are withheld for fellowships for traditional training programs, universities will likely be responsive to the message that the status quo is no longer acceptable. After all, a general medical practitioner has some knowledge of asthma and diabetes, even if he or she may turn to specialists in these areas for difficult cases. General practitioners in education often have a more difficult time because they start from such a limited base of facts on children with special needs and their proper treatment.

Because preservice education cannot be depended on to provide this experience and knowledge, some form of continuous TA and consultant help needs to be planned for to provide the knowledge and skill base that will enable these general educators to work together with special educators and other personnel such as school psychologists and speech-language pathologists. Although the general education teacher is a predictable participant in IEP meetings, how much he or she will understand and be able to use from that meeting may depend on his or her prior preparation.

Continued Professional Development

The professional field of special education has been changing so rapidly that even the well-prepared special educator may need to learn new knowledge and skills. This, in turn, means a systematic in-service training program to ensure that the veteran teacher understands such concepts as *functional assessment, theory of mind,* and other key ideas in special education. A general education teacher can be frustrated with a student like Bobby and his behavioral antics and will want to get something more than just advice from the special educator. This relationship can be made more difficult when the special educator assumes a level of expertise that can be resented by the general educator with 20 years of experience who wishes to be assured that this special educator really knows what he or she is talking about. Few special educators have been trained in the sensitive role of consultant and may need to add some communication skills through an organized training or TA program before they can play this new role effectively.

The decision making regarding personnel preparation for children with special needs has been made more difficult by the perception that such training additions are frills to be added in the unlikely event that a program ever has a budget surplus. Programs should understand instead that the absence of such personnel preparation decisions may doom them to unimpressive mediocrity. Special education professionals and other decision makers need to do more than recognize that personnel preparation and TA are an integral part of a high-quality program for children with support needs. They need to find ways to make personnel preparation and TA an integral part in ongoing general education systems.

CHAPTER 5

Research and Evaluation

R esearch and evaluation are two important components of a high-quality program for children with special needs, but they have to be carefully designed and promoted to be maximally useful. The distinction between research and evaluation often seems difficult to discern. Research represents a series of methods and activities designed to increase our knowledge on specific topics and help construct theories to explain current behavior and predict future behavior. Evaluation is the collection of knowledge used to determine the effectiveness or worth of a given program or treatment protocol.

Both research and evaluation can use the same instruments or tests to gather data, and both may use statistical procedures in judging the significance of the results. Ideally, the goal of research studies is to add to the knowledge about a given subject, whereas evaluation studies help to make a decision about a student, a program, or a curriculum. Research, in particular, is expensive and time consuming. How will it be supported, and who will conduct it? Where should research be carried out, in the schools or laboratories? One of the most extensive efforts in policy development has been made to provide the necessary funds to support research as a critical part of the professional scene for children with special needs. Support for evaluation is necessary to confirm or reject arguments for the value of various special education practices and programs. Because evaluation influences funding decisions for education programs and procedures, evaluation studies often become intensely political in their execution, implementation, and interpretation.

DECISION MAKERS IN RESEARCH AND EVALUATION

Decisions about research and evaluation are made by a wide variety of individuals and groups at varying levels of influence. Practitioners, researchers, and public decision makers have professional interests in research and evaluation efforts. Parents have more personal concerns that influence their individual desires for research and evaluation.

Triangle of Interests

The practitioner, the researcher, and the public decision maker form an interesting triangle of interests and diverse needs. The questions that each want answered are different, yet each needs the other two for effective programs for children with disabilities to be carried out. The researcher wishes to know whether a variation in the environment or in instruction makes a meaningful difference in student output or adds to the understanding of a child, family, or school. The practitioner wishes to know not only what makes a difference but also how it makes a difference. It is the sequence and process of the special intervention that the practitioner needs to know. The public decision maker is anxious to know how to invest scarce resources to create the most desirable outcome for the public. Often what satisfies one of these three members may not meet the needs of the other two, and different types of investigations may be needed to answer the questions of each of the three.

One of the constant needs in the work with children with disabilities is to find out more about the nature of a disability, its biological causes or social etiology, and what to do about it from a socio-educational standpoint. Researchers have relied on investigations from a broad band of disciplines, from neurology and biology to psychology and sociology, to design studies that will give them further insights into causes and cures.

Parental Concerns

The parents of individual children may have some specific questions that they wish research or evaluation to address. The stress that the family faces with a child with special needs stirs many different questions and calls on researchers to conduct a serious search for how to cope with the situation. What causes Arnie's autism and behavior? Why is Bobby slower to respond than other students his age? What can be the reason for Les's poor reading skills? Or Cathy's inability to use the technology that was designed for students like her? Why is Gretchen so bored with school?

The need to find answers to these questions leaves parents particularly vulnerable to any reasonable answer that might be provided. Parents are often bombarded with many different ideas about the causes for autism, learning disabilities, or mental retardation, and there is no shortage of professionals and others who would provide their own answers to these puzzles. So how is one to determine the most valid explanation among those that are available? This is the role of research, the conduct of careful investigations that try to sort out the evidence into defensible answers. Together with evaluation, which tests the effectiveness of treatment, evidence can be gradually assembled that will determine which factors are key to the conditions being studied and which can result in favorable outcomes.

For example, one proposed cause of autism is additives in the diets of children. Another is that autism results from the mercury in vaccinations for other diseases. A third is that a cold and unfeeling mother might be the cause. The National Academy of Sciences (Lord, 2001) has discredited these hypotheses in a research synthesis report. Parents need to know about such reports because supposed causes might keep some parents from having their child vaccinated or cause mothers to feel unjustified guilt.

DETERMINING RESEARCH NEEDS AND REQUIREMENTS

Legislation, court decisions, administrative rule making, and professional initiatives are all important engines of change in support of research and evaluation. Legislators authorize research and evaluation as important components of a commitment to children with disabilities. Another group of decision makers then must decide how much of the public money should be invested in research. Court decisions are often based on research findings. Administrative rule making shapes the way researchers structure their requests for funds. Professional initiatives generally determine what studies are going to be conducted with research money, how they will be conducted, and the uses of such research.

Legislation

The federal government has by far played the most important role in providing funds so that research can take place. The National Institutes of Health (NIH) represent an outstanding example of federal agency support in many different avenues of research. The federal agency was formally established by the National Institute of Health Act of 1930 (PL 71-251). The Social Security Act of 1935 (PL 74-271) represents the first modern attempts to improve public health through grants to states. Later, in 1944, the Public Health Service Act (PL 78-410) changed the National Institute of Health to the National Institutes of Health, and subsequent legislation established 27 centers that now operate within NIH and provide funds for the conduct of research in practically all domains of health. In the 1960s and 1970s, additional agencies were legislatively authorized in the social sciences and education fields in other departments (e.g., Office of Child Development) to provide research funds for investigation into the effects of poverty, family dynamics, and other child health factors (e.g., PL 88-164 for investigations into mental retardation and related areas). Later legislation such as IDEA and its subsequent amendments and No Child Left Behind continued the expectation that research and evaluation should play a critical role in the education of children.

The federal government has supported legislation leading to funding for research projects related to programs for children with disabilities since the 1950s. The vast majority of funds for research on children with disabilities comes from four major agencies: National Institute of Child Health and Human Development (NICHD), part of NIH; National Institute for Mental Health (NIMH), also part of NIH; the National Institute on Disability and Rehabilitation Research (NIDRR); and the Research and Innovation department in OSEP. Both Research and Innovation (OSEP) and NIDRR are part of the U.S. Department of Education. OSEP has administered separate funds for supporting research in special education. In 2004, these funds were transferred to the Institute of Education Sciences, which is the research organization for the entire U.S. Department of Education.

NICHD had a 2001 budget of $905 million. Because this funding covers biological and behavioral research studies of adults and children, the amount allocated to the study of children with special needs is small but meaningful. Within NICHD is a special Mental Retardation and Developmental Disability Branch, which provides support to 15 major Developmental Disabilities Research Centers around the country that conduct long-range research on the etiology, identification, prevention, and treatment of various types of developmental disabilities, including mental retardation, autism, and related disorders.

In NICHD, support is being given to a wide variety of biological and behavioral investigations, such as studies on family and community relationships following the deinstitutionalization of young people with mental retardation, the characteristics of children with fragile X syndrome and their responsiveness to treatment, and a variety of genetic factors related to mental retardation.

NIMH has experienced a major increase in total research funds, from $613 million in 1996 to more than $1.1 billion in 2001, with the largest jump in funding, proportionally, for research centers. This agency, like NICHD, covers both biological and behavioral studies of adults and children, so the amount spent on children with special needs would be a fraction of the total. Still, some ongoing, relevant investigations address the origins of mental illness; the genetics of schizophrenia, depressions, autism, and other disorders; and drug treatments for autism.

The history of early funding for medical research in the mid-20th century reveals that the funds were largely provided to individual investigators to support projects of the investigator's choice. As time has passed, three trends in the funding can be noted:

1. The available sums of money have increased as research projects have proven their worth in strengthening understanding and shaping the health and education of children with special needs.

2. A tendency to fund major research centers, often in higher education institutions, has brought together a variety of investigators to address complex problems over an extended period of time: "The culture of individual investigators working in isolation—stoked by competition, and fueled by ingenuity—is now being redirected to large teams that span university departments, disciplines, and geographic barriers" (NIH, 2004, p. 4).

3. Funding agencies have increasingly been anxious to get answers to some policy issues that might not be at the top of researchers' lists of interesting problems. The agency might put out a *request for proposal* on a given topic. For example, the agency might wish to know the prevalence of autism in children in a region. Those researchers who would be interested in answering such a question can then bid on a contract to accomplish the agency goals. In this fashion, the agency can answer questions of specific interest to policy decision makers that would not likely be addressed by the request for funds by the researchers in the field.

One of the many innovations pioneered by NIH has been that of peer review. In other words, a proposal by a scientist or group of scientists is reviewed by teams of other scientists in the same field or fields to determine its worthiness for support. Instead of administrators or politicians making such decisions, the researchers' colleagues judge the appropriateness of the research. These procedures have widely been credited with upholding the scientific merit of the research programs of NIH and have been widely copied in social and educational research.

Court Decisions

Research and evaluation have played an indirect role in many key court decisions related to children with special needs. They provide the rationale on which many court decisions are made. In the *PARC v. Pennsylvania* case, the court rejected state rules requiring a child to have a mental age IQ score of 5 years on an intelligence test before entering public school. Data on the learning abilities of children with mental retardation were used to solidify their decision that "no child shall be refused a free public education in this country" (Kirk et al., 2003). In the *Brown v. Board of Education* case, the Supreme Court outlawed segregation in education by using the data available regarding children's achievement to reject the "separate but equal" argument (Zigler & Styfco, 1994).

Because the courts are often faced with decisions related to equity in academia and the social development of children with special needs and their families, they often rely on the testimony of expert witnesses for their judgment.

These witnesses often rely on the knowledge available through accumulated research studies for their testimony. The courts are often dependent on the accuracy of scientific advice for the quality of their decisions. Justice Oliver Wendell Holmes, in a memorable decision allowing the sterilization of mothers with mental retardation, said, "Three generations of imbeciles is enough." Unfortunately, the genetic studies that lay at the base of that decision were faulty, and the court was misled (*Buck v. Bell*, 1927, p. 50). The basis for such a statement was the history of the Jukes and Kallikak families in which scientists concluded that poor intelligence was due to genetics and ignored the role played by the poor environments in which successive generations were raised.

Administrative Rules

The intersection between political decision making and educational research became much stronger as a result of legislation, such as No Child Left Behind. It puts additional testing responsibilities on the schools through administrative rule making. The act calls for "scientifically-based research," and one can wonder why anyone should be concerned about such a statement (Feuer, Towne, & Shavelson, 2002). Shouldn't researchers always be as scientific as possible in educational research? This is where administrative rule making can play a significant role because the rules must define "evidence-based research." Through administrative rule making, the phrase translates into a particular method of doing research, the use of the experimental–control group model.

The model is certainly appropriate to answer questions such as "Is treatment X effective?" but ignores many other valid means of investigation that can also be used to obtain useful results. If the government agencies in control of allocating funds for research restrict themselves to the randomized experimental–control model, then much useful research will be ignored or unfunded. Questions that are meaningful to some problems are not necessarily pertinent to others. Yin pointed out that

> Case studies are a preferred strategy when "how" and "why" questions are being posed (e.g., How does dyslexia affect the reading process?), when the investigation has little or no control over events, and when the focus is on a contemporary phenomenon within some real life context. (1994, p. 1)

In other words, randomized subject designs will not answer the questions that Yin identified. A successive case studies approach would seem to be the model of choice here. Dunst, Trivette, and Cutspec (2002) pointed out that maintaining a chain of evidence and replicating this relationship while ruling out other explanations increases the credibility of explanatory influences. The case study approach is the most useful to special education practitioners who can follow the sequence of events that is described by the intervention procedures.

Berliner (2002) identified some reasons why educational research is the "hardest science" of them all. The inability to control relevant variables in educational research would discourage many researchers in the hard sciences, such as biologists and chemists, who are used to controlling the relevant variables in their studies. Three major reasons for the complexity of educational research lie in 1) the contexts of the research, 2) the interactions that occur in variables within the research, and 3) even in the date that the research took place.

All educational researchers know the importance of context. The variation of results in multischool projects, such as Project Follow Through (House, Glass, McLean, & Walker, 1978), should alert researchers to the impact of local conditions on results. (Project Follow Through was designed to continue the stimulation provided to children making the transition from Head Start.) Student illness, a new teacher, a birthday party, or even bad weather might be said to have an impact on results from separate sites. Also, myriad interactions are present in any educational investigation. Certainly the nature and intensity of student disability, the training of the teacher, and the socioeconomic nature of the community all can have an impact on the results.

The date of the study is sometimes important. Studies measuring the impact of the regular classroom on students with disabilities done in the 1960s and 1970s would likely obtain different results than the same study conducted today because of the changed sociocultural atmosphere in the schools and the knowledge now available on the topic. These variables all create a condition in which attempts at generalization from a single study or place should be most carefully weighed.

Professional Initiatives

Once the legislative approval of research expenditures takes place, the actual content of the research is largely in the hands of researchers who design and carry out the wide range of investigations that result from that legislative mandate. American colleges and universities represent the largest source of investigators, who work individually or, increasingly, in groups or teams of investigators often coming from different disciplines, such as education, psychology, medicine, and sociology.

The available research money has made it possible for many psychologists, educators, pediatricians, sociologists, and other professionals to seek answers to the puzzling and complex questions that face special educators. In cases like Arnie's autism, one of the most useful goals for the professional community is to collect data that will put aside speculation regarding some of the presumed causes of autism or cast doubt on the dubious claims that have been advanced about the cures for autism and how to successfully educate students like Arnie in the classroom. Research does seem to point to some specific genetic markers as a contributing cause for this condition. It is in the narrowing of possible explanations for unusual behaviors that research contributes to the advancement in understanding of complex conditions.

Professional initiatives have clearly changed the educational landscape for children with special needs. Some of the many consequences of committed professionals' hard work and creative thinking are

1. The ability to change the developmental patterns of young children with delayed cognitive development through systematic interventions (see Ramey & Ramey, 1998)

2. The discovery that positive reinforcement seems to be more effective in changing the behavior patterns of children with behavior problems than do negative punishments and discipline (see Rutherford et al., 2004)

3. The discovery of intraindividual differences for children with learning disabilities through examining children across the full range of development (e.g., high on visual tasks, low on auditory tasks) (see Swanson, Harris, & Graham, 2003)

4. The discovery of the maintenance of superior performance on cognitive tasks into adulthood and later by children initially identified as gifted, making more important early educational stimulation, particularly for students from diverse cultural backgrounds

5. The importance of the continuing interactions of family, peers, school, and culture to the outcomes of the developing child with special needs (see Bronfenbrenner, 1989)

STANDARDS FOR RESEARCH

The insistence in No Child Left Behind on evidence-based findings and the importance of scientifically proven practices in the classroom has stirred discussion on just how such standards should apply to special education practices. A special issue of *Exceptional Children* (Winter 2005) was devoted to a discussion of the proper standards for various types of research that are used with children with special needs. The complexity of doing research with these children has been noted (Odom, Brantlinger, Gersten, Horner, Thompson, & Harris, 2005).

The first major issue has been the variability of the participants. Whether one treats children with learning disabilities, autism, emotional problems, or orthopedic challenges, one finds an extraordinary range of disability and characteristics within a particular category, which makes generalization from particular studies very difficult. Even more important, how does one cluster students for group statistical analyses when the students have few similarities besides a label (e.g., learning disabilities) that would justify such clustering? Also, finding a comparable comparison group is a special challenge, given the idiosyncratic nature of children with special needs.

A second issue in complexity is the educational context. Children with special needs often receive instruction in a wide variety of settings. When judging the effectiveness of treatment, it is not enough to report whether a practice in special education is effective: The report must specify clearly for whom the practice is effective and in what context (Guralnick, 1999). There is also the commitment to a free appropriate public education for all children with disabilities, so how does one, in the experimental–control model, assign some students to a nontreatment group?

A National Academy of Sciences committee on scientific research in education proposed the grouping of research questions into three groups 1) description (What is happening?), 2) cause (Is there a systematic effect?), and 3) process or mechanism (Why or how is it happening?) (Shavelson & Towne, 2002). Depending on which question is being asked, different research methodologies are called for, and each may have its own rigorous standards to be met to justify support and attention.

The special issue of *Exceptional Children* addressed the needed standards for four separate types of research:

1. Group experimental and quasi-experimental research (Gersten et al., 2005)

2. Single subject research (Horner et al., 2005)

3. Correlational research (Thompson, Diamond, McWilliam, Snyder, & Snyder, 2005)

4. Qualitative studies (Brantlinger, Jiminez, Klingner, Pugash, & Richardson, 2005)

Each of the articles focuses on what the particular standards should be to justify this type of research, and it is clear that many different approaches are appropriate, given the special issues noted previously. These and many other professional initiatives have served to make programs for children with special needs research based, rather than just tradition based.

ROLE OF STATES IN RESEARCH AND EVALUATION

Each of the 50 states still plays the predominant role in meeting the educational needs of its citizens, with help from the federal government, particularly
in special programs such as those for children with disabilities. Yet the amount
of money spent on research and evaluation by states is miniscule. The vast majority of state educational funds are spent on direct services, support of teachers,
administrators' salaries, materials, and so forth. State decision makers rarely get
the benefit of program analyses of the educational services being provided, and
the chances are quite substantial that considerable amounts of state money are
not being spent as efficiently as possible.

The reasons for this shortage of state resources for research and evaluation
are not hard to find. Most states experience chronic budget shortages for education. Educators or legislators rarely feel that they have the relative luxury of
funding evaluation studies when they are scratching around to pay, or help
local districts pay, teachers' salaries.

One strategy for breaking through this situation would be for budget decision makers to earmark a certain amount of funds for educational studies and
analysis. That is, whatever the amount of money spent by the state on educational services, a certain percentage (2% or 3% of those funds) would be reserved for educational evaluation or research. These funds would be indexed (or
linked to general education funds) so that they would increase or decrease as
the general education budget changes. In this fashion, studies to improve education would not have to compete with basic education needs for funds, and increasing information about more efficient ways of using the education dollar
would be available for decision makers and administrators.

TYPES OF RESEARCH

Research activities can be divided into two main types: *descriptive research,*
which aims to describe accurately the situation being studied, and *intervention
research,* which endeavors to insert activities that will change the conditions
being studied, hopefully for the better.

Contributions of Descriptive Research

One of the major emphases in the assessment of young children with special
needs is to find the extent to which their primary condition has changed children's development across a number of developmental domains. These assessments are done individually, through data gathered during IEP meetings, and
collectively, as investigators conduct longitudinal studies for common devel-

opmental patterns. One of the discoveries of descriptive research is that the effect of unfavorable factors can be muted by later favorable environmental conditions. Werner and Smith (1982) particularly noted the impact of the environmental context in a study of vulnerable children on the island of Kauai. They found that when children with prenatal complications were raised in a positive cultural and family environment that they became indistinguishable from children without such complications. However, in less favorable family contexts, the earlier problems predicted later developmental problems.

Sameroff, Seifer, Baldwin, and Baldwin (1993) identified 10 environmental factors that put a child at developmental risk. Based on a study of 215 4-year-old children, they concluded that it was the number of risk factors present, rather than the specific nature of a risk factor, that determined the degree of effect such factors were having on the children. These factors include such diverse dimensions as mother–child interaction, minority status, parental occupation, and anxiety. Because of the diversity of negative effects, a question surfaced as to where to focus useful interventions.

Table 5.1 shows the expected developmental delays and advantages for each of the five children followed in this volume, based on available research. Assuming their rating on these developmental areas represents a middle point of children with each condition, the pluses and minuses represent an expectation for other children with the same condition, with some caution taken when considering the wide variations within diagnostic categories.

Table 5.1 clearly shows Arnie, the child with autism, as being in the most difficulty. Arnie has mild to serious delays in all of the developmental categories, with truly serious delays in social development and language development and some delays in motor skills, cognition, and visual perception. With this wide array of problems, Arnie would seriously lag in academic achievement. This represents a composite portrait from summaries of the literature for other children with autism (Lord, 2001).

This is in high contrast with Gretchen, who seems to have positive to highly positive development, not only in cognitive and language domains, which would be expected with her classification of gifted, but also in social adaptation and visual perception domains. Only in motor skills does she not differ from her classmates. This, too, along with outstanding academic achievement, represents the pattern shown by the general population of gifted students, unless there are serious motivational problems or multiple risk factors in individual cases (Colangelo & Davis, 2003).

Les, whose learning disability has caused a serious reading delay, shows a sharp deficit in visual perception. His dyslexia has also interfered with his cognitive and language development but has not had any untoward effects in his

Table 5.1. Research-discovered characteristics of exceptional children

Child	Condition	Motor skills	Social development	Language development	Cognitive development	Visual perception	Academic achievement
Arnie	Autism	Mild delay	Serious delay	Serious delay	Mild delay	Mild delay	Serious delay
Les	Learning disabilities	Average for age	Average for age	Mild delay	Mild delay	Serious delay	Serious delay
Bobby	Emotional disturbance	Average for age	Serious delay	Mild delay	Mild delay	Average for age	Mild delay
Cathy	Cerebral palsy	Serious delay	Average for age	Mild delay	Mild delay	Average for age	Mild delay
Gretchen	Gifted	Average for age	Above average	Well above average	Well above average	Above average	Well above average

motor development or social relationships. Although there are widely varying developmental patterns in children labeled as having learning disabilities, the pattern Les shows would not be considered unusual, nor would his serious delay in academic achievement (Lerner, 2000).

Bobby has a deficit in his social development that carries over into problems in his cognitive and language development. He literally does not devote the time necessary to develop in these areas, and his behavior problems distract him from school-related tasks. This pattern of academic problems is consistent with children identified as having serious emotional disturbance (Kerr & Nelson, 2002).

For Cathy, the child with cerebral palsy, serious motor problems also seem to overlap problems in language usage and facility and cognitive development. This combination would cause problems in her academic achievement. Her social development seems to be typical, and she has no serious problems with visual perception. Again, depending on the severity of the condition of cerebral palsy, other children might show different patterns of strengths and weaknesses, but school psychologists would not find this pattern unusual (Kirk et al., 2003).

It is these patterns of development that special educators are trying to modify through IEPs and educational differentiation. Special educators must organize the program and instructional supports necessary to have a positive effect. The patterns in the chart represent midpoints for the conditions involved, and there is always a wide diversity of development within each of these conditions. Nevertheless, decision makers want to find general policies, which, if applied, will make a good adjustment for each of these students more likely. The accumulation of the findings of descriptive research projects have provided educators with developmental patterns that point to needed interventions and program differentiation for children with special needs. These general expectations always need to be checked with data on the individual.

Contributions of Intervention Research

It is easy to become impatient with the long time that research takes when there is so much to learn about children's learning, personality, and motivation. This impatience, in part, accounts for the great emphasis on intervention research designed to improve the development of these children with special needs, a major theme that can be identified in special education investigations. What benefits has the extensive body of intervention research (designed to introduce conditions in the life situation of the child in order to enhance the child's development) given to public decision makers and to practitioners? Certainly, the public decision maker wants some confirmation that the extra resources that are being devoted to children with disabilities have paid off in some measurable improvement (Gallagher, 2002; Ramey & Ramey, 1998; Shonkoff & Meisels, 2000). The practitioner is looking for specific ideas on how to improve the teacher–child interaction, increase the child's communicative skills, or improve his or her achievement. Guralnick (1997) addressed this issue in contrasting first-generation and second-generation research.

The first generation of intervention research was designed to answer the question "Does systematic intervention lead to developmental gains for children with disabilities?" Between 1970 and 1995, researchers attempted to answer that question, and several attempts have been made to synthesize this body of research (Guralnick, 1997; Guralnick & Bennett, 1987; Shonkoff & Hauser-Cram, 1987). These and other investigators concluded that early intervention programs are effective, producing average effect sizes falling within the range of a gain of .50–.75 of a standard deviation on those developmental dimensions under investigation. (*Effect size* is a statistic obtained by dividing the mean difference between the experimental and control group by the standard deviation of the sample. Effect sizes of .30 are considered small but real, .50 are modest, and .80 and above are quite impressive.) The effect size gains of .50–.75 would be equivalent to an 8–12 IQ point gain. Therefore, the answer to the first-generation question is that intervention can make a difference, which should reassure policy makers.

Because children with disabilities experience a wide range of conditions, the intervention justifications need to be summarized by category. The research literature shows a number of positive outcomes for children in many disability categories (Kirk, Gallagher, Anastasiow, & Coleman, 2006):

- Early intervention programs can give children with mild retardation substantial gains, and they can often successfully enter general education classrooms.

- Therapy can be effective in eliminating a broad spectrum of communication disorders or minimizing their impact on later speech and language.

- Deaf infants who are taught a manual communication system in the first years of life do much better as adults than those taught later in life.

- Social and behavioral problems can be modified with systematic interventions.

- Motor problems can be improved with systematic interventions.

Although the results from these interventions may be called modest and they never exceed typical performance (Farran, 2001), they are meaningful to the child and parents. The findings of a multiyear intervention program can now be predicted with some certainty (Gallagher, 1991):

- The treatment group, as opposed to the untreated or comparison group, would demonstrate modest developmental gains.

- A small number of children may gain appreciably in IQ scores and achievement results.

- A small number of children will show no effect from the intervention at all.

- If nothing is done to follow up on the program, many of the gains will be lost.

- One real advantage of these educational intervention programs may lie in the spirit of new optimism and encouragement within the family of the child in question.

In short, these kinds of expensive multiyear intervention studies are no longer necessary because they would only discover again what is already known. The range of studies and the consistency of results now available means that researchers can, with some confidence, tell public decision makers that well-designed intervention programs can result in modest but meaningful improvement in development for children with mild disabilities and children who are at risk for developmental problems. However, Guralnick pointed out that

> The first generation research literature contributed surprisingly little to the details of the design and implementation of early intervention programs, which curriculum approach to select, how quickly services should be initiated for children and families, at what intensity and with what degree of structure. (1997, p. 12)

These were all questions that were not addressed by the first-generation studies. Guralnick, therefore, called for a second generation of studies that are designed to identify those specific program features that are associated with optimal outcomes for children and families. These would include both program features and family variables and social contexts.

One of the recent topics addressing children who are at risk are intervention programs for children with low birth weight (LBW; 1500–2500 g) or very low birth weight (VLBW; under 1500 g). A major multisite study was undertaken to measure the effects of early intervention for LBW and VLBW children (Infant Health and Development Program, 1990). The combination of environmental disadvantage and LBW appears to create a greater likelihood for the appearance of later disability conditions. When a well-organized child care program was provided to children from ages 1 to 3 years and combined with parental counseling, the negative impact on children with LBW was much less. This positive interaction involved 377 infants randomly assigned to experimental and control groups in multiple sites and resulted in positive findings on intellectual growth and social behavior, particularly for those between 2001 and 2500 g at birth (Infant Health and Development Program, 1990).

Among the children who are at risk for emotional and developmental problems are those that have been subjected to persistent child abuse. More than a million victims of abuse have been identified, and the reported cases have been steadily increasing (Barnett, 1991). These children, of course, represent only the reported cases of abuse. Such abuse may interfere with the social and emotional development of the child and may even have an impact on the development of the child's cognitive abilities (Kazdin, 2002). Consequently, various therapeutic day-treatment programs have been established, and, in some cases, evaluations of their effectiveness have been conducted. In one study, after 9-month attendance in these programs, children showed significant gains in developmental areas such as cognition and language and motor, social, and emotional development, and they scored higher than a control sample of children drawn from a waiting list for these programs (Culp, Little, Letts, & Lawrence, 1991).

Another illustration of the importance of both duration and intensity of treatment in the attempts to modify behavior of young children is illustrated in a project that involved children at risk for behavior and emotional problems as identified by their kindergarten teachers (McConaughy, Kay, & Fitzgerald, 2000). The project called for the formation of parent–teacher action research teams. These teams consisted of the first- or second-grade teacher, one or more parents, and a parent liaison recruited from the local community. These teams worked together as equal partners to develop a portrait of the child's strengths and problems and to establish mutual parent–teacher goals. They agreed on how each would collect data to determine whether the goals were met. In addition to a random, matched-pair control subjects, all of the students participating in this study received social skills instruction.

Children treated in the program experienced significant improvements in problem solving compared with their control counterparts. The children benefited from treatment in year one of the study, but their improvements in year two were much more striking, indicating the importance of maintaining an intervention effort over an extended period of time in order to modify children's behavior patterns. The importance of beginning early in children's school careers was also noted in this study.

Once social competence is recognized as a major intervention goal, then specific strategies and techniques can be formulated. It is necessary to recognize that increased social competence will not emerge as a natural byproduct of cognitive instruction. It needs to be planned for, in its own right, with social techniques introduced and practiced in social situations in order for it to be effective.

Long-Term Effects of Cognitive Intervention

Even though early linguistic and cognitive intervention has positive effects, there is always the question of how long the effect lasts. It is important to look at the long-term effects of longitudinal intervention studies. One example of a major longitudinal research study was the Abecedarian Project (Campbell & Ramey, 1995), which is often cited as a model approach to answering the question, "Does early planned intervention make a difference?" By randomizing a population of 108 infants into experimental and comparison groups, Campbell and Ramey were able to demonstrate that the experimental group showed improved development in response to child care center intervention for 8 hours per day during the first 5 years of the children's lives.

But practitioners want to know what factors in such a complex and multi-faceted intervention program made the real difference. Was it the special lessons prepared for the young children (Sparling & Lewis, 1984), or was it the loving and consistent care given by the caregiver staff, or could it even be the increased optimism of the parents, which translated into positive interaction with the child in the home? The public decision maker, while intrigued by these results, is taken aback when he or she learns of the costs of such an extensive intervention program (about twice that of the ordinary preschool program), knowing that it can hardly be reproduced statewide at these prices!

In a similar vein, the Perry Preschool Project of preschool interventions with a randomized subject design discovered that the experimental group of preschoolers, 10 years later, had fewer referrals for criminal or antisocial behavior than the control group (Schweinhart, Barnes, Weikart, Barnett, & Epstein, 1993). But what was the causal mechanism here? The preschool program? The increased self-image of the children? The attitude of the parents? Even the most carefully designed project leaves causation up to speculation.

The Abecedarian Project also compared the experimental–control groups on crimes when the children became teenagers and found no differences in arrests or crimes between the experimental and control groups at age 19, with about 40% of each group charged with some offense by age 19 (Clarke & Campbell, 1998). The incidence of 40% of the sample charged with offenses compared well with the overall figures from the Perry Preschool follow-up (39%). The mechanisms by which the young child may be protected from such negative outcomes remain mysterious. Such studies, though illuminating for researchers, have practitioners and public decision makers uncertain about the next step.

The one long-term intervention study that reported substantially different results from other longitudinal studies is referred to as the Milwaukee Study
(Garber, 1988). This early intervention study also divided the sample into experimental and control groups. To children in the experimental group, it provided home care for the first 18 months and then a center-based care program
for the small number of children involved who were at high risk. Garber reported that under treatment, the students at risk for developmental delay at-
tained average or above scores in intellectual ability not only at the end of the
preschool but also at the age of 10 years. However, other social and behavioral
data were not as favorable to the treatment group. Garber reported, "Their
school behavior was poor, quite similar to the control children's deportment in
school." As other investigators also found, even a strong preschool program is
unable to inoculate children against unfavorable environments in school and
community at later ages.

Two of the questions that policy makers ask about special education are
"Is it effective?" and "Does the amount of extra time necessary for the education
of children with disabilities interfere with the education of other students?" In
these cases, the intervention is considered the special education program itself.
A research synthesis by Vaughn, Gersten, and Chard (2000) provided information on children, like Les, who have learning disabilities. This synthesis of 58
studies produced an effect size of .82, in favor of the intervention, which is
quite outstanding. A further analysis revealed the instructional strategies that
seem to pay off:

- Control of task difficulty (maintain high level of student success)

- Use of small interactive groups of six or fewer in teaching students with
  learning disabilities

- Directed response questioning (teaching students to generate questions
  while reading or working on problems)

Of equal importance is that these instructional strategies also seem to benefit
the other students in the classroom as well: "In all cases where interventions
have demonstrated significant positive effects for students with LD [learning
disabilities], they have resulted in at least as high effect sizes for all other students in the class, including average and high-achieving students" (Vaughn et
al., 2000, p. 108).

Concerns that special instruction for children with special needs may interfere with other students' learning were not justified in this instance. Studies
that use environment as an intervention variable and then test the effectiveness
of an inclusive classroom versus a resource room program, for example, without

specifying the instruction being used in either environment (Rea, McLaughlin, & Walther-Thomas, 2002) yield results that are difficult to interpret. Unless there is considerable clarity regarding the curriculum content and the instruction being utilized (i.e., the treatment or experimental condition), comparing schools or classrooms that are organized differently (e.g., special class versus inclusion) would not seem to be worthwhile.

Social Skills Intervention in Special Education

It has been increasingly apparent that the future adult adjustment of a child with disabilities depends not only on the cognitive skills needed to hold a job but also on the social skills necessary to get along with coworkers and adapt in the community. One of the advantages of the extensive attention to cognition has been that a measuring instrument, the IQ test, is easily available for assessing the child's cognitive development.

Now in the field of social competence, thanks to investments in instrument development, there is not only the Vineland Adaptive Behavior Scales (Sparrow, Balla, & Cicchetti, 1984) but also scales such as an Assessment of Peer Relations (Guralnick, 1992) and the Preschool Socio-Affective Profile (LaFreniere, Dumas, Capuano, & Dubeau, 1992). Even though the relationship between cognitive development and social competence is only modest, improvement in social competence may yet lead to improvement in the cognitive realm and vice versa (Kavale et al., 2004).

As is true in cognitive development, research on young preschool children has indicated that problems in social development appear to predict later social adjustment problems, and that discovery increases the importance of early intervention designed to develop social skills (Kerr & Nelson, 2002). Also, the consistency of social problems over time enhances the importance of early intervention designed to strengthen the attachment relationship between the primary caregiver and the child. This attachment relationship seems linked to social development and positive orientation to other children, and it is related to global social competence ratings at age 3, with fewer behavior problems and greater emotional health being noted (Guralnick & Neville, 1997).

The general assumption is that the social skills learned in the earlier positive parent–child attachment and the positive sense of self that such attachment generates are carried over into peer relationships. The importance of parental warmth and moderate parental control can hardly be overestimated. Similarly, children with behavior problems, like Bobby, have been noted as having poor earlier attachment and more negative input from their caregivers.

One should be careful not to attribute the cause of child outcome primarily to parent behavior when what may be happening may well be the result of a complex interaction factor. That is, children with challenging behaviors are less responsive to parents, and this often results in angry behavior on the part of parents, which in turn results in weaker attachment, and so forth. A downward spiral of child misbehavior, parental negative response, and more child misbehavior is a cycle that professionals want to break before it becomes an ingrained family pattern.

Intervention for social competence apparently requires more than just trying to modify specific behaviors. It involves the teaching of shared understandings to young children (Guralnick, 1992) or the design of scripts that lay out appropriate social behavior in reccurring situations (e.g., the lunch table, circle time, joint sandbox play). The direct training in common scripts appears to be effective, especially when followed up with caregiver prompts in subsequent interactions (Goldstein, Wickstrom, Hoyson, Jamieson, & Odom, 1988).

Casto (1987) reviewed the available intervention data from 74 studies on children with disabilities and reached the general conclusion that short-term benefits were clearly available in terms of positive effect sizes in cognition and motor and language development. He reminded readers that the interaction between the effects of intervention and the severity of the disability needs to be taken into account, with the children with more severe impairments being less likely to respond on developmental measures.

The Head Start program has become another longitudinal research base because many investigators wished to follow those young children into their early school years. Zigler and Styfco (1994) asserted that changes in intelligence in programs such as Head Start have not been a primary goal. The Head Start programs have a number of objectives, such as increased indicators of overall health (e.g., freedom from disease), ability to cooperate with others, ability to be socially empathic, and so forth. If the parents become more interested in their own education or more active in the community, that is also a positive outcome. Since the 1970s, some scholars have reflected on the poor decision making of investigators who tried to change cognitive development as a major goal in child development programs when cognitive development has proven to be the developmental channel that is most resistant to change in young children. It appears to be much easier to modify social relationships and positive attitudes toward learning.

Behavior Changes Through Intervention

Practitioners are often concerned with their students' lack of appropriate behavior and would value evidence of behavior improvement above all other variables. Webster-Stratton observed an appalling lack of comprehensive intervention programs for preschoolers with behavior problems:

These children are spending large amounts of time with untrained caregivers in the least adequate facilities where the child-to-caregiver ratios make it impossible to provide the degree of attention, affections, and emotional support required to meet the psychological needs of these children. (1997, p. 477)

By far, the number of intervention programs for young children with behavior problems are parent-training programs, and these have proven successful, in part. The child changes positively in the mother–child interaction domain, even though the benefits may not carry over into child care or school settings (Webster-Stratton, 1997). Such training obviously has to include the caregivers in school and child care settings if substantial carryover from the home to larger social settings is expected.

The programs that have tried to modify children's unacceptable social behavior have focused on early intervention with some tangible results. Yoshikawa (1994) reviewed programs for their effect on the eventual behavior of children considered at risk and came to two main conclusions:

1. The programs that demonstrated long-term effects on crime and antisocial behavior tended to be those that combined early childhood education and family support services.

2. Those programs that were designed primarily to serve adults tend to benefit adults more than children, and those designed primarily to serve children tend to benefit children more than adults.

The limitations of the cost–benefit model—the comparison of the increased costs of special programs with the economic benefits obtained—is that comparing money spent with positive outcomes does not take into account that small differences in child and family outcomes may result in large functional differences. For example, a small amount of gain in parental stress reduction may result in the cancellation of divorce plans that could, if carried out, have catastrophic financial and social implications for the family.

EVALUATION

As noted earlier, the purpose of evaluation is to provide data that allow policy makers to make a decision about an individual, program, or institution. Because such decisions have economic consequences for those involved in the programs, evaluation tends to have major political implications.

Educational Accountability

One of the current pressures felt by many school systems is that of educational accountability. This has been particularly true with the advent of No Child Left Behind, which places major importance on child outcomes. No longer will the public or decision makers accept the word of educators that something positive is happening in the schools. They want to be shown. Educators must deliver the results of educational programming to responsible authorities framed in terms of the growth of child developmental outcomes. As usual, there are special issues in relation to special education and its effectiveness because it must also be shown that children with special needs are progressing as expected.

One of the substantial movements in American education involves the use of tests to assess whether students and schools are performing to standards in key areas of the curriculum. One of the shortcomings of using test results is that the more objectively the tests are constructed (providing quantitative results), the more questions can be raised about whether such tests truly evaluate the impact of complex curricula. Even when gains are made in the objective test scores, they are often attributed to teachers focusing their instruction on what is on the test. As Berliner (2002) said, "You can train students to play *Chopsticks* better with intensive instruction, but he or she will still not be a pianist."

Special Education Evaluation Issues

The major effort to focus on child outcomes rather than on administrative process in general education has not been lost on special education. Wolf (2003) pointed out that much of what passes for evaluations in special education are really exercises in compliance monitoring, such as making sure that the student has a free appropriate public education or is instructed by a qualified teacher. The demands of compliance with laws and administrative rules also result in enormous amounts of time-consuming paper work for teachers and administrators. What is lacking, Wolf argued, is any evidence that all of this compliance has led to positive outcomes. He would like to change the slogan from a "free and appropriate education" to an assurance of a "free and effective education."

Turnbull and Turnbull (2003) responded to Wolf by noting that compliance with the law still is often lacking and that there should be a review of what outcomes the schools should be accountable for producing. In addition to academic outcomes, the Turnbulls suggested, schools should be responsible for emotional, physical, and developmental outcomes. The Turnbulls contended that the problems rest in the inadequate system for training teachers and for ensuring that teachers use research-based approaches.

Just what outcomes should be required? How should outcomes be measured? The questions return to testing and its adequacy in measuring outcomes. There remains the issue of how to best judge the educational progress of children with disabilities. Should they be judged by their performance on these broad achievement tests, or should they be judged on their ability to mcct the goals established in their IEPs? If Les has met the goals set down for him in his IEP, does it matter if he does not do well on the statewide tests? Or does that mean that his IEP goals were not appropriate in the first place?

The increasing popularity of high-stakes testing is a particular issue for children with disabilities because important decisions about the student and the school are made on the basis of the test results. As Ysseldyke (2001) observed, "When tests are used to make high stakes decisions . . . referral rates and dropout rates increase, and increasing numbers of students with disabilities are retained at grade level" (p. 304). The danger of too great an emphasis on testing is that attention may be taken away from the essential goal of helping the student to learn important academic strategies and conceptually complex academic concepts. Such goals are easy to state but hard to measure. To discover that students are two or three grades behind in reading may be useful information if positive steps are taken to adapt the lessons provided to them with that information in mind. But if all that is done is to retain the students in the same grade for the next year, little has been accomplished.

Alternative Assessments

The high-stakes testing procedures mandated by such legislation as No Child Left Behind have given rise to the development of alternative assessments for children with special needs. Alternative assessments are used when the student is unable to take the general education tests because of his or her disability. Although Bobby, Les, and Gretchen would be expected to take the same tests as their classmates, Cathy and Arnie can expect to have some changes in their examinations.

Cathy, for example, might take the same examinations as other students but have the time standards relaxed in recognition of her motor impairments due to cerebral palsy. The goal here is to not allow extraneous factors (e.g., time limitations) to prevent evaluators from knowing what Cathy has actually learned. Arnie, however, has had alternative assessments added to his IEP program. "Alternative assessments are data collection procedures used in place of the typical assessment when students cannot take standard forms of assessment" (Byrnes, 2004, p. 58). Because Arnie will be taking a program somewhat different from that of his classmates, a different approach is needed to answer the question, "Is he performing adequately?"

The most commonly used alternative assessments are performance-based portfolios, in which samples of the student's work are collected in various subjects over time and then rated for their quality. Even so, No Child Left Behind still insists that the content of the portfolios relates to the general curriculum. Alternative assessments are usually reserved for children with moderate to severe disabilities. This approach can help link the general and special education programs together by requiring collaboration to ensure that the special education assessment links to the general education curriculum.

Curriculum-Based Measurement

An alternative fruitful approach called curriculum-based measurement (CBM) has been initiated by Deno (1985). The CBM approach is a set of measurement methods for keeping track of how well students are learning basic skills (Fuchs & Fuchs, 2003). It has demonstrated its usefulness in charting progress for students with disabilities: The classroom teacher charts the student's progress in reading, arithmetic, and other basic learning skills by using a series of short assessments.

These 5-minute measurements are taken regularly and indicate the progress the student is making in oral reading of basic passages or learning subtraction skills, for example. Such procedures become more significant with the requirements brought on by No Child Left Behind, which included children with disabilities in the mandate that student performance be presented and assessed.

Standard achievement tests inadequately report the performance of students in special education services. After all, if they had been performing on a typical level for their grade, they would not likely have been referred to special education in the first place. A measurement taken once per year cannot convey the progress being made on specific curriculum goals for such students.

The success of the CBM approach for the measurement of basic skills (Shinn, 1998) has led to its being used to assess more complex curriculum goals, and this presents a challenge for educators who wish to assess progress in areas such as language arts and social studies because the construction of the short test passages is more controversial. This type of progress monitoring has been recommended by the President's Commission on Excellence in Special Education because it can show the progress that students can make on long- and short-term objectives. Progress monitoring can also be used to track the IEP goals in academic areas (Fuchs & Fuchs, 2003).

Importance of Treatment Fidelity

One of the difficulties facing program evaluation is a phenomenon known as treatment fidelity or treatment integrity, which refers to the degree to which a given treatment is implemented as planned or intended (Gresham, MacMillan, Beebe-Frankenberger, & Bocian, 2000). Treatment integrity is concerned with the accuracy and consistency with which independent variables constituting the treatment are implemented (Gresham et al., 2000).

In other words, if Bobby is being treated with ABA in the classroom but the manner of presentation did not follow the prescribed procedures for ABA, then how can one measure the effectiveness of the ABA treatment? All too often, no attempt has been made to ensure treatment fidelity in educational treatment evaluation studies, and the result of that lack is that researchers may be underestimating the true value of the specific treatment.

TOOL DEVELOPMENT

One of the purposes of research turns out to be the development of tools to extend further the value and scope of the research or evaluation itself. Science flies on the wings of its measurement instruments. The microscope, the telescope, and the protocol for analyzing deoxyribonucleic acid are simple examples of the important role played by the tools of the scientist.

The tools of the educator and the social scientist turn out to be software rather than hardware. The intelligence test and standard achievement tests are two examples of tools that have influenced the very nature of education itself. The development of the Early Childhood Environmental Rating Scale (Harms & Clifford, 1990) has been instrumental in defining the quality of child care environments, just as the Rorschach Ink Blot Test once dominated descriptions of personality.

Given the importance of the tools in expanding the scope of the fields of investigation, it is indeed odd that major funding agencies at the federal level have played such a small role in funding the development of valid instruments. Such projects would likely take several years and be somewhat expensive, and that may be the reason for the reluctance to further develop tools. It does seem short sighted, however, considering the lack of valid measurements for social development, behavioral deviance, family interaction, or community influence on the individual child and family, to mention just a few measurement needs.

There has also been a call for objective measures to use as indicators of academic progress. These are measures that lay people understand, such as a comprehensive achievement test like the Iowa Test of Basic Skills or the Scholastic Aptitude Test. Unfortunately, when such measures are used in evaluation studies, they can set up an unreasonable expectation. Namely, that broad general academic improvement can be expected from specific changes in school practice or curriculum. This expectation almost always results in disappointment because it is extremely rare for specific curriculum modifications to result in comprehensive changes in an individual's general cognitive abilities, temperament, or attitudes. It is just not easy to make major changes in the general makeup of human beings, although the results of specific instruction on tasks related to that instruction can be observed.

The best rule of thumb to use is that if an educator is trying to improve mathematics skills in multiplying fractions, the educator should test directly for the ability to multiply fractions. If an educator wishes to improve imagery in short story writing, he or she should provide a short story assignment and look for improvements over time on that activity, not whether the overall short story product has improved.

This is not to say that the growth in cognitive skills or the achievement of children is strictly limited to mastery of the specific instruction but only that the instruments that are available to measure such abilities are too crude to detect the specific changes that have been made. Observers can easily come to the conclusion that a special program has yielded nothing when, in fact, if they ask the teacher or the student, he or she will report substantial gains and mastery on the material taught.

To put it another way, one should not expect that

- Teaching problem solving skills in science will result in better problem solving in history.

- Teaching arithmetic skills will lead to improvement in algebra performance.

- Teaching astronomy will result in better performance on general science tests.

- Teaching divergent thinking skills will result in more imaginative essay writing.

The lesson is clear: evaluators should test for gains on the specific areas of instruction that have been emphasized in the curriculum. This can be done by analyzing student products, by measuring knowledge or skills gained on items directly relevant to the instruction, or by asking for the perceptions of a student and teacher on what has been taught. There well may be additional learning that has taken place beyond the specific information taught, but it will be learning that can hardly be anticipated in advance and will depend on the individual knowledge structures of particular students (Hyatt & Howell, 2003).

DECISIONS AHEAD

A number of decisions need to be made in order to determine future research and evaluation activities. A wide range of research studies and evaluation activities can be considered for support, and policy makers must determine which projects should be funded. They must also account for the funds that go to research and evaluation activities on the basis of whether these programs work.

What Research Studies Should Be Done?

Figure 5.1 presents some options of the range of research projects that might be considered for support. Some agency personnel or some advisory panels then have to make decisions as to which are the most valuable or most pressing. The supporting agencies mostly rely on outside panels of experts (i.e., peer review) to help them with their decision making.

The options in Figure 5.1 are merely samples of the diversity of studies that might be considered. Certainly one of the criteria that can aid the choice would be that the study has an excellent methodological plan and that researchers with good reputations and track records are chosen. Once that is confirmed, then the decision to fund may depend on one or a number of the criteria listed in Figure 5.1. The projects listed would vary markedly in cost, one criterion for choice. Some studies might take much longer than others. The longitudinal studies listed here would be expensive in time and resources while the meta-analysis might take only a year. The development of measuring instruments is also a lengthy process that would be likely to take more than 5 years before a valid instrument was available. The study of characteristics of a particular group (e.g., children with fragile X syndrome) would take less time and have modest costs, but would it contribute more to the development of the field?

The comparison of the relative effectiveness of ABA versus functional behavior assessment for children like Bobby could have both theoretical benefit and practical application but would be difficult to execute effectively. Obviously, there are many aspects to consider in deciding where scarce research dollars will go. The public would likely have interest in any studies that could provide immediate tangible aid. The early intervention study should be of interest, as would the meta-analyses of inclusion studies, a topic of public concern and interest.

There also has been a tendency to support or invest in centers of research, often in higher education institutions, that focus on particular topics, such as program evaluation on early childhood programs. Such centers assemble teams of multidisciplinary investigators interested in particular areas of investigation for a detailed and intense effort on a series of related projects. The agency decision makers usually support a mixed portfolio of research support, with some of the projects having short-range goals for rapid knowledge output and some with long-term goals but with potentially significant long-term contributions to make in the knowledge and treatment of children with disabilities.

Option	Criteria for choice				
	Cost	Theoretical benefit	Practical application	Length of study	Public support
Study of characteristics of fragile X, Down syndrome, and so forth	Modest	Possible	Minimal	Less than 2 years	Minimal
Early intervention study on effects of preschool	Substantial	Possible	Likely	2–5 years	Substantial
Longitudinal study (ages 3–8) of students with moderate disabilities	Expensive	Substantial	Likely	More than 5 years	Modest
Development of measuring instruments on social development	Expensive	Substantial	Important	More than 5 years	Minimal
Meta-analysis of studies on utility of inclusion	Modest	Possible	Likely	Less than 2 years	Substantial
Comparison of relative effectiveness of applied behavior assessment and functional behavior assessment on children with emotional disturbance	Substantial	Possible	Likely	2–5 years	Minimal

Figure 5.1. Decisions on research options. (*Note:* Ratings here are provided by the author based on research reviews, program reports, and personal experience.)

Who Evaluates the Evaluators?

In contrast to the rapid increase in research funds since 1995, funds for program evaluations have been in short supply and have not substantially increased despite the cries for accountability. The Rehabilitation Services Administration, for example, received only $1 million to evaluate the programs under their responsibility in 2001. OSEP found itself in a similar position of limited funds for program evaluation. Why?

Do public decision makers trust the evaluations that are currently being done? They know that the friends and colleagues of the program directors or the funding agencies are often carrying out such evaluations. Because evaluation studies can be quite politically sensitive, there is a suspicion on the part of many decision makers that they are not getting an unbiased report on the programs.

The decision makers themselves also have attitudes about such evaluations. These same decision makers put many of the education programs into place, accompanied by glowing statements of what they hope the programs will accomplish. The last thing they may want to hear is that programs they are responsible for initiating have been less than stunning successes. The political benefits for establishing the programs may diminish considerably.

What seems needed would be an equivalent of the Government Accountability Office (GAO), established to examine the use of public funds for the U.S. Congress. The GAO evaluates federal programs and activities and provides analyses, options, recommendations, and other assistance to help Congress make policy and funding decisions. There could even be a branch of the GAO established to look specifically at educational programs and provide a neutral or unbiased judgment on the usefulness of such programs. Some such mechanism needs to be found that will restore confidence that the education evaluation results are to be trusted.

It seems clear that the investments in research and, to a lesser degree, program evaluation have helped special education to become a respected member of the education community, with programs that are research-based for populations of students with special needs. I once testified before a congressional committee and was asked a plaintive question, "When is all this research business going to end?" I forget what startled answer I came up with on that occasion, but the right answer is, "Hopefully, never, if we are to maintain the quality of our programs."

As reported by the Education Commission of the States (2002), beginning in 2005–2006, states will be required to test all students annually in grades 3–8 in mathematics and reading or language arts with reasonable adaptations

and accommodations for students with disabilities and English language learners. Note that *all* students will be tested. Presumably that means that children
with disabilities will be tested along with their classmates. Recent rule making
allows local school districts to exempt 2% of the students from these tests, presumably the students with the most impairments. A press release by Margaret
Spellings, Secretary of Education (2005), stipulates than an additional 2% of
students with disabilities can take alternative assessments. Reasonable adaptations that can be made in measurement may allow Cathy to take the tests without time limits or even have a person transcribe her oral statements so that her
performance does not suffer because of her inability to write.

These testing requirements have garnered the attention of teachers and
administrators because they are high-stakes tests. The stakes are high not just
for students, about whom decisions will be made on the basis of scores, but also
for teachers and administrators. If the students in a particular school perform
badly, the teachers may be held responsible, and the administrators may find
their jobs in jeopardy. No wonder there are complaints that the teachers are
spending too much instructional time preparing their students for performance on these tests, which means that they do not spend as much time addressing the needs of children with individual differences.

Financial Support for Research and Evaluation

It is much easier to obtain funds to support direct services to children and families than it is to provide resources for support features such as research and
evaluation. Whenever there is a downturn in resources or budgets, it is tempting to cut those items that are not critical to direct service, so the funding of
research and evaluation programs often undergoes a rocky and unpredictable ride.

One way to avoid the roller coaster effect of financing is by indexing and
linking together the direct service funds and the research and evaluation funds.
This means that a certain percentage of the direct service funds will be set aside
(say 2%–3%) for research and evaluation. If the total budget goes up, then support for research and evaluation will go up and conversely will go down when
the total budget goes down. At least such an indexing strategy would keep efforts within reasonable limits and guarantee that efforts in research and evaluation will not disappear in bad financial times.

Both descriptive and intervention research have played a major role in increasing the understanding of children with special needs and the trust in the
utility of educational procedures. Policy research, which studies the rules and
standards by which legislation and court decisions are implemented, is in its
infancy but promises to help construct a more effective policy base for educa-

tion programs (Gallagher, 1994b, 2002). Research, in particular, is a long-term benefit that will help in the next generation. If decision makers want something that is research driven to influence educational programs tomorrow, they should have started 10 years ago. It is this long-term influence that per-suades some to cut the resources for research in hard times because its influence will not be immediately felt. If educators and decision makers have faith in the future, they need to keep these efforts in place so that the future can be better than the present.

CHAPTER 6

Finance and Data Systems

inance is the engine driving the special education train. Without the allocation of scarce resources to special education programs, educators would not be able to provide necessary services to children with special needs. Where and how the allocation of resources takes place should be recorded, and keeping track of the expenditure of resources for particular services requires a data system. The four engines of change—legislation, court decisions, administrative rule making, and professional initiatives—are all prominent in this key area.

HOW MUCH IS SPENT?

Let's look at some overall statistics on spending and reflect on how allocation of resources is determined. The Center for Special Education Finance conducted a nationwide investigation of how much money is spent on special education, using a stratified random sample of districts and schools in the school year 1999–2000. (In a stratified random sample, the sample is put in order along a key dimension, such as income, and researchers take a random selection from each resulting ranked classification. In this study, for example, districts were categorized as wealthy, average, or poor, and a random selection from each category was chosen.) Using a minimum of two districts per state, the Center for Special Education Finance was able to arrive at the most accurate figures yet available (Chambers, Parrish, & Harr, 2002).

They estimated that about $50 billion is spent on special education in total. The average cost of a student receiving special education services is estimated to be 1.9 times greater than a student in a general education classroom. This ratio is down from previous years, probably because more mild cases are being included. Also, the trend toward inclusion costs the district less than some forms of separate education.

During the same year, the federal government contributed $3.7 billion, or less than 10% of the total expenditure, a far cry from the 40% share promised by the federal government when PL 94-142 was passed in 1975. In addition, another factor often overlooked was the cost of transportation for students in special education who are unable to take buses used by other students. About 840,000 students receiving special education services were transported in fiscal year 2000 at the cost of $3.7 billion. In other words, the cost of transportation was as high as the entire federal government expenditure on these students. These costs approximate about 15%–20% of the total amount of money spent on students in the United States. It is no wonder that those who concern themselves with the money spent on education focus their attention on special education as a major element in the cost figures.

The always scarce resources expended on children with disabilities does not really depend on the "availability" of funds. Educators are used to hearing the phrase *we have no money available* for whatever is on their wish list. This does not mean that American society has suddenly run out of money, of course. The staggering amounts spent on amusement and recreation should make that clear. What the phrase *we have no money available* means is that the priorities for educators' particular needs (i.e., funding for educating children with special needs) are only so high. Indeed, some people will say that the amount spent now on children with disabilities is too much, not because the need is not great, but because educators have not demonstrated more convincingly that their efforts really pay off in a better life and future for the children and families being served by special education. (For more information, see Chapter 5 on research and evaluation.)

Previous chapters have provided the rationale for expenditure of public money for children with special needs, but where does the special education dollar actually go? Figure 6.1 provides a breakdown of the overall expenditures for 1999–2000. A majority of the funds (61%) is spent on programs for school-age children, and another 10% is spent on administrative and support services; however, there are a number of other costs, as well.

Some 200,000 students of the total 6.2 million students receiving special education services are placed in private school programs operated by public agencies or institutions other than the public school district in which they reside. The cost is estimated at $5.3 billion, or 11% of the total. Transportation takes up another 7% of the costs, and preschool services in public school and other settings amounts to another 9%. When other instructional programs, such as programs for homebound students and summer programs, which cost 2% of the total, are added, this represents the total expenditure for 1 year. These special education costs amount to about 14% of the $360 billion spent in elementary and secondary schools in 1 year (U.S. Department of Education, 2003).

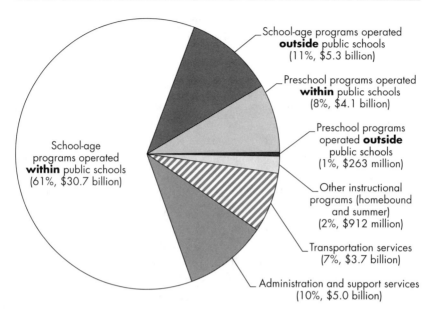

Figure 6.1. Allocation of special education expenditures, 1999–2000. (Reprinted from U.S. Department of Education, Office of Special Education Programs. [2003]. *24th annual report to Congress on the implementation of Public Law 94-142: The Education for All Handicapped Children Act.* Washington, DC: U.S. Government Printing Office.)

FINANCES AND PROGRAM CHOICES

One of the important decisions in special education financing is whether the method that is currently being used to provide finances for the education of children with disabilities has the unintended consequence of tilting the decision making regarding the choice of programs in one direction or another. This tilt can easily happen when the provisions for financing have been made at different times or with different children with specific disabilities (Parrish, 1997).

For example, Arnie, the student with autism, may be eligible in one state for a supplement of $10,000 when he is in a program that involves intensive communication and social skills instruction with a small number of other children with autism but a supplement of only $5,000 if he is included in the general classroom. Such a financial disincentive can cause decision makers to determine Arnie's placement on the basis of funding instead of a professional judgment about which situation meets Arnie's needs most effectively. If state formulas allow generous reimbursements for school districts when students with severe disabilities are placed in remote private or public settings but do not provide the same level of help when the child is included in the general public classroom, then there is a natural tendency for school administrators to choose the placement with the most financial advantage, everything else being equal.

Sampling is a strategy that educational policy makers have yet to adopt in their search for information to guide their decisions. If they want to know what attitudes special education teachers have toward inclusion, for example, they do not need to talk to every teacher in the state. A carefully done stratified sample of teachers can give them that essential information without enormous and time-consuming data collection. Similarly, they don't have to collect finance data from every school district in the state unless state law requires it.

The device of polling has been well accepted in political circles and in marketing. When well planned, a small, carefully selected sample of citizens can result in the essential information. This is because pollsters are not, strictly speaking, looking for total precision but only the important trends. Whether the exact percentage of citizens who dislike a particular policy is 47.2% or 45.6% doesn't really matter. The pollster learns that changes need to be made. In many questions about education policy, policy makers could tolerate a similar percentage of error as long as the essential trends are revealed in surveys of an appropriate sample. At the present time, there has been an insistence in collecting the information about every child and every family, and that has been terribly expensive in time and resources.

How would policy decisions be different if researchers found 1,230 children with autism in a state as opposed to 1,190? The chances are good that they would not have enough resources to take care of the total needs, anyway. The essential information is that many children with autism need help, and policy makers had better assemble the resources to provide that help.

DETERMINING FUND ALLOCATION

Because the allocation of scarce resources is the ultimate statement of priorities, it is important to use all available tools to enhance the financing of special education. The engines of change—legislation, court decisions, administrative rules, and professional initiatives—are all active in obtaining and distributing fiscal resources.

Legislation

Legislation has the biggest impact because it establishes the federal mandates to which schools and districts must comply. Also, federal legislation sets up agencies for distributing moneys set aside for educational services.

Federal Mandates

The role of the federal government in financing such programs has been controversial for many years. When PL 94-142, which mandated that all children with disabilities must be educated, was passed in 1975 and supported by subsequent court decisions, local educational administrators asked, "Who is going to pay for this?" Not surprising, they felt that because the federal government mandated the program, the federal government should pay for it as well. The federal government announced that it would pay a gradually increasing proportion of the total price tag, and that by the end of 10 years, it would shoulder 40% of the cost (Martin, 1989).

This goal of progressively increasing federal support for special education programs has not yet happened, however. For many years, the actual percentage paid by the federal government was less than 10% of the total, with the remaining fiscal responsibilities placed on local and state governments. The federal government has contributed an estimated 17%, according to the President's Commission on Excellence in Special Education (Branstad, 2002), which also called for the goal of 40% to be honored. The Congress's explanation for this default was that it had many other responsibilities (e.g., social security, national defense) that ate up limited revenue and scarce resources. Recent attempts have been made in Congress to increase sharply the federal financial role. In fiscal year 2004, a total of $11.6 billion dollars was spent, but it is not certain how this issue will eventually be settled (http://www.whitehouse.gov/omb/budget/fy2006).

PL 99-457 focused on the needs of children with disabilities from birth to 3 years of age and raised still more financial concerns. This time, the federal government mandated that services needed to be provided as an *entitlement* to every infant and toddler identified as having a disability. However, the federal government only allocated a small amount of planning and development money, with the vast majority of the funds needed to pay for services left to the states (Gallagher et al., 1989). So, once again, the federal government had announced a mandate that the states were going to pay for, with predictably bad feelings between the levels of government following that decision. Actually, the states pay more than three times the amount that the federal government does for the infant and toddler program (Barnett & Masse, 2003).

The states had an option as to whether they would comply with this act, and a number of states did delay their commitment to the program. Parents and advocacy organizations for children with disabilities were resolute about their states participating, and eventually all 50 states agreed to the mandate. Who would want to be the political leader known for saying that his or her state, alone among the other 49 states, has decided not to provide services for young children with disabilities (Gallagher, 2000a)?

One other aspect of PL 99-457, which is now part of IDEA 2004, is that states were allowed to determine whether to include children who were at risk for disabilities in the program as well. Such a provision made professional sense because it allowed for the early identification of children in developmental trouble and allowed states to provide treatment at the earliest possible time. However, public decision makers in many states looked at this provision and could only see an enormous rise in costs since the population of infants and toddlers who were at risk might even be higher than the total population of children with identified disabilities at this age level. The result is that only 10 states, each defining "at risk" their own way, took advantage of that provision.

Financing Support Services

In addition to providing direct service money to the states, OSEP (authorized through IDEA 2004) provides finances for an important infrastructure, which backs up the teachers on the firing line. The support program funding is significant particularly because issues such as research and innovation remain almost exclusively a federal responsibility. The $77 million spent on research and innovation is not all of the money expended for this purpose by the federal government either. Significant funds are added by NICHD and NIMH.

OSEP allocates about $80 million to personnel preparation, as noted in Chapter 5, which has helped to maintain leadership training programs and teacher preparation programs in the field of children with disabilities. Another $53 million goes to TA programs, and these two funds together make up the vast majority of federal support programs in the area of personnel preparation. Another $38 million are spent on technology development, demonstration, and utilization for special education. Together, the support programs spent more than $342 million in fiscal year 2001 to maintain the special education infrastructure that has proven to be an important part of the total program.

Court Decisions

Court decisions have been the source of fiscal decision making in special and general education. Early decisions such as *PARC v. Commonwealth of Pennsylvania* (1972) and *Mills v. Board of Education of the District of Columbia* (1972), which placed major financial responsibilities on the states, foreshadow legislative action designed to remediate the needs of children revealed in the court cases. Three separate decisions by state courts may begin a wholesale change or reform by the states because in all three instances, the special education financing system in the state was declared unconstitutional by state courts (Verstegen, 1998). In each of the cases in Alabama (*Campbell County School District v. State*, 1995), Wyoming (Opinion of the Justices, 1993), and Ohio (*DeRolph v. State*, 1997), the courts noted a fundamental inequity in how services were being provided to children with disabilities across the state. Although such decisions apply only to the state in which they have been made, other states have undoubtedly taken note of these decisions and are nervously reviewing their own systems. In short, the courts said the states are violating the principle of *horizontal equity*. Services provided within the state should be roughly equal from one community or school system to another. In each of these three states, the courts found that children with special needs in poor or rural districts had far fewer services available than children in more wealthy and urban districts.

In the Wyoming and Ohio decisions, there was an additional finding that the inadequate financing of special education programs was causing school districts to draw on general education funds to meet the needs of these children with disabilities, thus putting an additional drain on the general education funds for those districts. Although the courts provided no clear remedy for the states in these decisions, it is clear that the provision of basic special education and related services must be uniform across the state, regardless of whether a child is born in a more- or less-affluent area. Also, the provision of proper facilities was a state, not a local, responsibility. *Leaudro v. State* (1996) required the state to reallocate education funds to poor districts. Such legal challenges add weight to the opinion of many observers that the manner of financing the education of children is fundamentally flawed and that new efforts designed to be more equitable must be found.

Administrative Rules

No matter how detailed a piece of legislation might be, those who are responsible for implementing the legislation always have legitimate questions. Developing the regulations is the task of the responsible agency named to implement the legislation. In the case of IDEA 2004 and other legislation related to the education of children with disabilities, OSEP in the U.S. Department of Education drafts such regulations. Draft regulations are published in the *Federal Register*, which is the official communication channel between the government and the public, with a request for comments to be submitted within a publicized time frame. The drafting agency, such as OSEP, must answer the comments and then make whatever changes in the regulations that are called for. Once finally published, again in the *Federal Register*, the regulations have the force of law.

At the state level, similar tasks are carried out by the designated responsible agency or agencies. PL 99-457 required that all states appoint a lead agency for the coordination of services within an entity called the Interagency Coordinating Council (ICC), which the law carefully defined. Some states chose their state education agency as the lead agency, whereas other states designated one of their health agencies to be lead agency. Regulations can be the responsibility of different agencies from one state to another, resulting in different practices from state to state.

It would be a mistake to assume that regulations have little to do with financing. Take the eligibility requirements for PL 99-457, for example. In one state, the eligibility requirements can be written so that only children with moderate and severe impairments are eligible for funding. Depending on how each state defines "at risk," it enacts the final regulations and allocates the state dollars as it sees fit.

Administrative rules become particularly important to local districts as they try to assemble the reports necessary to inform their educational program decision making. A cap placed on local districts in terms of how many children may be eligible for reimbursement or what services the state will pay for has become one important administrative rule influencing expenditures. The states are unlikely to pay for cleft palate operations, for example, so the rules become extremely important to local directors to guide them in their expenditure decision making.

Professional Initiatives

One of the major contributions made by the professional community is to calculate the usefulness of the special education expenditures. Several methods of calculation are available, such as determining cost–benefit ratios.

Cost–Benefit Ratios

Cost–benefit ratios express the costs expended for a child with special needs in relation to the financial benefits that can be realized by such special services. Such benefits can be the lesser chance of grade retention, the reduced need for special education services in the future, and even the reduction of the uncertainty of the student in the future. Most of the discussions on the financing of special education have focused on the large amount of money that seems to be necessary to meet the needs of children with disabilities. However, there is another way of looking at this issue. Can early intervention actually save money that otherwise would have to be spent on needed services for children with special needs later on in their school careers or adult lives?

Barnett (1991) explored the cost–benefit ratios of early intervention in the Perry Preschool program, a program designed for children living in poverty in a major urban area. Because the study used a comparison group, Barnett was able to determine how much money was spent on the children who were enrolled in the special preschool program and how much was spent later in the life span of the children who were in the comparison group and who did not participate in the special program.

Barnett found that he could calculate a benefit of $70,876 for every $12,356 spent on a child in the special preschool program. These savings were obtained largely by the lesser incidence of incarceration among the experimental group in later life. Keeping a child or adult imprisoned is an enormous expense, and anything that can be done to reduce the number of youth who have to be in prison results in an enormous social and fiscal saving.

Based on his current pattern of behavior, Bobby, the boy with behavior problems, may well be at risk for some future incarceration unless his IEP team finds a way to meet his needs and reduce his tendency toward aggressive and antisocial behavior. Any costs incurred now to prevent that outcome represent a real societal saving in finances and in the potentially wasted life of children like Bobby.

Barnett concluded that

> The weight of the evidence establishes that early childhood intervention can produce large effects on IQ [score] during the early childhood years and sizable persistent effects on achievement, grade retention, special education, high school graduation, and socialization. Unfortunately, public policy decision makers often weigh their current expenses without considering the future savings that can be obtained through the intelligent planning and service delivery in the early years. (1991, p. 43)

It is ironic, however, that such long-term savings do not seem to impress many decision makers who must find the funds for early intervention now and are not concerned about savings to be gained sometime in the future.

Increasing Costs

Decisions related to special education funding have become increasingly difficult over the last few years. First of all, the special education student population has grown steadily from 3.7 million students in 1975 to 5.9 million students in 1995. Also, the scope and costs of services have increased more rapidly than general education costs. Lankford and Wyckoff (1995) found that costs grew 50% more rapidly for students with disabilities than for students without disabilities in New York during a 12-year period.

A case study report of special education finances in Massachusetts gave several reasons for the increasing costs of special education in that state (Berman, Davis, Koufman-Frederick, & Union, 2001). First, there was the increase in medical advances, which have saved the lives of many children who would have previously died at birth. Unhappily, these medical advances have not prevented serious motor and cognitive impairments in many instances, and these children with special needs are now showing up in schools (Berman & Union, 2003).

Second, since the 1990s, institutionalization of children with disabilities has decreased significantly, as has privatization of special education services. Foster care of children with disabilities can amount to a substantial figure. In addition, the percentage of children living in poverty has increased, and there is a correlation between children's living in poverty and having special needs in school.

The size of special education costs has now gotten the attention of policy makers, and there are allegations that special education entitlements are encroaching on funding for general education. In fact, more than half of the states did not even know what the total special education expenditure was in their state (Ladd & Hansen, 1999). The federal government stopped requiring the states to report their special education costs in 1988. Obviously, a better data system tracking finances is required.

Exceptional Costs

For children with extraordinary costs, such as Arnie, the child with autism, it has been proposed that a special fund be set up at the state level on which the local district can draw. A National Academy of Sciences report recommended a shared risk pool to which districts contribute, much as an insurance policy for children with unusual expenses, and also encouraged the state to take on greater responsibilities for special education costs (Lord, 2001). Wisconsin has established an emergency fund through its Department of Public Instruction, which provides funds for local school systems that have special costs due to children with severe impairments. Some states have used Medicaid funds, and others have used combinations of developmental disability funds, private insurance, and other sources to defray the large costs of serving children with severe disabilities (Lord, 2001). It has been suggested that the federal government might commit itself to these emergency funds, making it a national responsibility to meet the special programs and services that these students require

(Ladd & Hansen, 1999). Of course, the problem is that this money must come from somewhere.

State Strategies for Financing

Much of the significant legislation related to financing special education programs and services has been put into state legislation. States use several different models for financing special education. One of the decisions of substantial importance that a state must make is what strategy it will choose in providing fiscal resources to local districts. In what manner will the state provide for Arnie, Bobby, Les, Cathy, and Gretchen? Table 6.1 provides a decision matrix for four of the major strategies for funding, plus the advantages and disadvantages of each.

Table 6.1. State decisions on finance styles

Style	Description	Advantages	Disadvantages
Child-based funding (18 states)	Payment for each child identified Options of straight sum or weighted	Easy report on children served Political acceptance	Overclassification Conditions that are most heavily weighted get more students
Resource-based funding (10 states)	Payment by teacher or service unit	Easy to track special education funds Reinforcement of desired program alternatives	Difficult to determine units needed May hinder innovation Probably does not cover all service costs
Percentage reimbursement (11 states)	Reimbursement of excess costs up to an established ceiling per child or instructional unit	Maximum flexibility in programs Minimal labeling	Complex cost accounting Administrative burden at locating state levels
Fixed dollar grant per student (11 states)	Total funding available for special education disbursed by number of students for per pupil allotment	Convenient funding mechanism	Some students and communities short-changed True costs ignored

From National Association of State Boards of Education. (2002, July). *Policy update: Special education funding.* Alexandria, VA: Author; adapted by permission.

Child-Based Strategy

One of the models used by many states is the *child-based formula*, otherwise referred to as the head count approach. For every child with identified disabilities, the state provides a set amount of money to the local district to support
special services to the child. One of the natural consequences of this child-
based funding approach is overclassification. If the state provides support money
for children with learning disabilities, then it makes some fiscal sense for the
local district to find as many students whom they can diagnose with learning
disabilities as possible. The more students with learning disabilities, the more
money is collected from the state.

Weighted formulas recognize that it is more expensive to educate some
children with disabilities. Children with autism, like Arnie, may need support
that costs more than children with cerebral palsy, like Cathy, and an additional
problem arises. If a large amount of money is allocated to the district for each
child with autism and a smaller amount is allocated for children with mental
retardation, then one could predict that more children would be identified as
having autism and fewer identified as having mental retardation. These issues
related to weighted financial aid have become so widespread that funding agencies have often been forced to put a cap on the number of children for whom
reimbursement can be requested. That is, a district may be allowed to count
up to 5% of its students as having learning disabilities, but no more, no matter
how many students with learning disabilities they may count for their own purposes. This keeps the funding within some form of predictable cost for the state.

Resource-Based Formula

The second strategy in Table 6.1, the *resource-based formula,* places the emphasis on the extra personnel or service unit supplied rather than on the number
of students receiving services. A state might construct a formula in which there
is 1 teacher for every 25 students with a particular disability. This allows for
the calculation of the number of extra personnel that would be allotted to a
given district. The state must then figure out the number of personnel or service units to be assigned to the district, what the minimum and maximum al-
lowance of pupils per teacher should be, and so forth.

If the state provides a flat rate for each employee, it is unlikely that the
full costs to the school system of educating children with special needs will be
reimbursed. In addition, the resource-based approach does not include other
expenses incurred as part of a special education program. The approach does
provide a basis for tracking special education funds by counting the number of
personnel hired, however.

Percentage Reimbursement

The third model noted in Table 6.1, *percentage reimbursement,* recognizes that the state does not reimburse the local district for all of the excess costs that the special education program expends. Perhaps the state agrees to a percentage of excess costs (e.g., 70%) or agrees to reimbursement of excess costs up to an established ceiling per child or instructional unit. Although the percentage reimbursement formula does not require the district to label children in order to get reimbursement and also allows considerable flexibility on how the services are delivered, the accounting requirements are impressive and a clear administrative burden.

Fixed Dollar Grant

A fourth model, *fixed dollar grant,* begins with the availability of funds rather than the needs of a student. Given a set amount of money allocated to special education, that amount is divided by the number of students with special needs to arrive at an allotment per student. Whether such a formula actually works depends on the adequacy of the funds provided in the first place.

As can be seen in Table 6.1, each of the major formulas has advantages and disadvantages. States choose finance strategies on the basis of how they weigh the various advantages and disadvantages for each option. No matter which strategy is chosen, the local district can count on having to spend some of its own resources on the special education program for their district.

Financing special education requires a multitude of decisions, and traditionally, local, state, and federal levels of government have all been involved in complex formulas that add up to the finance package for children with disabilities. One of the key elements in calculating educational costs involves the teacher–pupil ratio: the fewer students per teacher, the more expensive the program is. If children who are deaf attend a separate class of eight students, then the costs will be high regardless of the other elements of the program. If Arnie, the child with autism, needs tutorial services, in which a specialist may work with only two or three students at a time, then the costs for Arnie's education multiply alarmingly.

Some Alternative Funding Proposals

Alternative proposals for funding special and general education are periodically suggested. The proposals also call for a realignment of power and authority in the process of changing the money allocation. Two of these proposals block grants and vouchers, have special significance for children with special needs.

Block Grants

One of the proposals for financing education is the *block grant approach*. In this approach, the money appropriated at the federal or state level for all kinds of specific educational purposes (e.g., remedial reading, vocational education) would be bundled together and sent to the states or school systems as one sum of money, without requirements that it be spent on particular programs or particular students. The argument for the block grant approach is that the state and local educators and decision makers are closer to the needs of the students and schools and are better able to decide the proper allocation of money than are bureaucrats in the federal or state government (Finn, Rotherham, & Hokanson, 2001). Also, the diverse number of programs supported by federal funds each have their own requirements and regulations and are often confusing to local educators, who become frustrated with trying to follow the accompanying rules and regulations for each of the separate programs. A block grant allows local educators to determine where funds are distributed on the basis of local needs, rather than on the basis of complex and exacting rules that sometimes work at cross purposes to what a school's students actually need.

The counter argument is that the block grant approach is bad news for children in minority groups, such as children with disabilities and children living in poverty, who find that local priorities for general education take precedence over the needs of small groups of children with special needs. Because the education money always runs out before *all* of the needs are met, who is going to be shortchanged? This is why many special educators view the block grant approach with suspicion.

Proponents of the earmarked special education federal programs point out that it was necessary to go to the federal government for help with their problems in the first place because children with special needs had often been ignored financially at the local and state levels. An additional reason for not supporting the block grant approach is that it takes priority setting out of the hands of the Congress and returns it, along with the power and authority that goes with it, to state leaders. Because federal decision makers receive praise and support for establishing and supporting these special programs, they are not likely give up that method of funding very soon.

Educational Vouchers

Another potential method of funding programs for children with special needs and other forms of education is the *educational voucher*. The voucher is, in effect, a promissory note for a certain amount given to parents who can cash it in at the school or program of their choice. The argument for vouchers is quite simple. Money spent on education should be placed in the hands of parents, who would then spend the money in ways they felt would best help their child get a good education. Power would be returned to the family, from educators who would not know what is best for individual children.

When there are unfavorable settings for children and their education, this voucher approach surfaces as a way for extracting children from schools that do not work or are harmful to the children involved. No Child Left Behind proposed that if a school failed to meet the standards of annual improvement 2 years in a row, then the parents of children in that school would be able to move their children to a school that was performing up to standard, allowing them a more favorable educational environment.

The counter argument to the voucher approach has been that the amount of money made available would inevitably not cover the total cost of special education and that the parents, or someone, would then have to pay the difference, a particularly difficult situation for parents living in poverty and parents whose children need very special treatment. Whether such an approach would satisfy the requirement of a free appropriate public education in the IDEA legislation would be a major question, as well. The courts would almost certainly become involved, as parents would likely have to sue to force the schools to provide services for free, as was promised in the IDEA legislation.

It is clear that how the United States funds its education is an issue that will be revisited many times in the future. Many states commit more than 50% of their total budgets to education, so how they attain and spend the money for such a huge enterprise is of great importance.

NEED FOR DATA SYSTEMS

If special education leaders or public decision makers are forced to make decisions about the expenditures of scarce resources, on what basis will they make such decisions? Suppose public decision makers ask how many special education teachers will be needed over the next 5 years or how many children with autism they should plan for in the next few years? Where do they find that answer? Unless there is a data system in place that receives data from local systems on a regular basis, the answers to these key questions will be, at best, an informed guess. The National Center for Educational Statistics (NCES) is a repository of data collected from the state and local systems, but unless the right questions are posed and the data are collected by the NCES, it cannot help special education.

Nor is it sufficient to count the number of children with disabilities that the individual districts have reported and then divide by the teacher–pupil ratio to obtain the number of qualified special education teachers needed. Decision makers also need to know the number of children who need very specialized help. Children like Arnie will require a special education teacher plus additional support—personnel who have specialized information about social skills training, behavior modification, and communication techniques that are related to the condition of autism. In addition, teachers of children who are blind or deaf must meet special requirements. Even well-prepared special education teachers often do not know how to teach a child to read or write in Braille. Travel and mobility training, needed by children with severe visual disabilities, is another special skill for the special educator. Therefore, decision makers need information on just what type of disabilities are involved in special education, the prevalence of students with a particular disability, and the intensity of the disabilities.

What are the chances that Les, the boy with learning disabilities, will have a qualified teacher of children with learning disabilities to help him with his special problems? When learning disabilities were first discovered, one of the treatment models proposed was a small classroom with 8–10 students so that the specialist could spend a great deal of instructional time with each student (Lerner, 2000). If that were the model in place today, then Les's chance of having a qualified teacher would be slim. Given the number of children with learning disabilities who are now being identified in the public schools, it would be impossible for educators to train enough specialists for this model. Fortunately, the treatment model has been modified so that many students like Les are in the general classroom with some special remedial lessons or tutoring being provided by teachers specializing in learning disabilities, who also provide help to the general education teacher.

In addition to the data available on the students with disabilities, decision makers also need information on the availability of special education teachers and other specialists, if proper planning is to be executed. They also need to know how many teachers remain to be certified. For example, a survey done with gifted students found that, in one southern state, more than 20% of the teachers now working with gifted students do not have certification now and are currently working toward certification (Gallagher & Bray, 2002). No Child Left Behind requires that only qualified teachers—those with proper educational certification—be employed. Because the number of special education positions far exceed the supply of qualified teachers, decision makers must make some adjustment by giving waivers to school systems or states or other administrative devices to allow special education programs to operate.

These data give some measure of information regarding the amount of personnel preparation resources that are needed to come up to standard. In addition, decision makers need information on the rate of attrition of teachers in special education, how many will retire or leave the program in a given year, in order to get a firm grasp on what the personnel needs will be in the future.

One of the ways that good planning can take place is to develop information concerning the needs of the program and the available resources to meet these needs. Table 6.2 shows hypothetical data for State X that can be used to determine the personnel requirements for a particular disability (e.g., learning disabilities). In order to put together a table like Table 6.2, a state would need data provided by each local school system regarding its student population and teaching staff.

The hypothetical data presented here is an illustration of what might be concluded from data. First of all, for a given state, the number of students with learning disabilities that need services can be arrived at by summing all of the reported students with learning disabilities from each district. Another way of calculating such needs would be to use a projected prevalence rate for students with learning disabilities in the school population and then calculate the projected number of students with learning disabilities on the basis of the total student population of the district or state. Table 6.2 uses a projected prevalence rate of 4%, which equals a project number of 40,000 students with learning disabilities.

Once the number of students who theoretically need service is known, State X can calculate the number of teachers needed by dividing by the projected teacher–pupil ratio (1:20), which equals 2,000 teachers. But how many certified learning disability teachers are currently at work in the state? To answer that question, the state would refer to the data from individual districts and add up the number of certified teachers available, in this case 1,400. So, State X appears to be short 600 learning disability teachers, but this number does not include teachers with temporary certificates who are working toward full

Table 6.2. Hypothetical data regarding children with learning disabilities in State X

A.	Public school enrollment K–12 (Cumulative local data)	1,000,000
B.	Projected number of students with learning disabilities (A x .04)	40,000
C.	Expected teacher–student ratio (administratively determined)	1:20
D.	Expected qualified teachers needed (B/C calculation)	2,000
E.	Number of teachers certified in learning disabilities (state records)	1,400
F.	Number of teachers temporarily certified (state records)	300
G.	Number of teachers leaving (5% attrition; state data)	70
H.	Number of teachers entering the profession (university records)	100
I.	Teachers needed (D − E − F + G − H)	270

certification (300), who can be counted as part of the available personnel pool. This reduces State X's deficit to 300 teachers. However, teachers leave the profession for a wide number of reasons, and yearly attrition must be taken into consideration. Previous attrition figures indicate that 5% of teachers typically leave each year. That would add another 70 teachers to replace. Finally, the higher education institutions in State X are graduating 100 teachers certified in learning disabilities this year, which brings the final estimate of needed qualified teachers to 270.

This is a substantial personnel preparation deficit and mirrors many existing personnel shortages in the field of special education. So, how does one deal with such a shortage in one's planning? Data can be made to look more palatable in several ways, even if the basic situation does not change. Decision makers could ignore the desired teacher–pupil ratio of 1:20 and say that perhaps 1:25 would be an acceptable figure if districts adopt a teacher consultation model in which the specialist provides suggestions to the general education teacher, with occasional tutoring for children like Les. Now, the state has a total deficit of only 70 teachers. This would almost eliminate the shortage by watering down the standards for a high-quality program.

State X could also try to increase the output of its training institutions by providing more scholarships for teachers in learning disabilities or by aggressively recruiting new students in this field. The state could even try to raid neighboring states for certified learning disability teachers. Certainly, it would have to adopt some alternative plan or settle for a continuing situation in which partially training or untrained personnel would be working with students with learning disabilities. Of course, by using statewide data, State X is also ignoring the particular needs of an individual community and the likelihood of an uneven distribution of certified learning disability teachers and students with learning disabilities across districts. More than likely, it would find the qualified teachers clustered in some areas and absent in other areas, which will complicate these figures and make it necessary to calculate local figures to identify the local imbalance.

One of the uses of a program analysis is to determine whether any of the solutions are even in the realm of possibility. At one point in the 1970s, the preferred differentiated program for children with learning disabilities placed a small group of eight students with learning disabilities with a trained professional. An analysis such as the one provided in Table 6.2 would quickly reveal that with such a program it would be impossible to meet the need for professionals: not in the next decade, nor in the next century, nor as far as one could see into the future. In short, the small-group model must be abandoned if a state has any pretense of providing needed services. It would be akin to asking everyone to have his or her own personal psychiatrist. It could never be accomplished for all who need it because of the numbers required. So, this type of planning analysis can help people see which program models lie within the possible parameters of money and personnel and which do not.

Because knowledge of the number of children in need of various services is critical to determining the projected cost of a program or services, a data system is a key element to comprehensive planning. A data system can also be useful for answering any number of questions, such as, "Are children with special needs who are part of minority groups being served in the same proportion as their demographic proportion in the state?" (Hebbeler, 1993).

Federal agencies have been aware of the need for such basic data for their own planning purposes. The NCES has added an early childhood education segment to its reporting (http://nces.ed.gov/fastfacts), and the National Child Care Information Center State Profiles have been helpful in gathering statistics on personnel status and development (http://nccic.org/statedata/statepro/index .html). Still, these federal data sources must rely on the capabilities of the states to collect accurate information from local communities.

The data system for young children must deal with more problems than school-age children, who can be conveniently found in one place—the schools. In the preschool years, children may be found in the home or in a variety of preschool settings (e.g., child care, Head Start, prekindergarten programs), which makes it difficult to be sure one has found all the 3- and 4-year-olds. Obtaining unduplicated counts of young children with disabilities receiving multiple services is an additional problem. That is, if a state counts the number of services provided instead of the number of children, it will overestimate the number involved because children like Arnie and Cathy could be getting services from a number of professionals. Confidentiality is also a significant issue because some mental health agencies are not able to share their files with other agencies due to confidentiality agreements with the families that do not allow the sharing of information without the parents' permission.

Although progress has been made in building some data systems at the federal level, many state and local districts still experience limitations in their data systems. A number of states have begun efforts to develop comprehensive data systems. It remains to be seen if such systems will receive the consistent financial support needed for their maintenance. States will likely need to assemble an interdisciplinary committee, with help from consultants with demonstrated expertise in data systems, to carry out the initial design and implementation of a comprehensive state data system. The people who will have to provide the data for the system—early care and early education personnel—should have input into the design of the system.

One of the disadvantages of data systems is the time required by service providers to do the necessary paperwork. Special education teachers estimate that they spend 5 hours per week on paperwork, as opposed to 2 hours per week for general educators. The data systems appear to be more complete for special education than for general education, but at a price (U.S. Department of Education, 2002).

The sizable technical problems in operating and upgrading data systems are not the only difficulties facing those wishing to establish a data system for children with support needs. Some policy makers do not wish to know some of the data that would come forth from such a data system because knowing such data (e.g., the number of children not being served) may force action that will result in expenditures that the policy maker might well wish not to make. The principle of *deniability* (e.g., "I didn't know things were in such bad shape!") is well established in the political realm, and a functioning data system may prevent the exercise of such denial.

DECISIONS AHEAD

Clearly, much work remains to be done, and many decisions have yet to be made. The following sections outline some of the most pressing decisions, including the design of defensible finance systems, the protection of support services, the possible consolidation of funds, and the combat of data systems' weaknesses.

Defensible Finance Systems

One of the most significant decisions immediately ahead for those in special education is how to design a system of financing special education programs that will pass constitutional muster in states. Existing financial systems in three states have been declared unconstitutional. General education has had parallel problems with its own financial strategies. The courts demand *horizontal equity* between communities in the state. That is, those services that are available in one part of the state should be similarly available in other parts of that state. Since the 1980s, the rural parts of any state have suffered from a lack of funding and resources because the finance system was not designed to provide them with equity with more affluent school systems in the state.

This does not mean that every district would have exactly the same services as every other district, but it does mean that some baseline of services should be available to every district. Whether the financial system is based on a head count or on census percentages, the rural districts in the past have lost out, and systems need to be adapted to meet the concerns of state courts very soon.

Protecting Support Systems

Much of this volume has been devoted to showing how important support systems can be for high-quality education for children with special needs. But how can educators be assured that such support components as communications, data systems, and personnel preparation are being funded appropriately? There is good reason to be concerned because the tendency of state legislatures faced with budget problems will be to not cut the direct services to children with disabilities and their families. Such direct service cuts would be guaranteed to result in anger from parents. The far easier way for the legislators is to cut the financing of the support system elements. These cuts will not be nearly as visible to the public but may well cripple the support systems. If money is diverted from TA programs, then who will know? The service programs will continue as before. A teacher may have to do without the help and assistance that he or she had been getting from the TA system, but public decision makers will be spared the criticism that they could count on if they decreased the budget for special education teachers.

The question is how these important support service entities can be protected in hard fiscal times. One suggestion has been to have the support elements *indexed* to special education services. That is, if the special education services increased by 5%, then the support services would get a similar 5% increase. Similarly, if the special education budget for services were cut by 5%, then the support services would be cut by the same percentage. In this way, the support services maintain a constant relationship to the service program, once it has been determined that the support services are adequate in the first place, and will not be the scapegoat when fiscal downturns inevitably occur.

Consolidation of Funds

One of the issues that is far from resolution is how funds for children with disabilities are to be handled at the local level in the future. Educational administrators urge support for greater flexibility of funds to enable them to produce a comprehensive education for all students. Advocates for children with disabilities remain uncertain about what would happen to these children if the earmarked funds designated to be used exclusively for children with disabilities were replaced with a single budget serving all students.

Parrish (1997) presented the need for a "seamless net of education programs and services to meet the needs of all students" and pointed out that the categorical separation of funds has led to fragmented and inefficient programs. But if the funds for children with disabilities are pooled with the other education funds, how does one guarantee a free appropriate public education for children with disabilities? Who will ensure that Arnie receives appropriate treatment for autism, or that Cathy has the technological help that she needs to adjust to her cerebral palsy, or that Bobby receives functional behavior analysis instead of suspension? One thing seems clear, however; the rapidly increasing special education funds cannot continue to grow as they have without some readjustment in the total educational financial package.

Combatting the Shortcomings of Data Systems

There is broad general agreement on the usefulness of data systems in a total program for children with disabilities. Nevertheless, data systems have a significant shortcoming that needs to be confronted: the time it takes to put the data into the system. If educators want to find out how many children have been suspended from school this year, then how can that information become available? Teachers and principals must fill out forms provided to them that allow them to enter the number of suspended students in their school and then send all of these forms to a central place to be aggregated and expressed in a useful manner. If that were the only piece of information needed, there would not be much concern, but educators and decision makers need a whole array of information— including achievement attainment, emotional status, and social skills mastery— and each of these data sets requires that somebody on the educational firing line provides the information.

Some are not impressed by the cost of such information gathering. After all, what is one more question? But it is the accumulation of questions that causes the problem. Those who report data and those who process data must reach an agreement that the information they are requesting from teachers, principals, and other administrators is crucial to the educational questions that need to be answered.

Public decision makers seem to split their time and complaints. On Monday, Wednesday, and Friday, they call for the programs to provide missing data that they need to make decisions. On Tuesday and Thursday, they complain about all of the paperwork that has accumulated and is irritating frontline educators. It is only through paperwork that the questions are answered. Yet too much filling out of forms and documenting behavior is actually reported to cause teachers to leave the profession. Where the necessary balance is remains a decision to be made. The issues of finance and data systems are likely to continue to be a central part of the decision making in special education that has to be made at all levels of government.

CHAPTER 7

Educational Planning for Children with Special Needs

I t has become increasingly clear that, in modern society, it is important to establish the means for planning to meet complex problems over an extended time period. This requires collaboration with other individuals and organizations. The corporate sector of society has long been committed to long-range planning, as has the military. Education is one complex activity that cries out for comprehensive planning. When planning for the education of children with special needs, educators need to set goals and objectives for special education programs, establish the sequence of activities needed to reach those goals, and, most important, allocate the resources necessary to fund that sequence of activities. Such planning needs to be done both for individuals, as with IEPs, and for larger subsets of students, such as children with autism.

The need for such collaboration actually runs counter to the American illusion of the primacy of the individual, that one person on his or her own can take on enormous problems and, by wit, motivation, and virtue, achieve important goals. Such a concept is frequently played out in American literature and entertainment. This is not to say that individuals do not play a significant role in motivating change or causing major events to happen, merely that they are unlikely to build a dam, create national economic policy, or reform a school system without substantial help from other individuals and organizations over an extended period of time (Fullan, 2001). The process by which these goals are achieved is called *planning*.

MAKING DECISIONS FOR PLANNING

The four engines of change have all been active in helping to make planning decisions about some of the major questions of past generations:

- How do decision makers set long-range goals and objectives for children with special needs and for the programs that support them?

- How do decision makers allocate and distribute resources most effectively for children with special needs?

- How do decision makers decide between alternate educational strategies?

- How can decision makers ensure that their plans were implemented, and how can they recognize barriers that stand in the way of achieving their objectives?

Planning requires commitment to goals over time and need help from our engines of change to establish a continuing process by which planning can become operational.

Legislation

IDEA 2004 and other legislation for children with disabilities mandated a number of planning processes for both individuals and organizations. For example, each state is required to develop a Comprehensive System of Personnel Development (CSPD) plan to ensure that competent personnel are available for children with special needs. The requirement for an IEP for each child with disabilities is also spelled out in legislation. An Interagency Coordinating Council (ICC) is required to help states coordinate the various resources in the infants and toddlers section of the legislation.

IDEA 2004 also provided clear expectations for the integration of children with disabilities with their age groups in general education:

> To the maximum extent appropriate, children with disabilities, including children in public or private institutions or other care facilities, are educated with children who are nondisabled, and special classes, separate schooling, or other removal of children with disabilities from the regular educational environment occurs only when the nature or severity of the disability is such that education in regular classes with the use of supplementary aids and services cannot be achieved satisfactorily.

There are similar protections for children with disabilities and their parents under Section 504 of the Rehabilitation Act of 1973, as amended (PL 93-112). Under this section, qualified people cannot be denied access to any program receiving federal financial assistance or any program or activity conducted by any executive agency.

The Americans with Disabilities Act (ADA) also extends the rights of people with disabilities to include the right of access to buildings, public transportation, and public accommodations. All of this legislation carries the message that children and adults with disabilities have the right to live in a society that provides a level playing field for them in education and in the society as a whole.

Court Decisions

One of the roles of court decisions is to reinforce or make more specific the language in legislation, such as the LRE clause in the IDEA legislation. In *Greer v. Rome City School District* (1991), the court noted that Congress created a statutory preference for educating children with disabilities in the same class-room as children without disabilities. Another court decision (*Sacramento City Unified School District, Board of Education v. Rachel H.*, 1994) raised the inclusion requirement to a *rebuttable presumption*. That is, the school must present evidence as to why a child with disabilities should not be educated in the general classroom. Such court decisions solidified the intent of the legislation and made clear to the schools just what is acceptable in this regard.

One of the most important rights of parents or individuals in American society is the right to due process. It is not enough to have laws or court decisions that say what should be done for children with disabilities. Due process provides a means for establishing that what should be done is, in fact, being done and in the right way. Procedural safeguards of IDEA 2004 include procedures for parents who wish to protest if they feel that their child is not receiving an appropriate education. They can ask for a hearing in front of an impartial hearing officer, they may appeal such rulings to the state education agency, and finally, if still dissatisfied, they can bring the issue to state or federal district court. If Cathy's parents believe that the IEP for their daughter is being mishandled or inappropriately applied, then they can move to request a hearing and eventually progress to the courts, if they aren't satisfied. If Arnie's parents think their child is being shortchanged in the IEP planning process, they, too, can ask for redress from the courts.

Administrative Rules

Legislative mandates require an enormous collection of rules that can be many pages longer than the original legislation. Rules and regulations are formulated to shape specific aspects of the process (e.g., how the IEPs and IFSPs are carried out, who should be in a meeting) so that professionals can carry out their responsibilities in the most appropriate fashion. OSEP has complex rule making responsibilities that include the regulations regarding the IEP, which is a cornerstone to planning for individual children with disabilities. Such rules detail the nature of the team doing the planning, the role expected of parents, and how the IEP should be developed (Jacob-Timm and Hartshorne, 1998).

The content of the IEP is specified as follows:

1. A statement of the child's present levels of educational performance

2. A statement of measurable annual goals and short-term objectives

3. A statement of the special education and related services and aids to be provided to the child

4. An explanation of the extent to which the child will not participate with children without disabilities in the general classroom

5. What modifications in the administration of statewide assessments are needed for the child to participate

6. The projected date for the beginning of the services and the locations and durations of these services

7. Beginning at age 14, a statement of the transition service needs of the child and the interagency responsibilities involved

8. A statement of the child's progress toward annual goals and how the parents will be informed of their child's progress

Each of these responsibilities involves many complicated steps and indicates the importance of the administrative rule making, which is often underestimated.

Professional Initiatives

The roles that professionals play in planning can be either individual or collective. Individually, professionals can be a part of devising an IEP for any individual child, and as a member of a professional association such as the CEC or NAEYC, they can develop policies related to planning for subgroups of children with special needs, develop manuals such as *What Every Special Educator Must Know, Fourth Edition* (CEC, 2000), or devise statements on professional ethics designed to protect the rights of children and families.

Time becomes a significant factor in developing policies for planning. The most important goals take years or decades to achieve. For example, when attempting a major effort in modifying personnel preparation for specialists in special education, professionals must first reach a consensus on the nature of change needed. Then, they must convince the institutions of higher education that colleges and universities should modify their existing personnel preparation program. The professionals then need to convince agencies at the state and federal levels that the funding reflects the changed personnel preparation emphasis (i.e., not continuing to fund obsolete programs).

A decade may be too short a time for all of these steps to transpire. During that period of time, funding should be consistent so that the changes can take place in a systematic fashion. Yet budget decision making often occurs on a yearly cycle and is subject to the vagaries of political power, tax revenues, and the call for resources of competing priorities. The rapidly increasing costs of Medicare, for example, can negatively affect long-term state education plans for change, not because decision makers are hostile to education, but because health care needs have drawn away the limited resources.

Of course, the more money is reserved for long-range priorities, the less money is available to meet current needs. This results in struggles between the long-range planners and those administrators just trying to meet current needs, which can often be seen as critical. Many newly elected mayors or governors can find, to their dismay, that the resources they had hoped to have available for their priorities have already been committed to other long-range purposes, and so a struggle is inevitable between the proposed new funding and the support of long-range interests. If the budget is level (i.e., no more money is available this year than last year), then something has to give, and it is more likely that long-term programs, which may have fallen out of favor, are the ones that are cut. That is why it is so difficult to maintain planning priorities over a number of years.

PRINCIPLES OF PLANNING

Planning may be shaped by a set of principles that guide current understandings of the developing child, with or without disabilities. One of these principles is that of the child in the societal envelope. Many diverse forces in the society affect children and their development (Bronfenbrenner, 1989). Not only is the development of children with special needs shaped by the members of their family but also by the cultural sea in which they swim from a very young age. How might Bobby's behavior be different if he and his family lived in a quiet community rather than the chaotic neighborhood in which they find themselves? The goal of Cathy's program is to create a normal and supportive environment so that she is able to cope educationally, with a minimum of extra stress. So part of the planning should involve a consideration of the environment surrounding the child.

Figure 7.1 shows a graphic depiction of the Bronfenbrenner model, indicating the impact and interaction of forces of family, peers, school, community, and the larger society. Although Bronfenbrenner (1989) did not reject the impact of genetics on the child, he asserted that various environmental forces, in interaction with one another, shape and determine the developmental outcomes of the child. From a planning standpoint, all of these environmental forces must be considered in developing an IEP for the individual child.

Multidisciplinary Efforts

Elder (1998) pointed out that individuals are shaped by their historical context (e.g., the Great Depression, World War II). Because the entire cultural environment determines the child's success or failure in school (Bronfenbrenner, 1989), the approach to help must be transdisciplinary. No one profession—sociology, psychology, medicine, or education—alone can claim expertise in all of the areas of action necessary to support children with special needs and their families.

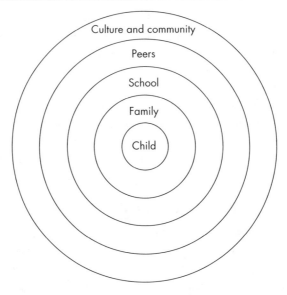

Figure 7.1. Bronfenbrenner's model of child development. (From Bronfenbrenner, U. [1989]. Ecological systems theory. *Annals of Child Development, 6,* 187–249; adapted by permission.)

Collaboration

Each of the five children with special needs has unique characteristics that call for the attention of more than one specialist with special training or agencies with their own responsibilities. Cathy needs an orthopedist, a special educator, and a general educator to work together. Bobby needs a psychologist, a special educator, an applied behavior analyst, and a general educator. Gretchen needs content specialists, a psychologist, a librarian, and a teacher of gifted students, among other professionals. Les needs a neurologist, a learning disability specialist, and a general educator. Arnie needs a platoon of medical personnel, family counselors, behaviorists, and special educators.

In all of these instances, people with diverse training and experience have to come together as some type of working team. The requirements of the IEP demand no less. The agencies or subdivisions in schools and communities that employ these experts have a special responsibility to be flexible to accommodate to the needs of these children. The requirement that individual professionals and organizations work together to create a plan broader than the mandate of any particular profession or agency is manifest but often unrealized. There are several levels of working together usually referred to as cooperation, coordination, or collaboration.

Cooperation implies that agencies or programs are aware of and promote the services provided by other agencies in the community but operate independently of one another. A state department of mental health may be aware that the department of education is concerned with children with emotional disturbances and may support its agenda but does little to blend the two agencies' efforts.

Coordination occurs when agencies or programs take into account the concerns of other agencies and programs. They work together to accommodate the others' services and schedules but continue to pursue individual program goals. Health and education agencies may work together on the diagnosis of learning disabilities but still pursue different program goals.

Collaboration implies a higher level of partnership to achieve ends that no single agency can accomplish. There is a sharing of values and priorities in the implementation of services that will resolve outstanding issues. Sometimes, infrastructure changes aid in such collaboration. The ICCs, for example, are charged with bringing about collaboration between a variety of agencies and interests.

Because public agencies are often organized by discipline (e.g., social work, health, education), a comprehensive approach to children and their families must include more than cooperation or coordination. There must be collaboration between personnel and existing agencies. Finally, modifying unfavorable circumstances surrounding the family and child requires continuous, and not just episodic, change if it is to be effective. Such calls for multidisciplinary collaboration to meet the requirements of children with special needs are almost clichés in daily conversations. Nevertheless, there are many factors to take into consideration before effective planning can take place.

STAGES OF POLICY INITIATION

Because planning often includes the initiation of new policies, it must also take into account the various stages of policy formulation. Table 7.1 shows the three major subdivisions necessary for policy initiation—policy development, policy approval, and policy implementation—and each stage requires a major planning and collaborative effort to be successful.

Actually, *policy development* turns out to be the easiest to accomplish. Policy can be designed by a relatively small number of experienced policy makers from various professional disciplines who can draft a major change in policy, such as inclusion for children with disabilities. However, for such policy change to be successful, large numbers of professionals and parents have to approve of the new set of ideas and practices. While the new policy is being developed and articulated, groundwork needs to be laid for the other two policy stages. This means that public decision makers who are crucial to the policy approval stage need to be aware of the policy development well in advance of their part in the process.

Table 7.1.   Stages for policy initiation

Policy development

The generation of a set of written rules and procedures that guide the allocation of resources, identify the eligible candidates for special services, delineate the system of services, identify who will deliver the services, and state the conditions under which the services with be delivered.

Policy approval

The series of actions and events necessary to obtain support or official sanction for the policies that have been developed. In some states, this may mean necessary action by the state legislature; in others, it may mean action by the governor; and in still others, it may mean actions taken by the lead agency. Some definite action is necessary, however, before draft policies become the official policy of the state.

Policy implementation

Once the policies have been given an official sanction, it is then necessary to implement them at the state level as well as the local level, where the actual service delivery takes place. At this point, it is necessary to determine if these rules are appropriate to the specific problems posed by both the state and local environments.

From Gallagher, J. (1994). Policy designed for diversity: New initiatives for children with disabilities. In D.M. Bryant & M.A. Graham (Eds.), *Implementing early intervention* (pp. 336–350). New York: Guilford Press; adapted by permission.

The *policy approval* stage depends on the decisions of people who are in positions of authority and power. They may be administrators, directors of programs, city council members, state legislators, or agency directors. They may not know very much about the specifics of the proposed policy itself, but they are in a key position to judge the impact of the policy on the people who will be affected by it. They also judge the need for new resources that may be required by the policy.

For example, in order to approve the policy of inclusion, people responsible for approving the policy had to be convinced that the policy worked for the children involved, and they had to judge the effect on the children's parents, classmates, and educational administrators. Would the new policy cost more money and personnel, or less? One of the attractive parts of the inclusion policy to decision makers is that it appears to be less costly than the alternatives of resource rooms or special classes. The public response to the policy of inclusion has yet to be fully judged, but it appears to be less negative than some of the critics would have thought (Salisbury & McGregor, 2002).

The practitioners who have the major responsibility for the *policy implementation* stage need to be aware of the new policy development and to have participated in the shaping of it. After having had to accept many policy initiatives that have been concocted by someone else, some teachers and other educators have often stated, "We wish to be in on the takeoff as well as the landing of this policy."

Finally, and probably most important for education, can policy implementation be carried out effectively? It does little good for an educational policy to be trumpeted by its proponents only to find that no one knows how to make it work at the local level. Major retraining of special educators and general educators may be necessary and technical assistance made available, at least during the initiation of changes in policies and procedures. Careful planning at all three stages of the policy change is essential to the eventual success of the new policy (Gallagher, 1994a).

SAMPLE PLANNING MODEL

How is systematic planning carried out? The development of specific plans for the delivery of services to children with disabilities becomes particularly important because of the need to hire specialized personnel or have special equipment available well in advance of the actual time for instruction. A number of models for planning can be entertained, but most of them contain similar elements.

Figure 7.2 displays a schematic representing one version of a planning model. Planning models are useful because the complexities of planning make it difficult to put all of the pieces together over a considerable time period without some systematic approach (Gallagher, 2002). Arnie is used in the example be-

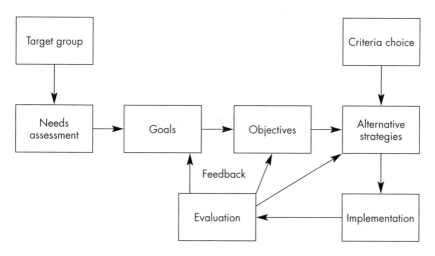

Figure 7.2. Planning model for children with disabilities. (From Gallagher, J.J. [2002]. *Society's role in educating gifted students: The role of public policy.* Storrs, CT: National Research Center on the Gifted and Talented; reprinted by permission.)

cause he represents the most complex set of issues of all the children—language development, social skills, academic performance, and peer acceptance.

Target Group

The first step in this model (Figure 7.2) is to identify which children are being addressed by specifying their age and condition. This example concentrates on children with autism, like Arnie, and limits the planning to the primary and elementary programs in the school district. Policy makers would want to know, at a minimum, how many of these children there are and the severity of their conditions. The example community has more than 100,000 citizens and 20,000 school children. If policy makers know the number of children in the primary and elementary grades in their school system, then they can estimate how many children with autism there might be in the school system. The prevalence rate has been reported as 20 per 10,000, or even 1 per 1,000, so it is likely that at least 20–35 children with autism spectrum disorders of varying ages are in that school system (Fombonne, 1999; Lord, 2001).

If, in fact, educators have positively identified only five children with autism in the system, they should wonder whether some children with autism have not been properly identified or have been characterized in some other fashion (e.g., mental retardation, behavioral disturbances) (Lord & Risi, 2000). Policy makers should conduct a review of children diagnosed with mental retardation or behavior disorders who also have symptoms of autism to identify misdiagnoses.

Needs Assessment

How would policy makers go about developing a needs assessment of this target group of children? Certainly multiple areas of functioning need to be assessed once children with autism have been diagnosed. These functioning areas would include communication, intellectual skills, behavior characteristics, and social development. Based on current knowledge of children with autism, policy makers should expect to find children with autism with serious delays in social development, with few if any friends (Mundy & Stella, 2000). Such children would reveal a limited *theory of mind,* meaning that they have a weakness in the ability to perceive what others are thinking or feeling (Lord, 2001). Children identified as having autism show a wide variation in intellectual development, but some children with mental retardation may be among the group. Policy makers would want to assess how the child is currently adapting in real-world settings. In other words, they would expect that IEPs be developed for each of these children, which would involve attention to the intellectual, social, behavioral, and communication areas. It would also probably need staff specially trained in autism because even people trained as special educators might not have the requisite training or skills to plan for and implement services for children with autism.

Goals

The next step in the planning process is to establish some major goals for the program for these students. Goals most often follow directly from the identified needs. That is, if a student has major communication problems, then one of the goals (spelling out the major intent of the program) would be to improve his or her communication skills. If the child has significant social problems, then one of the goals of the instruction would be to enhance the abilities of the student to interact reasonably well with his or her peer group. But goals that state broad general expectations for improvement are often not precise enough, particularly when trying to assess the effectiveness of the intervention program. After all, the children are growing older, and one would naturally expect some form of developmental progress on that basis alone. So how much growth should really be expected? This expectation should be quite individualistic because of the widely varying abilities of each student.

Objectives

Objectives are designed to transform goals into measurable expectations by stating specifically how much change is expected, on what dimensions, and in what time period. For example, a program objective might state, "We expect our program for children with autism to provide evidence that 60% of students with autism will show a 20% increase or more in social contacts with peers by the end of the school year." Thus, the policy makers specify how much increase, in what particular domain, and for how many of the students in the program. Objectives are measurable ways of determining whether the program is achieving what is hoped for it. Because many goals and objectives are at least partly qualitative in character, observers or judges are needed who show reliability of judgment (i.e., two or more judges rating consistently the same scene or videotape). When the actual results are fed back through a program evaluation (Figure 7.2), policy makers will know what new decisions they should be making in implementing the program.

Alternative Strategies

A wide variety of approaches can be considered in policy makers' attempts to reach their goals and objectives for young children with autism. The *decision matrix* shown in Figure 7.3 provides program alternatives together with the

Program alternative	Criteria for choice				
	Cost	Personnel needs	Track record	Public support	Legal issues
Inclusion in general classroom	Moderate	Consultation specialists needed	Program success reported	Ambivalent	Sufficient intensity of treatment
Special class—tutoring communication skills	High	Serious shortages	Improvements noted	Support	Accepted
Applied behavior analysis—behavior modification	Moderate	Special training needed	Improvements noted	Support	Accepted
Parent training	Low	Experience with parents needed	Some improvements needed	Support	Accepted
Status quo	Low	Current shortage serious	Uncertain	Ambivalent	Equity concerns

Figure 7.3. Decision matrix for children with autism. (*Note:* Ratings here are provided by the author based on research reviews, program reports, and personal experience.)

criteria that might be used to select between options (cost, personnel needs, track record, public support, legal issues). One of those alternatives can be inclusion within the general classroom with some professional support provided within that setting. This brings children with autism into closer contact with their peers without disabilities but might make it difficult for them to get the intensive therapies that might be required. The criterion of 25 hours of relevant programming per week, recommended by the National Academy of Sciences report, might be difficult to meet (Lord, 2001). The 25 hours represents a 5-hour school day for 5 days, meaning that the entire school day for children with autism should be designed to accommodate the various issues related to autism.

Lovaas (1993), one of the predominant experts in the field, suggested that children with autism spend at least 30 hours per week in an intensive program that would include home and parent activity. The National Academy of Sciences report members felt that this was too much but still wanted to express their desire for a serious intervention effort that would be necessary to achieve the positive results needed.

Another program alternative, as shown in Figure 7.3, is a small class with no more than 8–10 children with autism, in which specialists can provide a wide variety of small-group and one-to-one therapy sessions in communications and social skills. To use this approach, Arnie's IEP team would have to justify in writing the need for removing Arnie from the general classroom because of IDEA regulations that stress the general classroom as the desirable placement unless unusual circumstances are present.

Another option is to adopt the systematic application of ABA, in which the behavior issues of these children are met by a systematic and intense fashion with a well-established treatment strategy. Finally, one could commit oneself to a serious program of parent training in the hopes that the parents could continue the therapeutic approaches in the home and increase the sense of parent empowerment.

Choosing Between Options

As the decision matrix in Figure 7.3 shows, a wide variety of criteria should be taken into account in making a decision about which approach, or combination of approaches, to adopt. There is always the matter of cost, and the intense use of special therapists plus small-group instruction means high costs. Also, decision makers should consider whether special personnel are available. Can specialists be recruited in the education of children with autism? If not, they should remind themselves that the inclusion strategy is based on the availability of specialists to aid the general education teacher.

Track record in Figure 7.3 indicates available evidence regarding a strategy's effectiveness. Current emphasis on research-based strategies makes the track record criterion even more important as a factor for decision making. Various literature reviews or research syntheses can help establish an approach's track record. A body of research suggests ABA is particularly effective in coping with behavior problems.

Some studies on inclusion in action (Schattman & Keating, 2000) and as a policy in specific program descriptions (Levin, 1997; Salisbury & McGregor, 2002) report successful implementation; however, studies on the implementation of inclusion in public schools indicate a diversity of results (Hines, 2001; Lipsky & Gartner, 1997; Salend & Duhaney, 1999). Some report gains in social development (Guralnick, 2001), yet others do not. Some report academic gains in both children with disabilities and children without disabilities, and others do not. MacArthur (2003), who summarized a large body of research on inclusion of students with learning disabilities, stated, "The development of effective inclusion programs is a complex undertaking," including administrative support, personnel preparation, a team approach, and commitment by personnel delivering services.

These diverse findings can be accounted for by the many different operational definitions of *inclusion* being used in various school districts around the country. In addition, it is unclear whether the programs and principles of inclusion were being faithfully implemented. Such studies rarely incorporate measures of *fidelity of treatment.* The IDEA legislation has clearly established that inclusion is the preferred mode of educating children with disabilities, and until changes are made in the law, this practice will be the expected standard regardless of research findings to the contrary.

To what degree can decision makers gain public support for any or all of these strategies? This is another criterion to be considered in decision making. Local surveys and various town-hall meetings are ways to find out what the public opinion is on these choices. Legal issues may rule out the status quo if it includes providing only minimal services for students, and a special class would have to be justified with a detailed description.

Values

The values (e.g., low, moderate, high) inserted in the decision matrix in Figure 7.3 were developed out of literature reviews and my professional experience. The *cost* of the alternative options (one of the criteria for choice) are high for a special class or tutoring because of the high cost of specialists, whereas inclusion means keeping Arnie in the general class with some outside support. The value for the status quo is low because not much has been done for Arnie in the school. The cost of parent training is not very high. The behavior modification approach is between inclusion and the tutoring in cost. When one considers the *personnel needs,* finding a specialist in educating children with autism is difficult, due to serious shortages, whereas some consultant specialists might satisfy the inclusion and behavior modification approaches. The *track record* describes progress in the special application of skills, and some positive reports on inclusion, whereas the status quo has only uncertain results. *Public support* seems to be ambivalent because of some concern that the presence of a child with autism in the general classroom might upset the teacher and other children.

The *legal issue* noted in Figure 7.3 was whether the inclusion approach would allow for sufficient intensity of treatment to avoid a suit by parents or others on the grounds of insufficient treatment. The other approaches would seem to fulfill legal requirements. There are enough disparities in the available knowledge to allow for considerable local flexibility in the approach to Arnie's education.

The data that are collected to complete a decision matrix can look quite different from one community to another or from one state to another. Groups of activists may be convinced about the desirability of various options and their respective values. But a decision about how to educate children with autism or other disabilities must be made and then implemented. How effectively the implementation of the program is carried out may well determine the outcome of the options themselves.

Implementation

Once the choice of the particular program alternative has been made, there is the final problem of putting it into action with a proper curriculum and trained personnel. If policy makers decide to use ABA as a strategy, for example, then they must be sure that they have personnel capable of carrying out this approach. If they decide to use inclusion in the general education classroom, then the classroom teacher has to be prepared and made aware of the special issues that children like Arnie, Les, or Bobby will bring to his or her classroom. Many strategies can work to the benefit of the child with support needs if properly implemented, and few will work if they are not properly implemented, so it becomes critical to carry out the selected option effectively.

Evaluation

After a reasonable time, the program directors should evaluate the results of the program, another key element in the planning process. A properly conducted planning operation always includes evaluation as part of the total effort. An evaluation should include the standard quantitative measures of academic improvement but also qualitative measures such as child and parent interviews, observational rating scores, goal attainment scaling, and other measures that tap educational improvement.

Has it been worth the additional effort and expense put into it? Here, evaluators should look at the collective results of the IFSPs and IEPs, plus any unexpected results of the program. Perhaps a strong parent group has formed and now provides additional help to the program, or maybe clashes between students have angered and concerned parents. A comprehensive evaluation, publicly displayed, is necessary in order to maintain the trust of the general public and the taxpayers in the program itself.

With regard to the IEP, this means that some ways must be found to ensure that the goals and objectives have been met. Table 7.2 lists some of the elements related to the IEP plan for Arnie. The objective for Arnie to do addition requires that some tasks be constructed to make sure that he is performing with accuracy. Observers can note his social interaction with the small group that he is assigned to, and the hand flapping episodes need to be quantified.

Evaluation of a group of students can be done in a similar manner with goals and objectives set for the group and measurement strategies adopted to ensure that the group has been performing as expected. Depending on the results of the evaluation, feedback (see Figure 7.2) will be available to decision makers, which might cause a modification of the programs' goals or objectives or even a change in the basic program option itself. For example, one math program

Table 7.2. Individualized education program elements for Arnie

Area	Goals	Short-term objectives
Academic	Arnie will master reading sheets at a second-grade level.	Arnie will complete reading a high-interest, low-difficulty book.
	Arnie will master fundamentals of addition.	Arnie will be given a separate lesson in adding two numerals at a 90% correct level.
Social	Arnie will improve his social skills.	Arnie will work in a group setting with classmates primed to include him.
	Arnie will reduce his temper tantrums by 30%.	Functional behavior assessment will be done by a specialist to identify appropriate replacement behaviors.
Behavior	Arnie will reduce repetitive hand-flapping movements by half.	The teacher will give tools that require Arnie to use his hands in a constructive manner.

did not show the expected growth, and interviews and observations revealed that the program confused the students. An alternative approach can be adopted as a result of the feedback. Of course, a similar decision-making procedure could be carried out for other subgroups of children so that the decision matrix approach can give a clear portrait of the decision making that has gone on in the program of special education and the degree to which it is meeting the goals and objectives set for it.

CAPACITY BUILDING FOR COORDINATION

One of the important roles in comprehensive planning is the capacity-building aspect of the special education system. In the case of IDEA 2004, this has meant that funds are made available for the specific purpose of encouraging collaborative work among the components of special education such as state educational agencies (teacher standards), local education agencies (service delivery), parent training and information centers (TA), institutions of higher education (personnel preparation), and so forth. In addition to requiring funding for infrastructure components such as regional resource centers, clearinghouses and TA programs, IDEA 2004 requires competitive state program improvement grants (SPIGs) that allow the states to plan for systemic reform through collaboration. In particular, the SPIGs collaboration is expected to focus on personnel preparation because of the chronic shortages in personnel (Turnbull & Turnbull, 2000). By making additional funds available for collaboration, OSEP aided the capacity-building process substantially because any attempts at meaningful collaboration in special education efforts inevitably increased the costs of the programs involved.

How can planning for children with disabilities be coordinated with general education goals? The goals of inclusion assume that the academic goals of education for all students are somewhat the same, although some adjustments must be made for children with special needs. They also assume that the general education curriculum is standard, although different styles of presentation may be required. But how long in the development of these children with special needs does such an assumption last? Third grade? Sixth grade? Ninth grade?

Gallagher (1994a) discussed the Peter Pan phenomenon (i.e., the boy who never grew up) in planning. The temptation is to pretend educators can plan for certain activities assuming that all children will remain 10–12 years old forever. In that age range, some common educational goals, such as the development of basic academic skills and the mastery of social skills and experience, can be designed for nearly all children. But what happens after the age of 12? After the elementary school years, some key decisions have to be made on differential education.

How many children with disabilities eventually go to college (Wagner & Blackorby, 1996)? Somewhere in their developmental progress, children with disabilities who have vocational goals should be separated from peers for differential instruction. Research literature suggests that one of the goals for vocational success for children with mental retardation has to be a functional curriculum focusing on the world of work from middle school and beyond (Edgar, 1997). Such a functional curriculum cannot be planned for or introduced when the student is 17 or 18 but must begin when the student is in middle school. So, how can these vocational goals and the goals of inclusion be matched? For that matter, what are the specific developmental goals for children with autism, like Arnie, or other students with severe disabilities that may have to be planned for from kindergarten?

Regardless of the problems at the secondary level, if educators accept the arguments for a coordinated support infrastructure for young children (Gallagher & Clifford, 2000), then they face another issue: "Why hasn't such an infrastructure been put into place?" In other words, why do education professionals not do what they know they should? This puzzle is at the heart of why change is difficult and why the status quo retains so much power. The answer is considerably more complex than simple ignorance or malfeasance and requires a careful review of the barriers to change.

BARRIERS TO CHANGE

Planning is done with the full expectation that the differential plan that is put into place will be properly implemented. Yet, plans may face difficulties for many reasons. Gallagher and Clifford (2000) suggested that many barriers to change often go unnoticed yet stand in the way of comprehensive planning and collaborative action. Table 7.3 provides a brief description of the various types of barriers to effective action.

Institutional Barriers

To make tasks easier and ensure that complex tasks become simpler, policy makers have found it necessary to develop organizations and systems of care. Think of the many organizations that are involved in carrying out early interventions for children with disabilities: Head Start, child care organizations, and public schools, among others. These organizations may sometimes view collaboration as difficult and onerous. The various professional organizations, such as CEC or NAEYC, may look on proposals for collaboration in programs for young children with similar disquiet. All of these institutions and organizations must be reassured, in some measure, about the consequences of the col-

Table 7.3. Barriers to policy implementation

Institutional

These barriers arise when the proposed policy conflicts with the current operation of established social and political institutions. A call for interagency coordination might create difficulties in blending the existing policies and operations across health, social services, and educational agencies. If a lead agency is identified to carry out the policy, is that agency given sufficient authority and resources?

Psychological

A proposed policy can come into conflict with deeply held personal beliefs of clients, professionals, or leaders who must implement the policy. Perhaps some people resent the fact that they were not consulted before the policy was established. Any time someone loses authority or status, there can be personal resistance.

Sociological

Sometimes the new policy conflicts with established mores or cultural values of subgroups within the society. For example, it may be traditional in some cultural subgroups for family members to show deference to those in authority (e.g., physicians, agency heads). The notion of family empowerment might be a difficult one for them to entertain.

Economic

Often, the promise of resources to carry out a program is not fulfilled, not because of deviousness, but because of the multitude of issues to be met and the limited financial resources at the state or federal level.

Political

Some programs become identified with one or the other political party, and such programs become hostage when the opposing political party comes into power. There is a periodic overturn of political leaders through retirement or elections—changes that can cause disjunction in the support or understanding of the program on the part of political leaders.

Geographic

The delivery of services to rural and impoverished urban areas has long plagued those who have tried to provide comprehensive health and social services. Personnel resources tend to remain in large- or middle-sized urban areas, causing substantial difficulties in covering outlying areas.

From Haskins, R., & Gallagher, J. (1981). *Models for analysis of social policy: An introduction* (pp. 68–74). Norwood, NJ: Ablex; adapted by permission.

laboration and multidisciplinary cooperation before they will feel secure enough to give their endorsement and support.

Organizations often seem driven by one of the fundamental rules of bureaucracies: the first goal is survival of the organization itself. Then, they can concern themselves with the needs of their clients. When organizations face a call for interagency coordination, they must worry about whether their own organization might be diminished or even eliminated. Unless other compelling incentives exist, powerful stakeholders resist collaborative intervention so that they can preserve their individual control over the domain. This is not to say that these groups ignore the needs of the children who are their responsibility, but it is not hard to conclude that damage to the organization is damage to meeting the children's needs.

Psychological Barriers

Although there are institutional reasons for resisting change, substantial personal or psychological barriers can inhibit support for new ideas or practices as well. Professionals may have become increasingly wedded to their various procedures and are loath to put them away. Consider the suggestion that a child with disabilities should be diagnosed in an *arena assessment* setting in which all of the professionals involved (e.g., pediatrician, psychologist, social worker, special educator, speech-language pathologist) sit in a large room and observe as each professional in turn examines the child or interviews the family. Wouldn't seeing how the child responds to the various professionals be instructive to the other professionals watching by helping to inform them on the various procedures of the other professions? The arena approach might even shorten the discussion on possible action plans. Yet, it would also require the professionals not only to change their current practices but also to open themselves to comments or critiques from the other professionals in the arena assessment, such as "You mean that is all there is to a neurological examination?" or "So that is what is called an intelligence test?" One's professional ego has to be strong to undergo searching inquiry from one's colleagues.

One can predict how easy it would be to convince a pediatrician to give up her blood pressure equipment or a psychologist his IQ tests in favor of more advanced approaches. The potential reduction in status for individual professionals is always a powerful argument against change.

Sociological Barriers

The diversity of American society ensures that different cultural subgroups have a variety of values and approaches to child rearing and handling family problems. Consider the resistance to certain child care principles that suggest a child should never be disciplined by spanking when such discipline has been a regular part of the family life of many different cultures for generations. Nor does everyone share the values of education, competition, or personal responsibility that are often taken for granted by some teachers and educators. Some families have sincere opposition to many of the practices that are recommended without much thought (Harry, 1997). Considerable diplomacy and understanding will be needed to encourage families to accept certain policies that are alien or objectionable to them.

Economic Barriers

Every suggestion for change carries a price tag, and some taxpayers resist expenditures for whatever change that will result in more expense for them. The resistance is so strong that people proposing change may institute changes a little bit at a time to reduce the number of protesters. Gallagher et al. (2001) found that states moving forward on the development of prekindergarten policies all first focused on children at high risk, a target group for whom most believe early intervention is necessary. Such a decision to target children at high risk is designed, in part, to diminish the effect of critics on the new early childhood policies.

Also, public policy makers have found it much easier to establish programs for young children with disabilities than other children because the need is so obvious and difficult to argue against. Although the United States spends more than $7 billion annually in child care services, such amounts fall short of the need. A recent National Academy of Sciences report estimated that the United States spends one quarter of the money on children from birth to age 5 that it spends on children ages 6–17 (Ladd & Hansen, 1999).

Political Barriers

Each of the major political parties can well support very different policies addressing children with special needs. For example, one party may stress working directly with the child, while the other party may focus on the family and the environment. Public policies may well depend on which party is in ascendance at a particular time. Also, the adoption of such policies may depend on a political figure who has taken a particular policy as his or her own and has seen to it that the policy is supported.

But by age or election, politicians are vulnerable to disappearing from the scene or to suddenly finding the other political party in charge of policy making. That would be bad news for those depending too heavily on a policy supported by an earlier hero of the opposite party. Obviously, then, it is desirable to have bipartisan support so that the vagaries of particular elections do not deal a stunning blow to needed programs. Fortunately, many of the policies for children with special needs have received strong support from both major political parties, and that is one of the reasons that they have remained reasonably stable over time.

Geographic Barriers

As mentioned, resources are unevenly distributed on the basis of the geography of a particular state or a region in a state. Children living in rural areas or in the core of depressed urban areas can be virtually certain to receive less special care than if they lived in areas with adequate funding. These differences have been so dramatic as to even bring the constitutionality of the special educational finance system of various states into question (see Chapter 6). In addition, many professionals are less likely to wish to work in a rural or impoverished area, which will also reduce the likelihood of special help for those children with disabilities, despite pay incentives and other benefits. *Horizontal equity* (i.e., the equal distribution of services throughout a state) has been traditionally hard to implement and maintain.

Power of the Status Quo

All of the barriers noted above add up to some powerful forces, which make up, in part, the power of the status quo. Changing to new procedures always takes more psychic and physical energy than maintaining the status quo, and that fact alone can cause a lack of enthusiasm for new policy (Fullan, 2001). In order for change to take place, policy makers must overcome inertia in the form of a quasi-stationary equilibrium that is the main impediment to change (Schein, 1996). Weick and Quinn pointed out, "To understand organizational change one must first understand organizational inertia, its content, its tenacity, its interdependencies" (1999, p. 382).

Given all of these barriers, how is it possible to actually create change? Actually, there are some major imbalances in the society at this point, which appear to call for efforts to regain balance and stability. One of the most dramatic of these imbalances is the rapid growth in the workforce of mothers of young children, which heightens problems with out-of-home child care. This brings many different organizations and groups into the discussion.

The successful implementation of interorganizational consensus relies on the legitimacy of the project involved and the ability to involve all key stakeholders. What type of interorganizational arrangement is made depends on the "exchange relations" between groups (Cook, 1977). Two important elements in the state of service to young children are specialization and scarcity. Specialization may mean that an agency representing the health field may be needed in comprehensive planning because of its specialized knowledge, and scarcity comes into play when interorganizational cooperation has the advantage of creating economies of scale. The manifest shortage of well-prepared service personnel can force collaboration between agencies and the training institutions, such as colleges, universities, community colleges, and professional associations.

DECISIONS AHEAD

Many comprehensive planning decisions remain to be made. These include the challenges of 1) establishing comprehensive, multidisciplinary, long-range planning for children with disabilities and their families; 2) navigating the difficult terrain of the human side of professional relations; and 3) integrating services for young children. The following sections indicate the difficulties with each need of comprehensive planning.

Establishing Comprehensive, Multidisciplinary, Long-Range Planning

Given the unfinished nature of much of the comprehensive planning in many states, establishing comprehensive, multidisciplinary, long-range planning is a significant issue. The blending together of many different disciplines is certainly not done without some stress caused by the threatened status of the various disciplines involved. There seems to be a clear hierarchy of professional disciplines, which can be played out in interagency committees or task forces to the detriment of objective information or effective models of service delivery. Hierarchies of status and influence do play a role within the professions involved in solving the problems of young children. Education, for example, is widely perceived to be near the bottom of these professional hierarchies, while medicine often is at the top. So, the comments by educators in task force meetings may not carry the weight that they might deserve.

Another problem that such groups as ICCs have in serving young children with disabilities is what authority do they actually have to get things done in the state? If they have the ear of the governor, then the decisions of ICC members might well be crucial to next steps, but if the members of the multidisciplinary group all have to report back to their various agencies for approval of recommendations, they can easily be ensnared by bureaucratic processes and rivalries. It is not enough to establish instruments of collaboration between agencies; these entities should have a clear line of authority so that their recommendations are heard and enacted.

Recognizing the Human Side of Professional Relations

This volume notes a number of times that fundamental human emotions on the part of the relevant players are a significant portion of the process. When barriers unaccountably appear to block progress or impede decision making, at the root of the problem is often the bruised self-image of one of the parties involved or sometimes the bruised image of an entire professional group. The thought that issues of professional jealousy, pride, or anger would interfere with providing good services to children with disabilities strikes parents with horror, but, nevertheless, it can be true in some instances.

One of the reasons for demanding that parents have a seat on commissions or task forces is so the most egregious of these emotions are not played out in the meetings. After all, what professional would want to reveal his or her petty grievances in the presence of deeply concerned parents? Personnel preparation programs need to pay more attention to the role that personal emotions play in group endeavors so that fledgling teachers are not taken aback when they encounter negative reactions in their professional lives.

Integrating Services for Young Children

Many of the problems raised in this chapter highlight the current situation regarding young children. In the absence of overall planning, four influential groups have developed, each with their own funding streams and organizations and overlapping claims on how to help young children develop. These are 1) the child care community, composed of personnel and centers that provide child care for children, many from families with low incomes; 2) programs and personnel serving young children with disabilities; 3) Head Start, a program directed at helping the development of children living in poverty, many of whom are part of ethnic and cultural minority groups; and 4) Title 1, representing efforts by the education community to provide help for children at risk for academic failure once they enter school. Each of these four groups have their own legislative mandate but do not often communicate with each other about the needs of their programs. Consequently, there is much redundancy in their efforts, even if the players are unaware of such redundancy. For example, each of the four groups commits itself to a program of personnel preparation and is accountable for the progress of its programs when one coordinated program of personnel preparation with specialties extending off of the core programs might be possible (Gallagher, Clifford, & Maxwell, 2004). Certainly, the complex nature of assessing developmental progress among young children does not have to be repeated four times over. Each group has an impressive set of rules and regulations that govern its operations. How can they be blended into one set of rules?

Yet, each group also has its own coterie of advocates who have fought long and hard for the scarce resources that they have obtained and are reluctant to cede their authority. They are justifiably suspicious of what would happen to them in some form of merger into a seamless comprehensive preschool program. As one professional said, "I am all for cooperation if we cooperate them, but I am not sure about it if they cooperate us."

The goal of a comprehensive program is easy to understand. For one thing, removing some of the redundancies in these programs would lead to a considerable savings of limited resources; this is a real attraction to public decision makers. But how can they get from where they are to the goal that all policy makers and educators seek? It may take one or more imaginative governors to set up a commission or task force committed to the goal of comprehensive planning for young children for their own state and to give the authority to the task force to bring groups together and demand their commitment to an overall plan.

As society becomes increasingly complex, policy makers face the necessity of engaging in comprehensive planning to meet outstanding needs. Their skills in mastering these tasks will have much to do with the health of services in the future. This chapter makes the point that high-quality programs for the education of children with disabilities requires thoughtful planning and the presence of many support components. Many professionals are currently committed to design the institutions and service delivery practices that make comprehensive planning work.

CHAPTER 8

Technology and Children with Disabilities

Technology has played an important role in the education of children with disabilities for many decades. It is one vehicle by which children with disabilities can maintain contact and communication with the world around them. The image of technology is often that of some complex machine with moving parts doing many new and wonderful things. But *technology* means any device that makes instruction more effective and can include many low-technology devices such as pencil grips, simple switches, and head pointers. Low-technology solutions can include devices to aid a student in organizing his or her thoughts and work, such as outlines or flow charts. For example, a student might use a learning issues board by first identifying what he or she knows about the problem at hand, then determining what he or she needs to know, and finally proposing how to go about learning what he or she needs to know.

The rapid explosion of information technology in the 1990s and the professional community's subsequent acceptance of technology may surpass any other major change in education since the 1950s. In 1994, only 3% of U.S. classrooms had Internet access. By 1997, the number of connected classrooms rose to 27%, and by the fall of 1999, 80% of U.S. classrooms had Internet connections (Means, 2000).

The utilization of technology is considered so important that IDEA 2004 requires special education teachers to show mastery of technology so that they can provide appropriate instruction to children with special needs (Lahm & Nickels, 1999). Despite such mandates, large numbers of special education teachers are uncertain about their abilities to use technology for their students. Extensive staff development is clearly needed, as is the modification of preservice personnel preparation programs for greater inclusion of technology (Wahl, 2004).

DIFFERENT USES OF TECHNOLOGY

Technology has two quite different uses for children with disabilities. The first is *assistive technology,* which covers a wide variety of devices that are designed to enhance the basic functioning of people with disabilities. Assistive technology includes the use of augmented communication for children who cannot speak, hearing aids for children with hearing impairments, Braille readers for students who are blind, and walkers or wheelchairs for students with mobility impairments. Use of assistive technology to aid instruction content mastery is increasing (Edyburn, 2000). Table 8.1 provides examples of assistive technologies.

The second use of technology is *instructional technology,* the use of technology for the delivery and support of instruction. This includes special adaptations of computers, telephones, and access to the Internet that allow students with disabilities to learn in a similar fashion to students without disabilities. When children like Bobby, Arnie, or Cathy can use technology in the same manner as other students, their inclusion in the general classroom is reinforced in their minds as well as in the minds of the other students.

The distinction between assistive technology and instructional technology is that assistive technology helps the child's readiness to learn, and instructional technology helps them in the actual content learning process. Cathy, the student with cerebral palsy, has problems of mobility that extend not only to locomotion but also to her ability to perform tasks of fine motor coordination.

Table 8.1.   Uses of assistive technology

Problem	Purpose	Devices
Daily living skills	Sustaining life—eating, grooming, elimination	Dressing aids Adaptive toilet seats
Communication	Receiving, internalizing, and expressing information	Hearing amplifiers Picture boards Captioned videotapes
Body support	Stabilizing, supporting, and protecting the body	Support harness Head gear Furniture adaptation
Travel and mobility	Moving horizontally or vertically—navigating the environment	Wheelchairs, walkers Orientation and mobility services
Environmental interaction	Operating equipment and gaining access to facilities	Remote control device Door openers Driving aids
Education/transition	Using instructional materials effectively	Computer adaptation Educational software
Sports, fitness, recreation	Participating in games, leisure activities, and hobbies	Modified rules and equipment Special Olympics

Source: Blackhurst and Edyburn (2000).

When she faces a computer, she has to cope with a mouse or keyboard, which can prevent her from inputting information. Even a supposedly simple matter as turning on the computer becomes a serious challenge. She needs help from assistive technology to gain access to information sources.

Les, the student with learning disabilities, can use technology to systematically develop and organize his reading skills, skills that have developed automatically in children without disabilities. Students with learning disabilities, like Les, may have difficulty mastering keyboarding skills (Pisha, 1993). The goal is to provide visual and auditory cues that help Les gain an understanding of the reading process that he has been unable to detect without assistance.

Although the use of computers in general education has rapidly increased, the same cannot be said about computers' availability for children with disabilities. Students without disabilities are significantly more likely to use computers and the Internet than their peers with disabilities, and students with intellectual disabilities are least likely to have access to and benefit from technology. The barriers to such use appear to be the high cost of technology devices combined with lack of funds, lack of time for training students and teachers how to use the equipment, and lack of time to prepare the equipment for use (Wehmeyer, Smith, Palmer, & Davies, 2004). More action is clearly required than merely issuing a statement that students with disabilities will have access to the general curriculum.

One of the principles of inclusion of children with disabilities within the general classroom is that such a placement would provide students with disabilities access to the general curriculum. Just being in the same room where curriculum is presented, however, is no guarantee that the student with disabilities can master the general curriculum without considerable help. This help can take the form of accommodations, adaptation of the curriculum (i.e., what students learn), modified methods of instruction (i.e., how students learn), and assessments (i.e., how well students have learned and schools have educated them) (see http://www.beachcenter.org/).

Accommodations help a given student to gain full access to the subject matter and instruction without changing the content of instruction or teacher expectation of performance (Nolet & McLaughlin, 2000). For Cathy, whose cerebral palsy makes it difficult for her to use a computer, a paraprofessional could be assigned to make sure that Cathy has effective physical access to the computer. Adaptations may modify how the teacher presents curriculum content, and multiple methods of presentation through verbal and visual channels may be used (Wehmeyer, 2002). Augmentations may focus on teaching learning strategies so that the student can learn to self-manage his or her learning process. Les, for example, may be given special instruction in how to decode passages and, thus, bypass his reading problems. Some systematic ways of developing these accommodations, adaptations, and augmentations have been made available through some of the new centers and institutes supported by the U.S. Department of Education.

DEVELOPING TECHNOLOGY USE

All four engines of change—legislation, court decisions, administrative rules, and professional initiatives—have played a significant role in developing the use of technology in the education of children with disabilities. The following sections outline the contributions of each engine of change.

Legislation

Legislation makes it possible to authorize and fund major projects devoted to the development of hardware and software. Because the assistive technology and equipment can be quite expensive and the number of children using the equipment is often small, it is necessary to have a source of funds that allows for the purchase of such equipment so that children with disabilities can have a free appropriate public education. Such tools as those noted in Table 8.1 have become a part of the necessary tools for an effective education. Legislation plays a very significant role in ensuring the availability of technology for children with disabilities, as in the other areas of support services planning for such development. In 1958, federal funds were first made available for the purchase and distribution of captioned films for children with hearing impairments. This program has had a long and distinguished role to play in the education of children with hearing impairments and was the forerunner of television closed captioning.

The need for support organizations to produce and distribute technology, such as the American Printing House for the Blind, was also learned early. Starting in the 1960s, the federal government began to support the special education instructional materials centers to make instructional technologies more accessible to special education teachers (Blackhurst & Edyburn, 2000). These centers lent instructional media and materials, developed and evaluated instructional materials, provided in-service training for teachers, and helped in the development of locally assessible instructional materials centers. The 14 centers provided organizational support for TA until other commercial and state resources became available. PL 90-247 expanded the instructional media program to include the production and distribution of educational media. The first legislation to focus on assistive technology was the Technology-Related Assistance for Individuals with Disabilities Act of 1988 (PL 100-407).

In 1997, the IDEA Amendments mandated that every IEP team consider assistive technology when planning the IEPs of students with disabilities. This provision ensures that attention will be paid to technological issues for each child. Also, the CEC established the Center for Special Education Technology, supported by federal funds, which serves as a national clearinghouse and information source. All of these organizational and legislative initiatives are devoted to providing needed support to teachers of children with disabilities.

The importance of legislation to support the development and organization of instructional materials for children with disabilities has been generally recognized for many years. Such support has been crucial because the small number of children served make the developmental costs of technological innovations financially prohibitive for private companies. The reauthorization of the Assistive Technology Act of 2004 (PL 108-364), with strong bipartisan support, shows that public policy makers recognize the importance of coping with the digital divide, the gap between those with access to technology and those without, and providing an infrastructure to produce continuing technological support to children and adults with disabilities.

PL 108-364 provides grants to all 50 states to help them establish 1) a support program of assistive technology; 2) alternative financing programs (to provide loans for more effective access to individuals with disabilities); 3) protection and advocacy for assistive technology designed to provide information; 4) support and representation to individuals with disabilities and their families; and 5) national TA in areas of information dissemination, program evaluation, interagency coordination, and program development. This law requires states to spend at least 60% of their funds in direct services to make sure that students with disabilities actually receive assistive technology. It also authorizes funds for TA, program development, and information dissemination. It eliminates the *sunset provision* included in an earlier version that was designed to eliminate, over time, the state grant program. This legislative move indicated the intent to keep the federal support of states on a continuing basis. Despite the wide general support for the purposes of the act, the funding of the act has been modest (less than $30 million), and that level of funding is not expected to improve very soon (see Chapter 6).

Three major forces are delaying the more extensive expansion of technology in the educational programs of the schools. The first is the heavy burden placed on state budgets by other expenses, such as the increase in Medicare commitments, during the times of budget stagnation or recession. The increasing costs cause school systems to draw back from more investments in technology for the classroom (Hurst, 2005).

Another factor delaying the instructional uses of technology is the challenge of accountability, brought on largely by No Child Left Behind. Facing increasingly heavy demands for data from the student performances on state tests, many schools have reassigned some of their technology capabilities to the task of generating more and more data reports to satisfy the requirements of federal legislation (Hoff, 2005).

One final source of uncertainty is the lack of consistency of funds needed to conduct major technological development. Technology funds seem to depend on fluctuation of economic forces in the states and vacillation of interest from the federal government and private sources. Their interest seems to ebb and flow from one year to the next, leaving educators uncertain about the resources they can commit to technology (Trotter, 2005).

Court Decisions

Court decisions have played a role in ensuring that children with disabilities have all that is necessary for a free appropriate public education. There are equity issues here, as well. If all of the children in a class are using computers, but Cathy and Arnie are unable to use them because of motor problems or attention difficulties, then advocates can petition for equipment accessible to students like Cathy and Arnie.

The *Rowley* decision (*Hendrick Hudson School District v. Rowley,* 1982), which determined that a child with disabilities is not necessarily entitled to the best possible education but merely a meaningful addition to the general education, raised many questions about how much assistive technology needs to be provided to satisfy the free appropriate public education principle. The Office for Civil Rights in the U.S. Department of Education has made a number of quasijudicial procedures and decisions that focused mainly on evidence of discrimination and the limitations of the use of assistive technology to allow the student with disabilities a free appropriate public education. These procedures yielded judgments indicating

1. Modification and adaptations of a computer to enable a student with quadriplegia to use the computer without assistance

2. Use of computer for students with mobility impairments to gain access to the library (The district was not required to install an elevator to make the library accessible.)

3. Use of tutorial software and a laptop computer for a student with narcolepsy

4. Use of an Arkenstone scanner to scan and read text for a student with learning disabilities (The Office for Civil Rights determined that Section 504 was not violated when the student was not allowed to use the device for a state reading exam.)

5. Use of a computer with a keyboarding program for written assignments for a student with attention-deficit/hyperactivity disorder.

These judgments, after the Office for Civil Rights conducts hearings and review, set policy for schools related to a variety of assistive technology issues.

Administrative Rules

Administrative rules have established, among other things, the role that technology can play in the development of the IEP:

> Assistive technology may be included (a) as part of the student's annual goals or short term objectives; (b) in a list of specific accommodations needed for the student to function in the least restrictive environment; and (c) as a related service necessary for the student to benefit from special education. (Parrette, 1998, p. 217)

The rules governing the access to and use of technology have played a large part in allowing children with disabilities to perform effectively in the least restrictive environment. The requirement that assistive technology be considered in each IEP as written in the IDEA Amendments of 1997 has stirred a number of regulations that explain just how this requirement will be fulfilled. For example, §300.308 of the 1997 amendments states that school-purchased assistive technology devices can be used in the child's home if the IEP determines that it is necessary for a free appropriate public education. The regulations of these amendments also make it clear that parents are to receive training that can help the student with disabilities to use the available technology more effectively. IDEA 2004 has continued the mandate that the IEP consider the potential uses of assistive technology for each child.

Professional Initiatives

Of course, the rapid expansion of technological development depends heavily on the creativity of a multidisciplinary community of professionals who have taken on the challenge of meeting the needs of children with disabilities through technological development. The importance of assistive technology has been recognized both by professional associations such as AAMR and parent and citizen organizations such as The Arc of the United States. These organizations have released a joint position on assistive technology: "People must have access to devices, services, and training that improves independence, mobility, communication, environmental control and self-determination. Designers, manufacturers, service providers and our constituents with their families should be educated about the benefits of technology." These goals are well represented in the Assistive Technology Act of 2004 (PL 108-364).

One of the reasons for the upsurge in the use of technology in special education is not only due to the leap forward in many technological developments but also because technology is increasingly seen as one way in which students with disabilities can meet the requirements of the general education classroom in inclusive settings. As Puckett (2004) pointed out, "Assistive technology has an increasingly important role to play in helping special education students achieve these general education outcomes."

How can special education fit into the general education curriculum? As Hitchcock and Stahl pointed out,

> The general curriculum is simply not designed for those students. In fact, students with disabilities have generally not been included during any phase of their design, research, development, adoption, or validation. As a result, most general curricula are demonstrably ill-suited to achieve or measure results for students who have disabilities. (2003)

Under such circumstances, then, it becomes important to think about the Universal Design for Learning (UDL) as a key to successful inclusion. Flexible media options that can be embedded within the curriculum adjustments can help to meet the needs of each learner. With options that depart from the standard printed material, students like Les and Bobby can master lessons that otherwise would have sunk them further below the expected performances.

There is good reason to believe that such UDL innovations have a meaningful effect on learning. Means (2000) reported that through the use of inquiry-oriented software, middle school students manipulated simulations and visualizations of concepts of velocity and acceleration to the point that they outperformed high school physics students in their ability to apply the principles of Newtonian mechanics to real-world situations (White & Frederiksen, 1998).

Such results emphasize the importance of pressing to see that children with disabilities do not face a widening achievement gap (e.g., the *digital divide*). Some federal agencies have made a major effort through the use of Title I funds to provide computer labs for needy schools with some success (Means, 2000). The challenge now is to educate teachers in the proper use of these new tools so that the students can make maximum use of their capabilities.

ASSISTIVE TECHNOLOGY

Blackhurst and Edyburn (2000) provided a catalog of the uses of assistive technology (see Table 8.1). Computer adaptations are typically used to strengthen the use of instructional materials, but mobility devices, such as walkers and wheelchairs, and remote control devices, such as door openers, should also be used so that children with disabilities are able to get to the place where educational activities are happening. Also, children with disabilities need recreation and fitness as much as other students, perhaps more. Modified play equipment can allow Bobby, Les, and Cathy to enjoy the same advantages that other students have while participating in sports and recreational activities.

Remote control devices and controls can take the place of the computer mouse for a child like Cathy, who cannot manipulate a standard computer mouse successfully. Arnie can also profit from devices that would augment communication, such as picture boards or other devices, designed to bypass Arnie's lack of verbal skills. Table 8.1 provides a good portrait of the extensive range of human activity aided by assistive technology.

Grabe and Grabe suggested some ways for coping with mobility impairments:

A power strip that can be used to turn all equipment on and off with a single switch

Alternative keyboards that position the keys further apart and disable repeat keys so that users with slower and less precise movements have less difficulty

Special software that causes the cursor to scan across a screen representation or across program choice buttons, allowing individuals with the capacity to control a switch (using a knee, the mouth, or the head) to make selections (2001, p. 417)

With these additions, Cathy can be a part of the larger classroom group by using the available equipment.

A number of adaptations are available that can help Cathy to use the keyboard with efficiency and without embarrassment. For example, keyboard guides separate the keys, and repeat functions can be turned off when the keys are held for a period of time (Nelson, Bahr, & Van Meter, 2004). If handling the mouse is a problem, the keyboard can be used as a pointer instead of the mouse (Cochran, 2005). Such simple additions can help bring reality to the goal of UDL.

Often, special education teachers are not aware of the availability of many hardware and software sources. One source is an appendix in a volume by Cochran (2005), *Clinical Computing Competency for Speech-Language Pathologists,* which provides the names, addresses and web sites for more than 80 sources of software and hardware. Such sources can help the student and the teacher feel less isolated from the potential of technology.

The computer's role is shifting from tutor to supporter for the learner. Education software was designed on a linear model, in which instruction is presented in sequence, but it is now being designed on a hypermedia model. In hypermedia, the user is presented with choices so that he or she can take greater control over the flow of information. For example, which reading a passage, Les can select a word in the text and hear the word pronounced, or he can see a graphic illustrating the meaning of the world. In this way, the computer serves as a supportive function for learning. The learner is able to demand aid and assistance, which are no longer delivered automatically.

INSTRUCTIONAL TECHNOLOGY

Perhaps the greatest challenge for special educators in the area of technology is the great advances that are being made in instructional technology, which provides access to knowledge for children with disabilities. Instructional technology allows for a different kind and level of content to be presented. In the field of education, the term *digital divide* traditionally refers to poorly equipped schools, but it can also describe students with disabilities who do not have access to technology, even in schools with instructional technology.

Means (2000) described some of the more interesting technological developments:

- The ThinkerTools software allows middle school students to manipulate simulations and visualizations of the concepts of velocity and acceleration.

- Global Learning and Observations to Benefit the Environment involves students in real scientific investigations with detailed data collection protocols for measuring local atmosphere, soil, and vegetation.

- The JASON project uses the Internet to allow students to communicate with scientists while they explore coral reefs, rain forests, and other interesting ecologies.

- The KidSat project allows students to direct a camera's movements on a NASA space shuttle. The pictures are made available for study over the world wide web.

Gifted students like Gretchen can have adventures in technology that are considerably ahead of those who do not have an understanding of scientific concepts and a grasp of the world around them. It is the challenge for special educators to narrow that digital divide for children with disabilities.

One of the most common uses of existing technology is word processing. Children with disabilities often have substantial difficulty with handwriting their ideas. Computers and word processing software enable students to put ideas on paper without the dreaded paper and pencil. Word processing software can offer some help with grammar and punctuation, and the spellchecker device can bring some clarity and neatness to the final version of the story that a student is trying to tell. Using the Internet to find sources of information can provide students with behavioral problems additional help without the necessity of going to the library. Bobby's teacher is not always sure that Bobby will arrive at the library even if he sets off in that direction, so having the resources accessible at the computer becomes an extra aid to the teacher as well. (Students should be monitored carefully when they are using the Internet, which is largely unregulated and can be dangerous or misleading.)

Distance Learning

One of the rapidly developing areas in technology is *distance learning,* defined as a process of teaching and learning in which the teacher is separated from the students by distance or time. It can either be *synchronous,* which means that the teacher and student experience and communicate interactively in real classroom time, or *asynchronous,* which means that communication can take place at any time or any place. Access to the teacher is available 24 hours per day, 7 days per week through the Internet, although instant teacher response is not, of course, expected (Churton, 2002).

Distance learning can allow children who are homebound to be a part of the learning situation, even if their participation is asynchronous. If Cathy is homebound for a period of time, she can maintain contact with her teacher and her class, and the teacher can give Cathy an assignment that she can do when she is able. Les also can be freed from the time demands on performance, which have affected him negatively in the past. As long as he has a generous amount of time to get the work done and he feels no pressure to respond immediately, he can perform well.

The benefits of distance learning are not reserved for the student. Teachers can profit from such education as well, particularly teachers with little experience with students with disabilities who need additional instruction about how to plan effectively for children with special needs. General education teachers can use the Internet to gain access to free, on-line modules for independent learning, such as the ones provided by the IRIS Center at Vanderbilt University (http://iris.peabody.vanderbilt.edu).

One of the limiting features of distance learning is the cost of equipment, so it is necessary to provide additional funds to allow distance communication to take place. Like many other special education support system devices, distance learning cannot suddenly become activated. Communication networks have to be established, special lessons have to be created, and the equipment must be on hand. Also, resources must be allocated before distance learning can take place, and these tasks all again call for comprehensive planning.

Utility of Computer-Assisted Instruction

Little doubt exists about the potential usefulness of technology for practitioners in instructional programs. A large sample of administrators and special education teachers responded to the technological benefits in instruction (Lewis, 2000):

- Immediate feedback was provided (77% of respondents agreed).

- Students could proceed at their own rate (77%).

- Computer-based instruction could be varied for individual students (73%).

  In terms of the affective advantages, the following were reported:

- Students' self-concepts improved (74%).

- Enthusiasm for school in general increased (65%).

- Engaged time and time on task increased (61%).

In the view of these practitioners, the academic performance improved, and students learned things more quickly. The research results on these issues were less enthusiastic. Word processing had a small but positive effect on quality and quantity of writing in students with disabilities (Slaven & Masse, 2002). They experienced modest improvements on time on task and rates of learning, but technology is clearly not a panacea nor does it eradicate the effect of a learning disability (Lewis, 2000).

Lewis summarized the limitations as follows:

> One of the more common fallacies about instructional technologies is that students will be able to make academic strides by working independently at computers. For students with learning disabilities that is simply not the case. . . . Students who are distractible may fail to direct attention to the instructional task. Others may attend to inappropriate aspects of the task ignoring the text in talking storybooks to interact with the graphical and game components of the programs. (2000, p. 13)

Arnie can benefit from using a communication board, with which he can point to his needs or interests without verbalizing. The Internet can be used by all five of the children—Arnie, Bobby, Cathy, Les, and Gretchen—to broaden their content mastery and to help them seek information on their own without waiting for the teacher to present them with information.

The extensive use of technology requires institutional support, and two key agencies in the federal government have provided strong leadership. Created in 1978, National Institute on Disability and Rehabilitation Research (NIDRR), located in Washington D.C., is one of three components of the Office of Special Education and Rehabilitative Services. It operates in concert with the Rehabilitation Services Administration and the OSEP. Its mission is to generate, disseminate, and promote new knowledge to improve the options available to people with disabilities.

The Rehabilitation Services Administration administers PL 108-364 by providing grants to states to help bring about change and to increase the availability of, access to, and funding for assistive technology. It also helps states provide services to rural and underrepresented populations and provide legal advocacy to individuals with disabilities in regard to assistive technology issues. OSEP has been generously funded for technological development with an appropriation of $34 million in fiscal year 1998. It uses some of these funds to support organizational units that can construct instructional materials and multiple uses of technology. In order to obtain complicated software for technology or for the development of the hardware itself, some organizational units have to be supported that can carry out the multiyear effort that such products require.

Universal Design for Learning

Modifying existing buildings to allow access for students with disabilities has resulted in expensive and architecturally awkward additions. It would be better to design new buildings for access in the first place. This is similarly true with curricula. Hitchcock, Meyer, Rose, and Jackson observed, "The UDL framework helps us to see that inflexible curricular materials and methods are barriers to diverse learners just as inflexible buildings with stairs as the only entry option are barriers to people with physical disabilities" (2002, p. 9). Instead of the creation of new technologies that are then retrofit to fit the needs of children with disabilities, Rose (2001) proposed the encouragement of UDL technology from the start. Rose specifically recommended, "Congress should require that any educational technology developed, maintained, procured, or used by the federal government should be universally designed."

The development of digital curricula would be an example of the application of UDL. A computer can present a single curriculum as a variety of versions, all with identical content. For example, the text can be presented in very large font for children with visual disabilities or even printed out on a Braillewriter for students who are blind. With some assistive technology, students who have difficulty using a mouse can turn pages in a text by an eye blink. Other students can click on a difficult word to have the computer read it aloud or link it instantly to a context-based definition. Table 8.2 provides a UDL example in mathematics illustrating the flexibility possible with the use of technology so that every student, regardless of his or her personal characteristics, has a chance at mastering the key knowledge and skills.

Table 8.2. Math example for universal design for learning (UDL)

Suppose a math teacher uses the UDL approach to convey the critical features of a right triangle. With software that supports graphics and hyperlinks, he prepares a document that shows:

- Multiple examples of right triangles in different orientations and sizes with the right angle and the three points highlighted
- An animation of the right triangle morphing into an isosceles triangle or a rectangle, with voice and onscreen text to highlight the differences
- Links to the reviews of the characteristics of triangles and of right angles
- Links to examples of right triangles in various real-world contexts
- Links to pages that students can go to on their own for review for enrichment on the subject

The teacher could then project the document onto a large screen in front of the class. Thus, he would present the concept not simply by explaining it verbally or by assigning a textbook chapter or workbook page but by using many modalities and with options for extra support or extra enrichment.

From Hitchcock, C., Meyer, A., Rose, D., & Jackson, R. (2002, November/December). Providing new access to the general curriculum: Universal design for learning. *Teaching Exceptional Children, 35*(2), 8–17; adapted by permission.

In 2002, members of the Congress introduced bills (H.R. 4982 and S. 2246) proposing the establishment of a national repository of digital curricular content and a single national electronic file format that publishers can use when creating electronic versions of texts. The idea here is to make the adjustments early, instead of belatedly realizing that some special adaptations have to be designed for children or adults with disabilities. Support for program development has meant not only support of individual research efforts but also of organizations that bring together important resources needed to attack difficult problems, such as the design and development of curriculum material. One such organization is the Center for Advanced Technology in Education (CATE) at the University of Oregon. CATE designed a computer-based study strategies project that prepares teachers and students to use computers effectively while studying for content area classes (CATE, 2000).

The rapid development and growing popularity of technology use in the schools has put considerable pressure on the producers of software to produce materials quickly. As a result, many publishers rush materials out without fully testing them, especially for software for children with disabilities. Many publishers have been unwilling to respond to questions about formative or summative evaluation on their products (Higgins, Boone, & Williams, 1999), and others have admitted that they did not conduct evaluations of the materials prior to publication.

Higgins, Boone, and Williams (2000) produced a checklist for evaluating educational software for use with children with disabilities (see Figure 8.1). The survey contains sections on student needs, teacher options, appropriate instructional options, and instructional and screen design. In Figure 8.1, the appropriate instructional options category helps determine the degree of adaptation in the particular software being analyzed. The instructional and screen design category provides a rather complete description of how the instructional input is provided and the degree to which it can be modified. The sound and feedback categories provide other key elements of the software under consideration. The authors pointed out that such a checklist could allow "the educator to ascertain if the software publisher, at the very least, incorporated information concerning the learning characteristics of students with disabilities into a particular piece of educational software" (p. 114). The checklist by Higgins and colleagues provides the guidelines for professional standards to be applied to software, and such standards are strongly needed in a field that has many different products and a wide variance in quality or appropriateness.

Much can be done beyond supporting UDL as a concept. OSEP has provided long-term support for the Center for Applied Special Technology (CAST), which has accepted the responsibility to generate products that exemplify the UDL approach. Thinking Reader, designed in cooperation with a commercial company, provides students with instruction and practice in key reading strategies. Using core literature such as *Roll of Thunder, Hear My Cry* (Taylor, 1976) or *The Giver* (Lowry, 1993), this universally designed resource enables struggling readers to read the same high-quality books as their peers.

CAST eReader combines talking and reading software to make any electronic text accessible to struggling readers. This approach uses the spoken voice, visual highlighting, and document or page navigation to help those who have difficulty with mastering reading. In addition, CAST established the National Instructional Materials Accessibility Standard (NIMAS), which guides the production and distribution of digital versions of textbooks and other instructional materials so that they can be converted to accessible formats. NIMAS works with states, school boards, and publishers to raise awareness of the benefits of accessible materials. Building an effective infrastructure through major centers makes the development and distribution of instructional materials aimed at UDL more possible.

Also important for accountability is the ability of the software to record the students' responses and keep score of their performances so that the teacher

COMPONENTS	Yes	No
Appropriate instructional options		
Built-in learning guidance for complex tasks		
Consistent screen design features (student can predict)		
Hints		
Includes optional game format		
Identical navigational elements on every screen		
Readability of software corresponds to identified users		
Sound		
Can be disabled		
Speech capabilities		
Utilizes appropriate sound		
Verbal directions have corresponding on-screen text		
Feedback		
Consistent		
Provides corrective feedback		

Figure 8.1. Educational software checklist for children with disabilities. (From Higgins, K., Boone, R., & Williams, D. [2000]. Evaluating educational software for special education. _Intervention in School and Clinic, 36,_ 109–115; reprinted by permission.)

COMPONENTS	Yes	No
Immediate		
Appropriate duration		
Obvious and overt		
Relevant to input/task		
Instructional and screen design		
Errorless learning		
Input is not automatic entry		
Multiple-choice answers		
Opportunity for ample practice to reach mastery		
Provides for overlearning		
Opportunity to review concepts		
Option for competition		
Provides for cumulative review		
Small instructional sets		
Software keeps score		

(continued)

Figure 8.1. *(continued)*

COMPONENTS	Yes	No
Software records student work		
Math problems are in vertical format		
Information presented in multiple media (print and spoken)		
Content and materials can be modified		
Provision for alternative means of expression and control		

can see quickly when the software is not having a good match with the student. The importance of consistent and immediate feedback gets lost once student responses stray from the basic theme of the lesson.

One of the tangible advances possible with the advance of technology is the practical implementation of the concept of zones of proximal development (Vygotsky, 1978). Most teachers respond instantly and positively to Vygotsky's idea that teachers should concentrate on those concepts in which the student has some familiarity with the instructional task but has not yet mastered it. Providing instructional material that the student has already mastered is a waste of time, and material that is difficult and beyond the current reach of the student merely frustrates and discourages. The task of the teacher is how to find that zone of proximal development for an individual student. When the teacher organizes the instruction presentation on the computer, he or she can track the performance of the student, whose responses are instantly recorded and can be printed out. The teacher can discern the student's *zone of proximal development* and adjust the next presentation to the student accordingly.

CHANGING THE LEARNING ENVIRONMENT

The remarkable development of technology tools such as the computer and the Internet are actually changing the relationship of teacher and student. Just as the automobile and television have changed people's relationships to one another, so has educational technology. Teachers and professors have become accustomed to the role of gatekeeper of knowledge, doling out information as and when they deemed appropriate. Now, students with independent access to the Internet have alternative paths to learning, including a much wider range of knowledge than any individual teacher could provide. Also, the teacher is no longer the exclusive gatekeeper of knowledge, deciding what the student should learn and when. All of this has led to new learning environments. Learning is now in the hands of the students, who can use multisensory stimulation and become active and exploratory minds instead of passively waiting for information delivery. Students can do collaborative work and use multimedia more easily, rather than operating in isolation on a single line of study. Table 8.3 shows the shift from traditional learning environments to new learning environments made possible by technological growth and development.

Technology has become a vehicle of educational reform of major proportions, and special educators are responsible for ensuring that children with disabilities do not get left behind (Bolick & Cooper, 2003). Children with disabilities now have some tools that, if properly learned and used, can help them be far more independent. Educators must combat the potential growing *digital divide* between children without disabilities and those with disabilities. A national survey of assistive devices used by students with cognitive impairments found that more than twice the number of students who currently use assistive devices could potentially benefit from them but did not have access to them (Wehmeyer, 1999). Arnie, Bobby, Cathy, and Les need support and assistance in using new technology so that they do not fall farther and farther behind their classmates. The concern here is policy implementation, not only policy development.

Table 8.3. Establishing new learning environments and incorporating new strategies

Traditional learning environments	New learning environments
Teacher-centered instruction	Student-centered learning
Single sense stimulation	Multisensory stimulation
Single path progression	Multipath progression
Single media	Multimedia
Isolated work	Collaborative work
Information delivery	Information exchange
Passive learning	Active/exploratory/inquiry-based learning
Reactive response	Proactive/planned response
Isolated, artificial context	Authentic, real-world context

From Bolick, C.M., & Cooper, J.M. (2003). *An educator's guide to technology tools.* Boston: Houghton Mifflin; reprinted by permission.

Rose (2001) described the uses of powerful new technologies to do new things, such as

- Engage students in active experimentation at a level impossible in traditional classrooms

- Encourage students to communicate about learning with other students all over the world

- Allow students to evaluate their own learning

- Challenge students to create solutions in social groups

- Create new kinds of assignments in which students produce and edit new kinds of media, well beyond the limits of writing text

Teachers who are comfortable with the uses of technology can help children like Les or Bobby to imitate a search of the Internet for important information. Once a student can imitate his or her teacher, the teacher can gradually reduce his or her assistance one step at a time, a strategy called *scaffolding,* until the child is able to do the process on his or her own without the teacher's direct guidance.

SUPPORT ISSUES IN TECHNOLOGY

Incorporating assistive and instructional technologies presents a number of difficulties. Challenges include difficulties in personnel preparation, funding, and accountability.

Personnel Preparation

The rapid development of technology creates a special problem in personnel preparation. It is not enough to insert technology as a part of personnel preparation for special educators, although that certainly should be done. Thousands of special education teachers who received their training before the massive influx of new technologies need to upgrade their skills. General educators involved with inclusion also need instruction on how to use new tools with children with disabilities. As Lewis pointed out,

> Students with learning problems do not belong alone, in the back of the classroom, seated in front of a computer. Instead, teachers must become the mediators between the learner and the technology, that is, the ones who interpret the task for the student and help him or her acquire the skills needed to accomplish it. Extensive skill development is often required. For example, word processing should be taught within the context of an instructional program that is based on the writing-as-a-process model and includes teaching strategies for planning, editing, and revising. (2000)

TA (see Chapter 4) is one approach whereby short-term training institutes can be presented that focus on the special uses of technology. Teachers who are already on the job can use distance learning to gain access to special lessons on technology through video clips or other illustrative ways. Just as the student no longer must depend on the teacher and the standard curriculum but can search for new knowledge on the Internet, the same is true of teachers. The self-directed teacher can design a self-taught program. Numerous web sites include training materials, tutorials, and information about assistive technology applications.

How can one retrain the majority of existing teachers and modify the existing preservice programs for both general and special educators? Whether through established workshops or formal course work, in-service programs or self-taught lessons, the modern teacher needs to be aware of the knowledge and skills necessary to help his or her students learn through technology. Loeding gave thought to one area of concern: "For preservice educators to become technologically competent, it is important that their professors model the use and integration of technology in their courses. Educators tend to teach as they were taught" (2002, p. 38). Hasselbring (1997) summarized the state of affairs: "The cost is high, but the greatest barrier is not the cost of the technology, it is in educating teachers and students to rethink what it means to learn and use existing technologies in useful and meaningful ways."

Funding

Despite the almost universal acceptance of the need for technological advances to be provided to children with disabilities as an essential part of their special education, educators face a continued lack of funding for technology, which represents a formidable barrier to acquiring needed tools and services (Cochran, 2005). Although many special educators focus on federal sources of funds (see Table 8.4), private sources (e.g., insurance, low-interest loans) and community-based sources (e.g., civic clubs, church groups, foundations) can be explored. Table 8.4 shows the concepts and funding sources that can be brought into play from the federal level, including technology as necessary for a free appropriate public education, equal access, preparation for employment, and restoration of a child to his or her functional level. IDEA 2004, vocational rehabilitation, and Medicaid can all be called on for support.

Accountability

The more that funds are committed to technological aids, the greater the call becomes for accountability. Is the state getting its money's worth, or are these tools going to be placed in a closet and never seen again? Such questions have

Table 8.4. Examples of concepts and key phrases associated with the priorities of various funding sources

Funding source	Concept	Keywords
Education—IDEA and state special education funds: Early intervention (Part C), preschool and school-age children (Part B)	Necessary for a free appropriate public education	Device or services required to implement an objective, allow the child to benefit from special education (related aid or service) or to support participation in the general education class
Government employer, agency, or educational institution—compliance with Section 504, Section 508, or Americans with Disabilities Act of 1990 (PL 101-336)	Equal access, effective communication, consumer preference	Auxiliary aid or service required to ensure participation in programs and access to resources at least as effective as those offered to others
Vocational rehabilitation	Preparing for or maintaining employment, increasing employability	Rehabilitation technology devices or services to render an individual with a disability employable
Medicaid	Reduction of physical or mental disability, restoration of the patient to his functional level	Medical necessity must be for use in the home. *Note:* School or educational benefit should not be mentioned.

Key: IDEA, Individuals with Disabilities Education Act of 1990 (PL 101-476).

From Cochran, P.S. (with Appert, C.L.) (2005). *Clinical computing competency for speech-language pathologists* (p. 411). Baltimore: Paul H. Brookes Publishing Co.; reprinted by permission.

to be addressed if educators are to receive the support needed. Evaluating the results of technology use over groups of students is difficult because technology is highly individual, depending on the specific needs of the children involved. The establishment of rubrics (i.e., standards for specific tasks) to judge performance, the development of baselines from which one can measure the growth in student production, and the statement of clear objectives in the IEPs can all help to answer the legitimate questions of the decision makers and resource providers. Such answers have to come, in large part, from case studies of individual students (Nelson et al., 2004).

DECISIONS AHEAD

The rapid advancements in the field of educational technology have often hidden the difficult decisions from view that are just ahead of us. The following section discusses several problems that must soon be addressed.

Meeting the Costs of
Assistive and Instructional Technology

It is one thing to demonstrate how one can use assistive technology to allow children with disabilities to gain access to information previously denied them. It is quite another to say that *every* child who has problems with access should have the technology available to him or her. Often schools can underestimate the true costs of a device, which can include assembly, special batteries, parts, maintenance requirements, and so forth. When one multiplies the cost of digitalizing a curriculum by the number of classrooms in which there is a child with disabilities, the cost problem becomes apparent. School administrators may invoke the court's decision in *Hendrick Hudson School District v. Rowley* (1982) to deny an obligation to provide an optimum education for every child, as long as they make an honest effort to improve the child's performance.

Affording the Time to Make Technology Work

Although many of the technological advances can now be made accessible to children with disabilities, children like Arnie and Les may need more time than their classmates in proceeding with a lesson. The teacher must consider the additional time that a child like Cathy may need to use the computer. Cathy's assignments should take into account that difference in time or Cathy will become frustrated again.

Even as remarkable a technology as Braille, which can introduce literature to children with visual impairments, still requires much more time than reading the text in the conventional way. The student with visual impairments has to either work longer than other students or have assignments adjusted to account for the time needed to master material. The expectations of how much a child with disabilities can do have to be adjusted with experience so that reasonable goals and objectives can be set and met (Kirk, Gallagher, Anastasiow, & Coleman, 2006).

Deciding Who Does the Development

The development of technological hardware and software can be measured in years of design and development. The question is who will do that work and what type of setting will be needed for the work to get done. Federal research and development money clearly must be allocated to organizations such as the CATE in Oregon or the Education Development Center for Children and Technology in Newton, Massachusetts, or the American Printing House for the Blind in Louisville, Kentucky, if many of these technological advances can be made accessible to children with disabilities.

Financial support must last over a long period of time for developers to create software that is available to large numbers of children with disabilities. This necessitates commitments from organizations that provide resources, such as OSEP and the Rehabilitation Services Administration, to fund research and development and then spread the word on the development and availability of the products of such technologies.

In the near future, decision makers may have to face the question, "Should we do everything in technology that we now know how to do?" Many hard choices—driven by economics, practicality, and the needs of students—lie ahead. As decision makers think about the future of special education, the provision of an enriched environment for the uses of technology is one of the criteria that needs serious consideration.

CHAPTER 9

The Education
of Gifted Students

Among children with special needs, gifted and talented children stand
out. Some people believe that gifted students are so different from other
exceptional children that they belong in their own category, but the
practice of tying the groups together has a long history. Twenty-two states still
include gifted students in their definitions of exceptional children, although
the federal government does not. All of the major textbooks on exceptional
children (Hallahan & Kauffman, 2000; Heward & Orlansky, 1994; Kirk et al.,
2006; Smith, 2001) include gifted students as a kind of exceptional children.
The definition of exceptional children, noted in Chapter 1, gives a clue. It includes all children who are sufficiently different from typical children that they
need special educational adaptations to reach their potential. If that phrase is
taken seriously, then gifted students clearly should be included.

Gretchen, the gifted student in this volume, has problems that are different from those of Arnie, Les, Bobby, and Cathy, who are not able to respond to
educational demands without some help. Consequently, without special attention, these children fail or achieve significantly less than other students. That
certainly does not describe Gretchen, whose enthusiasm for learning and her
ability to learn have put her far in advance of the other students. In her case,
the problem is not the inability of the student to meet the standards of the
school. It is the inability of the school to meet the standards of the student.

MEETING EDUCATIONAL NEEDS

Gretchen has already mastered the skills and much of the content expected of
students at her grade level before the fall semester even begins. Her general
education teacher must cope with meeting the needs of students with more
typical achievement and students with disabilities and has little time to design
a separate educational experience for Gretchen, whose negative response to the

intellectually inappropriate lessons is predictable. So what should the teacher be doing with and for her, and what help should the teacher have?

Two research studies described the consequences of failing to meet the needs of gifted students. An investigation of 871 gifted students in nine separate school districts in North Carolina found that more than half of the students said their courses lacked challenge and that they.were bored (Gallagher, Harradine, & Coleman, 1997). Boredom is one of the recurring complaints of gifted students, who are asking for more challenge from their schools. Westberg, Archambault, Dobyns, and Salvin (1993) performed an observational study in 46 third- and fourth-grade classrooms across the United States. In each of the classrooms, they looked at the teacher's interactions with one gifted student and one student with typical ability for a 2-day period. They found no instructional or curricular differentiation for the gifted student in 84% of the instructional activities. Only math seemed to provide an opportunity for forward movement for gifted students. So what have been the past attempts to provide something special for these students?

One of the inhibitors of effective educational action is public and educator misunderstandings commonly held about gifted students. Table 9.1 shows various popular myths about gifted students that have been spread over the years. Note that in each case the gifted students are supposed to have some negative characteristic (e.g., emotional disturbance, snobbishness) that would seem to balance off their presumed cognitive superiority. Note also that in each case these statements are incorrect and, in many instances, the exact opposite of what research indicates. Of course, individual gifted students may have some negative characteristics, such as poor health or emotional disturbance, but such characteristics are not typical of this group of students.

DETERMINING POLICY FOR GIFTED EDUCATION

The field of special education for gifted students is a good example of what can happen when only a limited support system is available for aiding teachers in meeting the special challenge of gifted students. Although previous chapters illustrate the strong support system for children with disabilities, much less support is available to teachers of bright students through the policy tools of legislation, court decisions, administrative rules, and professional initiatives.

Legislation

In order to obtain significant legislation establishing an educational support system for gifted students, strong public support for spending the scarce resources necessary is crucial. Such public support on behalf of gifted students is not present at this time.

Table 9.1. Myths about gifted students

Gifted students are physically fragile and sickly.

Identified gifted students tend to be freer from physical ills and are generally large and physically mature for their age (Subotnik & Arnold, 1994; Terman, 1925).

Gifted students do not maintain their giftedness in later life.

Such an attitude is characterized by the inelegant phrase *Early ripe, early rot.* Several longitudinal studies have shown conclusively that such students generally achieve high status in science, politics, and the arts and entertainment industry in later life (Subotnik & Arnold, 1994; Terman & Oden, 1959).

Gifted students tend toward emotional disturbance.

Although some forms of creativity in the arts seem to be linked to emotional disturbance, the vast majority of gifted students are reasonably stable emotionally, with fewer divorces and hospitalizations for mental problems (Neihart, Reis, Robinson, & Moon, 2002; Terman, 1947).

Gifted students, if placed together for instruction, will develop feelings of superiority and inflated self-concepts.

Although this may be true of specific individuals, the research evidence notes that the self-concepts of gifted students actually go down as they meet and compete with students who are their intellectual equals (Gallagher & Gallagher, 1994).

Gifted students, if accelerated in school, will become socially maladjusted.

Four decades of studies on the impact of educational acceleration on gifted students fail to find any serious problems. To the contrary, they appear, as a group, to perform better than matched nonaccelerants (Lubinski & Benbow, 2000; Colangelo, Assouline, & Gross, 2004).

By far, the largest amount of legislation concerning the education of gifted students can be found at the state level because the states are largely responsible for education in general. Practically every state has some language in its education legislation that addresses gifted students (Karnes, Troxclair, & Marquardt, 1997; Stephens & Karnes, 2000). In 22 states, gifted students are included in the broad category of exceptional children (Baker & Friedman-Nimz, 2001). This categorization of including them in exceptional children has been both a benefit and hindrance to programs for gifted students. The benefit clearly comes from the legislative budgets that have been made available to the education of exceptional children, which are mainly targeted at children with disabilities. Programs for gifted students have profited from raises in budgets for the general category of exceptional children. Almost all of the states with the largest budgets for educating gifted students tie gifted education to the broader area of education for exceptional children (e.g., Florida, Georgia, North Carolina). In other states, programs for gifted students may be administered in the state department of education under curriculum, school psychology, or other sub-departments, largely because of history and local conditions. Such state programs for gifted students have not done nearly as well financially as those placed under special education (Gallagher, 2000b).

The categorization of programs for gifted students under the broader category of special education has some drawbacks, however. These programs must follow the rules of special education even when those rules are not appropriate. For example, federal legislation requires the design of an IEP for each child in special education. Many states put considerable pressure on schools to comply with this standard for gifted students, as well as for children with disabilities for whom the IEP provision was originally designed. The sheer number of IEPs that are mandated, as well as the time involved in constructing them, is a substantial burden for special educators (Gallagher & Desimone, 1995).

The one piece of identifiable legislation at the federal level currently aimed at gifted students is the Javits Act. The law and its regulations made a small amount of funds available ($11.25 million in 2002) but put specific requirements on its use, with an emphasis on aiding high-ability students from underserved populations, such as students with economic disadvantages and students with limited English proficiency. In this regard, the Javits Act has stimulated increased efforts on behalf of gifted students from special populations (O'Connell, 2003).

The Javits Act also established the National Research Center on Gifted and Talented (NRC/GT), which is a collaborative effort of the University of Connecticut, the University of Virginia, Yale University, 54 state and territorial departments of education, more than 280 public and private schools, more than 135 content area consultants, and stakeholders representing professional organizations, parent groups, and businesses (Renzulli & Gubbins, 1997). Since its inception, the NRC/GT disseminated a significant amount of information about the education of gifted students.

Court Decisions

Another major source of policy statements and decisions are court decisions. Some may assume a lack of major court activity regarding gifted education because the disputes have mainly been handled at the state level and are not very visible nationwide (Karnes & Marquardt, 2000). A number of issues are currently being played out in the courts, such as early admission of gifted learners, racial balance in programs for gifted students, and the responsibility of the schools to provide special services for the gifted (Karnes & Marquardt, 2003).

Organizations such as the National Association for Gifted Children (NAGC) have attempted to link programs for gifted students to federal disability legislation and to argue that federal court decisions on exceptional children also cover gifted children, but these attempts have largely failed, leaving a miscellaneous set of court decisions that seem to be determined by local circumstances rather than by broad legal principles (Karnes & Marquardt, 2000).

The Office of Civil Rights (OCR) participates in various discussions with school systems because of the observed limited participation of children from minority groups in programs for gifted students (Gallagher & Gallagher, 1994). The OCR has decided in the favor of the local schools in more than half of the cases in which the charge was discrimination against students and families from minority groups. The key element in most of these cases was whether the local schools took definitive steps to ensure that the procedures they were following for identifying or placing gifted students were free of discriminatory actions or rules (Karnes et al., 1997).

A National Academy of Sciences report recommended that when a family and a school has a dispute, it should be settled at the lowest level possible through mediation or negotiation (Donovan & Cross, 2002). The first level of addressing a dispute is mediation; the next level is a due process hearing; and only when resolution seems impossible does the dispute becomes a full-scale court case, which almost always leaves behind empty purses and hard feelings.

Administrative Rules

Administrative rules and decisions established by local schools and state education departments constitute another source of policy statements. Many of these rules have the effect of limiting the opportunities of gifted students. For example, some schools have a policy that no child can enter kindergarten prior to his or her fifth birthday. This interferes with the early admission to school of younger gifted students who have clearly shown the intellectual capabilities and social maturity of an older child. This kind of rule frustrates many parents looking for a place for their bright child who may already be reading or doing arithmetic at a third-grade level before the age of 5. Local schools can establish their own criteria for eligibility to a local program for gifted students as long as it does not conflict with state rules or state law.

Administrative rules about identification or placement in special programs for gifted students can be a source of difficult relationships between parents and school. Many policy decisions regarding the education of gifted students fall to educational administrators at the state and local level. All too often these administrators know very little about the education of gifted students and make decisions that seem to be best for the school and the education department at the moment.

Professional Initiatives

Professional groups want to set their own standards for treating gifted students. NAGC developed a set of standards related to dimensions such as teacher certification or ability grouping. These standards, with the weight of a professional organization behind them, can influence or change local or state regulations. Although many schools follow a policy of inclusion regarding the education of gifted students, as well as for students with disabilities, inclusion conflicts, in part, with the NAGC's set of standards:

> NAGC maintains that gifted students, like other children with special needs, require a full continuum of educational services to aid in the development of the students' unique strengths and talents. One such option in that continuum of services of gifted students can be the regular classroom (inclusion). In such an inclusive setting there should be well-prepared teachers who understand and can program for these gifted students, and sufficient administrative support necessary to help differentiate the program to their special needs. (Landrum, Callahan, & Shaklee, 1999)

This statement reveals a consensus of educators of gifted students that the policy of inclusion for gifted students is only one alternative to be considered in planning for gifted students and that other alternatives need to be considered.

CEC has contracted with the National Council for Accreditation of Teacher Education (NCATE) to review higher education programs for accreditation in the areas of exceptional children. The Association for the Gifted (TAG), a division of the CEC, produced a set of standards that lists the fundamental knowledge and skills that special education teachers of gifted students should possess. This section has become part of a larger publication of *What Every Special Educator Must Know* (CEC, 2000), which contains the standards for each area of exceptional children. The major categories for gifted education include philosophy, assessment, instructional content and practice, and management of the teaching and learning environment. Examples of items under instructional content and practice are:

Knowledge Needed
K1. Research-supported instructional strategies and practices (e.g., conceptual development, accelerated presentation pace, minimal drill and practice) for students with gifts and talents.

K2. Sources of specialized materials for students with gifts or talents.

Skills Needed

S1. Design cognitively complex discussion questions, projects and assignments that promote reflective, evaluative nonentrenched thinking in students with intellectual or academic gifts and talents.

S2. Select instructional models appropriate to teaching topics, content area or subject domain.

The nine categories represent a comprehensive portrait of the knowledge and skills expected of a specialist in the area of gifted education. Both TAG and NAGC support these standards, which play an important role in shaping the educational programs for gifted students in public schools.

EQUITY VERSUS EXCELLENCE: COMPETING AMERICAN VALUES

A majority of the public overwhelmingly approves of providing support for special education for children with disabilities instead of for those students who are gifted. The fundamental value underlying this attitude is *vertical equity,* or the unequal treatment of unequals in order to make them more equal. This value lies at the heart of progress for children with disabilities and children from disadvantaged circumstances.

The disparity between programs for children with disabilities and programs for gifted children may be most easily seen in federal funding of the programs. The amount of money directly allocated for programs for gifted students does not exceed $50 million, whereas programs for children with disabilities have several billions of dollars of funding. For every dollar spent at the federal level for gifted students, roughly $1,000 is spent on children with disabilities. Public policy almost invariably reflects some of the fundamental values of the American society, and this is particularly true of the decisions regarding gifted students. For many years, various advocates have been conducting a tug-of-war between the key values of *equity* and *excellence* (Gallagher, 2002).

On the one hand, American society values fair and equal treatment of all students and is repelled by suggestions that favoritism is taking place in the division of resources to school systems or in the admittance of students to higher education. Americans are also keenly aware that some groups (e.g., Native Americans, African Americans, children with disabilities) have historically been denied their right to a free appropriate public education. Such recognition stirs feelings of resentment about any sign of favoritism to a particular group of students. One sign of favoritism is the perceived special privilege given to students like Gretchen who are already performing well in school and elsewhere. This resentment has resulted in opposition to special programming or services for gifted students on the grounds that it violates the principle of *equity* (Margolin, 1996; Oakes, 1985; Sapon-Shevin, 1996).

On the other hand, Americans also have a fundamental commitment to great achievement and excellence, and the United States honors the individual contributions of scientists, captains of industry, artists, and particularly those who have struggled against great odds to achieve (e.g., Abraham Lincoln, Helen Keller). Americans attribute the global power of the United States to its educational system, which has encouraged, or at least allowed, the emergence of greatness and excellence among American children.

These two principles, *equity* and *excellence,* are in conflict over the allocation of scarce resources. The pendulum favoring programs and services that reflect one value or another has swung from side to side, depending on what other forces were influencing society at the moment, but both values of equity and excellence are always there in the schools.

The value of equity comes into play in the education of gifted students when some educators insist that programs for gifted students contain the same proportion of students from minority groups as their prevalence in the larger population. This can encourage or force the schools into looking more intensely for gifted students who do not fit the common standard for admission into special programs but who have outstanding capabilities in some areas.

The value of excellence comes into play when educators pick students for the National Honor Society, a school chorus, or a state competition in soccer or basketball. Under these circumstances, it is performance, not aptitude, that counts the most. The older the student becomes, the more important performance is as a criterion for membership in advanced classes, honors programs, and other evidences of academic excellence.

Another argument to support excellence in the public schools is academic competition with other nations. When the Soviet Union launched Sputnik in 1957, great concern suddenly emerged that the United States was not adequately supporting excellence in the sciences. In the next decade, the National Science Foundation initiated expenditures for building challenging curricula designed to bring the U.S. space program back into a competitive position with the Soviet Union's program (Tannenbaum, 2000).

The threat from abroad—encapsulated in the phrase "The Russians are coming; the Russians are coming!"—strengthened the school programs designed to support excellence and outstanding accomplishment in the schools. The decline of the Soviet Union as a world power lessened the usefulness of this argument for receiving special funds for gifted students from public policy actions (Gallagher & Gallagher, 1994). An alternative argument is that the 21st century world exists in an age of information and that it is in the best interests of the United States to have as many superior students leading the way in this new age as possible. Occasionally, major publications try to stimulate the public's interest in excellence. In 1983, Gardner published *A Nation at Risk* to warn the public that ignoring excellence is a risk to the society. Another report, *National Excellence* (Ross, 1993), made the same point. It seems that a major scare or concern every 10 years or so is necessary to focus national attention on these students.

The political weight of the equity argument is very heavy and is felt powerfully in the public schools. Emphasis on the No Child Left Behind Act has led to the educational neglect of the students whose ability is superior or better. Renzulli (2005) and Gallagher (2005) presented editorials on the topic in *Education Week*. Both pointed out that of the doctoral students finishing in mathematics and science, only a minority of them are native born and that earlier education at the elementary and secondary levels does not seem to stimulate bright students to further effort in the academic fields. The risk of losing world leadership in information technology and related fields is a very serious matter for the United States. Gallagher concluded,

> If we believe, or act as if we believe, that our national security depends on how many nuclear weapons we have stockpiled or how many divisions under arms we maintain, instead of our commitment to nurturing the intellectual resources of coming generations, we may well tremble for the future of our nation. (2005, p. 42)

Tomlinson pointed out that No Child Left Behind seems to have proficiency as its goal, with scant attention being paid to the development of excellence, which should be another clear goal for American education: "An equity initiative that discourages attention to excellence—no matter how laudable its goals may seem cannot take us the full distance we need to go as a nation" (2002, p. 59). From the standpoint of education of gifted students, legislation should proclaim, "No child shall be held down," to encourage the schools to seek out and stimulate those students who represent excellence in achievement and creativity.

FINDING GIFTED STUDENTS

One of the key steps in the education of gifted students is initial identification. School systems have no difficulty identifying students like Gretchen, who are clearly gifted. For others, whose talents are less obvious, decisions must be made that can cast long shadows on students' careers and lives. One of the challenges for identification of gifted students emerges from the disproportionate numbers of students from minority groups who are *not* included in programs for gifted students. In some early studies, no evidence of test bias was found on individual test items, and the predictive ability of IQ tests was effective for all groups regardless of race or ethnicity (Jensen, 1980; Heller, Holtzman, & Messick, 1982). Other studies found evidence that changing the same test questions from abstract problems to concrete problems linked to cultural circumstances resulted in meaningful improvement in the performance of groups from racial and ethnic minorities (Ceci & Laker, 1986; Sternberg & Gregorenko, 1997).

The National Academy of Sciences assembled a panel to provide insight on this issue and reported on the complexity of identification (Donovan & Cross, 2002). It suggested that the basic tools may be compromised and that "many have begun to turn attention to more academically meaningful assessment approaches, such as performance-based assessment, and other approaches more closely tied to instruction and classroom practice" (p. 283). There is now a strong movement away from using a single index to determine giftedness, such as the IQ test score, in favor of using multiple indices and a decision made by a school committee in possession of a wide variety of information about the student.

As noted earlier, when policy is established, a number of assumptions are made that may not be true. An earlier assumption was that a student was gifted because of genetic characteristics present at birth and that the environment experienced by the student had little or no effect on the developing abilities of that student. This assumption turns out to be wrong (Shonkoff & Phillips, 2000) and has caused a good deal of shuffling around for alternative identification methods (e.g., teacher ratings, portfolios of products, aptitude scores on unbiased tests) (Callahan, Tomlinson, & Pizzat, 1993).

As a result, the number of children identified as gifted has increased to include more children from economically disadvantaged homes and a range of other students who had been earlier overlooked. Prominent among students previously unnoticed are those labeled as *twice exceptional:* gifted students who possess another exceptionality as well. These students may have a specific learning disability such as dyslexia; emotional disturbance; or Asperger syndrome, which can combine high ability and many of the characteristics of autism (Attwood, 1998). Each student who is twice exceptional needs an IEP tailored to his or her highly individual characteristics so that he or she can also receive special education services.

Creating an Educational Environment for Gifted Students

One standard method for schools to respond to student excellence is to bring the brightest students together and have them interact with a well-prepared teacher using an advanced curriculum (Colangelo & Davis, 2003; Van Tassel-Baska, 2003). Such attempts include grouping gifted students in special classes, placing them in resource room or pull-out classes, organizing them in cluster grouping in the general classroom (i.e., assigning 8 or 10 gifted students to one classroom), and placing them in special residential schools for students outstanding in subject areas such as math and science (Kolloff, 2003). Occasionally, *magnet schools* have been used, in part to draw groups of gifted students together around specific topic areas (e.g., art, sciences, math) so that these students have a greater opportunity to interact with other bright students and have special instruction in specific topic areas related to their special interests and talents.

Another method of adjusting the educational environment is to accelerate gifted students to another grade level. A wide variety of strategies from early admission to grade skipping to advanced placement courses can be used to speed gifted students through the long and often unstimulating years they will spend in school. If they seek advanced training in medical school or doctoral programs in the arts and sciences, they can literally spend a quarter of a century or more of their life in school (Gallagher, 2002). Educational acceleration is designed to reduce that time somewhat and also to place advanced learners in a more challenging educational setting with students who are closer to their own mental level. Yet, there are many misconceptions abroad in the educational community about this practice. Many teachers feel that acceleration results in social disruption and emotional stress on the student and thus counsel parents against consideration of this acceleration approach.

A major report, *A Nation Deceived,* summed up 50 years of research on the effects of educational acceleration:

> Students who are moved ahead tend to be more ambitious, and they earn graduate degrees at higher rates than other students. Interviewed years later, an overwhelming majority of accelerated students say that acceleration was an excellent experience for them. Accelerated students feel academically challenged and socially accepted, and they do not fall prey to the boredom that plagues many highly capable students who are forced to follow the curriculum for their age peers. (Colangelo et al., 2004, p. 1)

The many researchers reporting in this volume found no support for the ideas that acceleration causes social problems, that it hurries children out of childhood, or that gifted students need to be kept with their own age group. Individual students may suffer these ills, but the vast majority of gifted students who are accelerated are free of these problems. Any strategy that reduces the time spent in the educational system without negative effects could be of substantial benefit to students and to society (Benbow & Lubinski, 1996; Gallagher, 2002).

Talent Search

The Talent Search model originated by Stanley (1996) achieved national attention with a big idea but only modest resources. Stanley asked the question, "How can we find the most talented youth of our generation?" (Lupkowski-Shoplik, Benbow, Assouline, & Brody, 2003). More than 300,000 students from every state now participate in the talent search program, and nine national centers and three international centers help to carry out the program (www.jhu.edu/gifted/index.html). The basic idea of the program is to find talented youth and provide educationally challenging experiences for them. Students who have shown high performance on standardized tests are screened using special high-level tests. Through the talent search program, the extraordinary range of student performance has become better known.

A quite different approach would be to provide *educational vouchers* to parents and give them the opportunity to seek special assistance for their gifted students whenever they thought best, using the voucher to pay for the special services. Parents and the general public have mixed views on this approach. Although vouchers give choice to parents for the placement of their child, the vouchers do little to improve the special education facilities in the new school to support education of gifted students (Gallagher, 2002).

At the institutional level, one might wish to develop special schools for students who are excellent in mathematics and sciences to give them a running start into higher education. Eleven states have currently used this option as one approach to providing special education for gifted students (Kolloff, 2003). Summer programs such as governor's schools, which provide an enriched curriculum, are also popular in many states and are the only special program for gifted students in some states. Their popularity lies, in part, with the fact that in a summer program, there is no requirement to change the general school program or curricula. Olszewski-Kubilius (2003) reported on fast-paced classes provided in summer programs for gifted students. Intense instruction in a given subject such as mathematics has proven highly successful. Getting schools to accept the student's summer work for credit in the general school program has been somewhat more difficult.

Long-term planning could involve the development of an infrastructure that might include regional TA programs, accountability measures, data systems, and personnel preparation posing such questions as "How many specialists will be needed over the next 5 years?" Such an infrastructure would still face uncertain public support and meaningful cost increases.

Decision Matrix

Figure 9.1 shows a decision matrix for educating gifted students. This chart presents a number of major policy options available together with the criteria that can be used to weigh the options against one another. Given current circumstances, what are the decisions available to policy makers and educators of gifted students? Many options are available to be considered. This is where professionals in the field can weigh in with their expertise. The state department of education could provide funds to support differentiated programming for gifted students or content themselves with supporting personnel preparation programs geared to matching certified teachers in gifted education with gifted students. Figure 9.1 shows heavy costs and personnel needs for the option of special classes, despite a good track record of positive achievements. The public remains mixed over its options for such a major step.

In terms of *cost,* direct subsidies of gifted programs probably represent the most expensive of all the options listed. Direct subsidies of gifted programs also raise considerable *personnel needs* that would have to be planned for and funded. Summer programs, an alternative, probably put very little pressures on finance because special summer programs can be staffed by faculty who are already in the system.

Less is known about the *track record* of these options because of the shortage of research projects that are policy oriented. No one knows, for example, what parental vouchers will accomplish for gifted students who choose them. No research studies have examined how supporting the infrastructure actually improves the education for individual gifted students. Recent meta-analyses of studies in acceleration (Kulik, 1992) and in measuring the effects of grouping (Kulik & Kulik, 1997) have yielded positive results for these program options.

Decision makers, however, are very sensitive to the criterion of *public acceptance.* Does the public feel that gifted students are already doing well and do not need additional programs to make them even better? Public acceptance is quite mixed on the issues of vouchers as well. The public's attitude may have a great deal to do with which options are eventually chosen. This does not mean that any option that has a negative public image should be summarily abandoned, but it does point to the need for further public education on the range of options.

The *parental support* of the various options can play a significant role in their acceptance or choice. For most additional programming, parents appear positive. There are mixed feelings about the use of vouchers or educational acceleration.

Options	Criteria for choice					
	Cost	Personnel needs	Track record	Public acceptance	Parental support	Other
Subsidize gifted programs	Heavy	Heavy	Good	Mixed	High	
Subsidize personnel preparation for gifted	Modest	Modest	Good	Good	High	
Support parental vouchers	Heavy	Modest	Uncertain	Mixed	Mixed	
Math and science schools, residential schools	Light	Light	Good	Good	High	
Summer programs, governor schools	Light	Light	Good	Good	High	
Support infrastructure	Modest	Modest	Probably good	Uncertain	Moderate	
Educational acceleration	Light	Light	Excellent	Mixed	Mixed	
Status quo	Modest	Modest	Moderately good	Mixed	Moderate	

Figure 9.1. Decision matrix for gifted education. (*Note*: Ratings here are provided by the author based on research reviews, program reports, and personal experience.)

The advantage of such a decision matrix, such as this one shown in Figure 9.1, is that it provides a quick overview of the range of options and criteria that come into play in the decision making to be done in the education of gifted students. The decision matrix reveals something else, too. It is not sufficient to have data on the effectiveness of a program. Other criteria in the matrix, such as public attitudes or costs, must meet with favorable responses. In many policy decisions, values can trump facts when the final decision is made.

Of course, there is no educational policy, no matter how sound, that cannot be butchered in its implementation. Accelerating gifted students who are outstanding academically but are socially immature is not an optimal implementation of a policy of acceleration. Who would want to accelerate a child who is not physically or socially mature in his or her own age group?

SPECIAL ISSUES IN GIFTED EDUCATION

As with each exceptionality, a number of special issues in gifted education require particular efforts to obtain solutions. The following represents my choice of the most pertinent problems.

Missing Support System

Teachers are often admonished to be "professionals," but one of the characteristics of other professionals is that they have a support team to help them. Lawyers have paralegals and secretarial help. Physicians have nurses, laboratories, technicians, and other support staff to help with diagnosis and treatment of patients. In contrast, teachers are often left to their own devices and are often their own assistants and secretaries. An appropriate support team for teachers of the gifted would mean, at least, the availability of a school psychologist to help with assessment and available consultation with content specialists on differentiated curriculum for gifted students for particular subjects. All too often, the individual teacher or specialist can feel very alone, wishing for a support system that does not exist but that would aid him or her in the work with gifted children.

In programs for children with disabilities, as earlier chapters outline, federal funds enabled the development of some extensive support systems. These include TA and regional resource centers, demonstration programs, major support for personnel preparation, a national clearinghouse for information, and substantial funds for research and evaluation. All of these strengthen the effectiveness of the specialist working with children with disabilities (Kirk et al., 2003). Specialists working with gifted children also need support because these students are exceptional in ways that also require accommodations and special curricula. As with other education specialists, specialists working with gifted children should not be required to invent a new curriculum to supplement the general curriculum.

Perhaps the greatest shortcoming of the missing support system is the absence of support for personnel preparation (Gallagher, 2002). Because the preparation of specialists in this area usually involves a relatively small number of students and faculty within a college or university's school of education, a personnel preparation program for gifted teachers is unlikely to survive economically without some form of state or federal subsidy. In tight budget times, higher education institutions are less enthusiastic about adding a program of personnel preparation for teachers of gifted students that might increase their own deficits. Personnel preparation for this specialty then becomes the responsibility of state departments of education, professional associations like NAGC or TAG, and ad hoc arrangements with consultants for short-term training at local or regional sites.

Another support system shortage is in the availability of TA centers. In Texas, New York, Iowa, and other states, schools can call on regional service centers for individual consultation or short-term training. Few of these service centers are staffed with personnel specializing in gifted students. When the specialist or teacher in gifted education at the local level has a special problem or crisis and does the educational equivalent of calling 911 for emergency help, does anyone answer? All too often the answer is no.

The current data systems in most states fall far short of collecting key data that would aid those planning programs for gifted students. If one wanted to know the answer to simple policy-related questions, such as "How many teachers are certified to teach gifted students in this city or state?" and "How many more are needed?" the embarrassing response is that no one knows because those data have not been collected on a systematic basis.

When one looks for the available research, evaluation, and demonstration money, the current federal source of funds for gifted education is the Javits Program in the U.S. Department of Education. NRC/GT represents one of the few continuing centers to provide some help in this area. The center also is paid out of the federal Javits legislation. Those wishing to do serious research in the education of gifted students must seek funds from private sources, programs focusing in content areas such as science or mathematics, or agencies such as NICHD that support research on broad areas of child development.

Accountability

Issues of accountability are as relevant for gifted students as for children with disabilities. The problem of assessing Gretchen is somewhat different, however. If schools are restricted to grade-level tests, then it will be difficult to find out just how much Gretchen knows. If she scores in the 99th percentile on a test, the school personnel only know that she has mastered what is in the test. Because she is not tested on knowledge beyond her grade level, they cannot peg her lessons at the appropriate level of challenge because they cannot know how much beyond her grade level she really is.

Two levels of decisions are used in accountability efforts: political decisions and educational decisions. By dividing the testing into these two categories, one can see how much testing is being done for political purposes and how much for educational decision making. Table 9.2 illustrates the different measures involved in these decisions. The political decisions determine whether a school system is doing well or whether some corrective measures should be applied, if the student scores are too low. They may be of use to public decision makers who wish to improve basic education but not necessarily the education of students like Gretchen. The results of the end-of-grade tests are of little use to the current teacher because the academic year is almost over before the results are known.

National Assessment of Educational Progress tests have been used to see how schools are achieving in a state or region of the country. They, too, are of little use to the individual student or teacher. The same can be said of the international comparisons in content mastery. The Scholastic Aptitude Test may help get a student into a college or university but may not be of any help in modifying the student's curriculum or the instructional strategies of the teacher.

The educational decisions, as shown in Table 9.2, deliver information that is potentially useful to the teacher of an individual student because these decisions reveal how well the student is able to apply his or her knowledge in situations of *authentic assessment* or *performance assessment*. A *portfolio analysis* can yield a great deal of information about the strategies the student is using to search for knowledge or the degree of insight he or she has about the topic at hand. In performance assessment, for example, the student may be asked to apply a mathematical formula or theorem to a practical problem so the evaluator can

Table 9.2. Two levels of decisions used in accountability efforts

Political decisions	Educational decisions
Scholastic aptitude test	Authentic assessment
General achievement test	Performance assessment
International comparisons in math and science	Teacher-made tests
End-of-grade tests	Portfolio analysis
Competency tests	Student journals
National Association of Educational Progress (NAEP) tests	Teacher journals

Reprinted from Gallagher, J. (2003, March 8). *Accountability*. Address given at College of William & Mary conference, Williamsburg, VA.

test the student for more than just the memory of mathematical formulae. Such information is of limited value to political decision makers, however. In one talent search conducted at Johns Hopkins University, 22% of seventh-grade boys and 45% of eighth-grade boys exceeded the average scores of graduating high school seniors in verbal ability. These figures are matched by the talented girls in those grades (Center for Talented Youth, 2001). All of this tends to underline the lack of challenge presented to gifted students in general education and indicates the need for acceleration and greater content sophistication in their programming.

A Cool Problem

One of the influences in the allocation of resources in public policy has been the perception of the immediate nature of the problem itself. Gallagher (2002) made the distinction of cool versus hot problems in the public perception, with the hot problems demanding immediate attention. Table 9.3 provides a brief collection of cool and hot policy problems. Problems such as national defense, terrorism, violence in the schools, and the education of children with disabilities present society with issues that call for immediate action. The failure to manage these issues would create serious political crises right away.

The cool problems are those that are seen as important in the long run for the society but do not demand immediate attention. Air and water pollution, global warming, and the needs of gifted students are a few cool problems. Unfortunately, scarce resources usually run out before state or federal legislatures allocate significant funds to the "cool" problems. The advantage and disadvantage of democratic society policy making is that 1) immediate crises do get a hearing, but 2) long-range problems are often put off for another day.

Table 9.3. Public policy: Cool and hot problems

Cool policy problem (We should act sometime.)	Hot policy problem (We must act immediately.)
Air and water pollution	Violence in the schools
Mass transit	Children with diabetes
Children with gifts and talents	National defense
Universal health care	Cancer
Global warming	Heart disease
	Terrorism

From Gallagher, J. (2002). *Society's role in educating gifted students: The role of public policy* (p. 24). Storrs, CT: National Research Center on the Gifted and Talented; reprinted by permission.

Policy Recommendations

Gallagher (2002) conducted an extensive review of state and federal policies for gifted students and made several policy recommendations:

- The level of support for the development of differentiated curricula at various age levels should be greatly increased. This would mean substantially increasing the funding for the Javits Program and/or greater support for state initiatives in this direction.

- At the state and local levels, the programs for gifted students should be expected to generate periodic reports on their results. Plans would include measurable objectives and a method to evaluate the plan and services offered. Such evaluation should focus on improved student performance on high-level tasks.

- Either state or federal legislation needs to be passed to establish the elements of support systems. Professional associations must accept a crucial leadership role in pointing out the need to decision makers and staying with these issues until some new public policy is created.

- Various professional standards should emphasize the expectation for cultural diversity in student participation in gifted programs. If gifted programs lack diversity, then local schools must be asked to explain. The OCR has sensitized local school systems to set up rules about diversity of participation in special programs.

The implementation of these recommendations would bring special programming for gifted students into a rough parity with programming for other students with special needs.

DECISIONS AHEAD

Several serious issues must be settled regarding the education of gifted students, and until they are resolved, a number of groups will not be provided with the educational equity they require.

Issue of Race

There is considerable confusion about what to do about the clear disproportion of students from racial minorities who are identified or enrolled in programs for gifted students (Colangelo & Davis, 2003; Donovan & Cross, 2002). The percentage of African American and Hispanic students enrolled in gifted programs is less than half of their general population prevalence. Asian students participate at disproportionately higher rates than their percentage of the population would suggest. The racial and ethnic disproportions have been ascribed to some very different causes. One theory suggests a bias in standard measures of intelligence against minority groups. This theory proposes that there is really no difference in intelligence among cultural subgroups and that the cause of the observed disproportion is the cultural bias of instruments and educators (Ford & Harris, 1999). A second theory is that unfavorable environmental conditions that students from some racial minorities often experience (e.g., low socioeconomic level) contribute to poor performance on tests and in education.

Familial and cultural values have also been theorized as influencing achievement. As people who have been historically subjected to both individual and institutionalized racism in the United States, African American and Hispanic people sometimes view the school system with suspicion and even hostility, contributing to a perception of academic achievement as culturally alien (Fordham & Ogbu, 1986; Ogbu, 2003). Asian American students' high achievement on standardized tests has been attributed to the high value that many Asian American families place on education and achievement (Kitano & DiJiosia, 2002), which creates a favorable climate for academic attainment. As researchers continue to explore these issues, it is crucial that they remain aware of the power of dominant stereotypes and work to examine their critical assumptions carefully.

Another unsettled issue is whether a quota system should be used to equalize the proportions of students in minority groups who participate in programs for gifted students or whether an improvement of the environments from which some of these students come could gradually reduce the disproportion in that fashion. Of course, society cannot be easily reformed to eliminate racism.

Options for Parents of Gifted Students

As long as the only option for parents in educating gifted students is the public schools, then educational administrators do not need to pay much attention to parental complaints. Now, a growing number of options increase parents' power to influence the schools. Are there alternatives to the public schools that do not include the expenditure of huge sums of money that the family would spend on private schools for their gifted child? One of the options, noted previously, is vouchers, which would give a freedom of choice to families who could choose a school that will challenge their child. The use of vouchers, linked to No Child Left Behind, seems to be currently limited to schools that are not performing well. Parents of gifted students can also choose to send their child to *magnet schools* that have an emphasis on particular content fields, such as mathematics, science, or art. This would allow the further development of interests in gifted students who would wish to specialize in these fields.

Charter schools are free from the requirements and rules of the regular public schools, and they also have attraction for the gifted student because teachers and students have more flexibility to pursue their own interests in charter schools. Finally, *homeschooling,* noted previously as a potential choice for parents of children with disabilities, can also be used by families of gifted students. Homeschooling can allow a gifted student like Gretchen to advance at his or her own pace and seek out issues of interest (Kearney, 1999).

Distance Learning

The Internet and computer use represent another option in increasing use in the education of gifted students. The Education Program for Gifted Youth (EPGY) at Stanford University developed a series of distance learning courses (Ravaglia, Suppes, Stillinger, & Alper, 1995). In a pilot study using EPGY material, a group of 18 eighth-grade students mastered 1.5 grade years in 5 months of instruction (Pyryt, 2003). On-line courses and distance learning courses will multiply for gifted students in the coming years.

Public Support

Finally, decision makers must confront the general lack of public financial support for these programs for gifted learners. The payoff for gifted education programs—students much better prepared to play a significant role in future societies—seems far off to current policy makers, who are more concerned with immediate crisis issues. It is the low priority placed on programs for gifted students that has prevented greater public investment in support features such as personnel preparation, data systems, and TA. Until there is a comparable support system infrastructure for the nurturing of excellence as now exists for the nurturing of children with disabilities, it will be difficult to allocate and maintain sufficient resources for educating gifted students, despite the view that such resources represent the most cost-effective use of money spent in education.

CHAPTER 10

Outside Forces that Affect Decisions in Special Education

M any of the changes taking place in special education originate in forces that lay outside the boundaries of the field of special education. To complete the portrait of 21st-century special education, this chapter includes some of the outside forces that impinge on special education and special educators from various parts of the societal compass. This chapter focuses on two types of forces: forces outside the boundaries of education itself (e.g., economic forces, development of parent groups, cultural differences) and forces within the broad framework of education but apart from special education (e.g., testing policies, certification, curriculum standards, graduation requirements).

As noted in previous chapters, Arnie, Bobby, Les, Cathy, and Gretchen each swim in their own cultural and environmental seas that tend to affect their social adaptations and their learning. The same can be said for actions of the public schools. Much of what the schools do or do not do is related to other forces outside the schools themselves. Forces such as immigration, the war on terror, the state of the economy, and the value society places on each individual all play significant roles in shaping the public school agenda and priorities. Some of the more important of these forces and the changes in the environment affect all five children. This is a prelude to the final chapter, which considers major changes in special education.

FORCES OUTSIDE EDUCATION

Educational Reform

Some of the most serious decision making in American education today revolves around the issue of educational reform. A widespread belief is the educational enterprise is broken or seriously impaired, and that belief has stirred many in the fields of education and political policy making to propose changes to address the perceived deficits. Unless schools meet their annual yearly progress (AYP) goal, incremental improvements in tested achievement, they face a series of sanctions designed to bring them up to standard. An unstated assumption underlying this policy is that the schools are responsible for most, if not all, of students' achievement. Otherwise, why punish or reward teachers for their students' performance? Why threaten educational administrators or schools boards with drastic consequences if their schools do not perform up to some standard?

But is the assumption that schools have almost total responsibility for students' achievement really correct? Other factors have long been recognized as equally or more important. Jencks (1972) said that "the character of a school's output depends largely on a single input, namely the characteristics of the entering children." A family's socioeconomic status and the cultural background of the family and neighborhood play a dominant role in a student's performance.

Gallagher (2000a) estimated that the schools contribute, at most, 25% of student variance on achievement; self-variables, family variables, community values, and other differences account for 75% of student variance. Bronfenbrenner's (1989) theoretical model suggested major inputs from outside the school affecting the child. The special education decisions regarding Arnie, Bobby, Cathy, Les, and Gretchen are affected by a multitude of forces that they and their teachers may be only dimly aware of.

Parent Groups

One of the major social phenomena of special education is the formation of parent groups, citizens seeking ways to help their children with special needs to meet the challenges of the public schools.

The Arc of the United States

One of the most powerful of forces that lie outside the education community that has affected special education is the organization of parent groups, particularly in the 1960s and 1970s. The parents of children with mental retardation quickly discovered that their ability to negotiate with their local school system was extremely limited. The Arc of the United States (http://www.thearc.org) was established in 1951 as the National Association for Retarded Children, bringing together more than 100 local groups. During the 1960s and 1970s, The Arc played a major role in shaping legislation and educational policy and making parents a major player in policy development.

The Arc, with its current membership of 225,000, continues to advocate for people with mental retardation by

1. Acting as a watchdog on programs providing services and making sure that the money is wisely spent

2. Assisting in standard setting and evaluation of programs

3. Providing services in the community on an interim basis

4. Initiating demonstration programs for innovation

5. Implementing research projects to add to the knowledge base

To understand the impact that a parent organization has, one can only imagine a conversation between a parent and a legislator about whether the state can afford to provide programs to meet the needs of children with special needs. The legislator would have a difficult time explaining that there was not enough money to provide such services when the parent can easily point to current expenditures of a dubious nature. In fact, many legislators do want to help. This scenario, repeated in many communities across the country, resulted in increased funding in special education.

United Cerebral Palsy

An advocacy organization founded in 1949, United Cerebral Palsy (UCP; http://www.ucp.org) provides direct services for people with disabilities and their families in addition to providing information and referral services and legislative advocacy. Every year, more than 30,000 children and adults receive UCP assistance in therapy, assistive technology training, early intervention programs, and family support. UCP has now joined forces with The Arc of the United States and other advocacy groups to form a collaborative advocacy effort that has helped to support the passage and improvement of disability legislation. Cathy's parents are members of UCP and are pleased with this collaborative effort with The Arc because of The Arc's history of impressive advocacy in Washington, D.C.

Learning Disability Association of America

Another organization that serves parents and students in the largest group of children with disabilities in special education is the Learning Disability Association of America (LDA; http://www.lda.org). It has more than 60,000 members and more than 775 local chapters. As with the other parent organizations, LDA wishes to create public awareness and acceptance of people with learning disabilities, to work with the schools to improve programs, and to promote legislative assistance at the national and state levels. Because of the relationship between learning disabilities and school dropout and delinquency, LDA works with schools and legal authorities to develop comprehensive approaches to education and employment.

Autism Society of America

The Autism Society of America (http://www.autism-society.org) was established in 1965 and currently has more than 50,000 members and a network of more than 200 chapters nationwide. It is a leading source of information and referral on autism and has been active in impressing on Congress the special needs of children like Arnie. It is also active in encouraging increased appropriations for programs devoted to improving services to children with autism, particularly working through NIH and its agencies that conduct research on the condition.

The blossoming of organizations designed to meet parents' needs for information and for influence in the education community signals the growing influence of parents in education decision making. Their willingness to devote time and resources so that their organizations are strong and effective is a key to the influence of special education. Several professional advocacy organizations also have parent members and offer information or services to parents. For example, NAGC has a special journal for parents, *Parenting for High Potential,* and holds a special parents' day at their national convention, which helps Gretchen's parents to become an active force in gifted education.

The Achievement Gap

Ever since schools have been accumulating results on achievement tests and dividing them by gender, race, social class, and other categories, clear evidence of major differences in assignment to special education by the race of the student has been evident. The National Assessment of Educational Progress has been charting the performance of samples of children in each state since 1967 and has been used as one of the reliable indicators of the achievement gap between mainstream and minority children. The gap was reduced in the 1970s and 1980s but has remained relatively constant since that time. African American and Hispanic high school students have an average achievement of about the same level as a Caucasian student in the lowest quartile, and they are much less likely to graduate from secondary school. They are likely to be referred to special education because of low achievement (Education Commission of the States, 2002).

Concerns about an achievement gap stem from sensitivity to possible racial and ethnic inequity in the school system. Most education professionals and policy makers are so committed to respecting each student's civil rights and providing nondiscriminatory education settings and programs that racial differences in measured ability or performance are distressing. The causes of the achievement gap have created concern within school systems. Most of the causes have been sought within the academic community. Social status, teacher attitudes, and policies for tracking students have been identified as potential causes for the gap. The result is that researchers propose school-based solutions. For example, Thernstrom and Thernstrom (2003) claimed that good schools could close the gap.

Although the forces within schools have been held responsible for the creation of the achievement gap, there is reason to believe that many of the multivariate causes lie outside the school boundaries. The achievement gap between races and ethnic groups is present prior to the entrance to school (Kober, 2001), suggesting societal forces at work in children's early years. Some of the social factors identified as linked to the achievement gap have been low parental education, lack of access to high-quality prekindergarten programs, and peer influences. Many current theories recognize a combination of factors, such as institutional discrimination, poor schools, and poverty. Older hypotheses about intellectual differences among races have been debunked.

Many observers have noted that there are more children from minority families in special education than is indicated by enrollment in general classes. As noted in Chapter 2, the National Academy of Sciences panel confirmed the disproportion of minority children in special education programs and called for early identification and programming for these students (Donovan & Cross, 2002). Special educators also face difficulties posed by the immigration of Hispanic children into the United States. Many of these children speak English as a second language and must also cope with problems of poverty and differing cultures. It is certain that a number of these children newly arrived in the United States will be referred to special education, increasing the need for greater understanding of cultural differences by school personnel.

Ogbu (2003) did a comprehensive study of the Shaker Heights, Ohio, school system to find the possible reasons for the achievement gap found there, as well as in many other communities in the country. Ogbu identified two major forces that seem to interact with one another. The first is the system, which includes all of those ways in which the society treats and has treated minority groups. Second, Ogbu identified cultural forces, which include

> Factors that arise from how the minorities themselves interpret and respond to their treatment; that is, their adaptations to U.S. society and to their minority status, which depends on their unique history or how they became minorities in the United States. (2003, p. 45)

Such attitudes, when present, create an additional challenge for special educators to overcome.

Ogbu pointed out that many of the proposed solutions, such as educational vouchers, charter schools, performance contracts, cooperative learning, and merit pay, are school related and have little to do with cultural forces. Consequently, they have been only moderately helpful in this situation. He suggested that African American communities and families need to assume a proactive role in increasing the academic orientation, effort, and performance of their children through enhancing the vision of successful African American citizens in business, the arts, and sciences; organizing supplementary education programs; and encouraging parental monitoring of student work.

Still others point to the early upbringing of children in minority groups and children living in poverty as the key to poor academic performance. Hart and Risley (1995) showed huge differences among children from differing social classes in the amount and kind of language that they hear and use daily. The argument for targeted preschool experiences focusing on language development relates to attempts to compensate early for such deficiencies (Clifford & Gallagher, 2001; Neuman, 2003).

Finally, some continue to believe, despite overwhelming evidence to the contrary, that because Americans now have equality by fiat, any differences in achievement must be due to race-based intellectual abilities (Hernnstein & Murray, 1994). Legal equality is a long way from practical equality, and there remain significant societal barriers to performance for children from minority groups.

Policies have been set in place to narrow the achievement gap (Donovan & Cross, 2002). The raft of legislative initiatives for children with disabilities owes some of its success to its linkage to the antidiscrimination arguments for children from minority groups. Policy makers should make a comprehensive effort to address school- and culture-related problems that lend to the achievement gap. Similar conclusions have been made about the multifaceted factors concerning the school adaptation of all children with disabilities.

Scientific Advances

Educational programs and institutions are responsive to major scientific discoveries in this country and the world, although with some time lag. Many times, these discoveries are made without special notice or concern about exceptional children, until later problems can emerge requiring adaptations in policy and programs. Many agencies have established a research-to-practice unit to speed up the translation of research to the classroom.

Genetic Discoveries

There are many other professions besides education in which decisions are being made that affect exceptional children. One of the areas certain to influence special education decision making in the immediate future is the rapid progress made in medical practice and biological research. Perhaps the development with the longest lasting influence is the Human Genome Project, whose fantastic goal is to chart all of the genes and chromosomes of human beings. In the process of doing that basic research, many discoveries will pinpoint some previously unidentified genetic links to a variety of disorders that cause children to need special education services (U.S. Department of Energy, 2003). The *Human Genome News* is a newsletter that reports current developments from the U.S. Department of Energy, Office of Science, Human Genome project.

Arnie, Les, and Bobby have disabilities that have been attributed to environmental causes (autism, learning disabilities, and emotional disturbance, respectively). In the case of Arnie, cold and distant mothers were considered as a possible causal agent to autism (Bettelheim, 1974). In Les's case, poor education in the early years was considered a cause (Swanson, Harris, & Graham, 2003). For Bobby, his environment and dysfunctional family were pinpointed as the cause for his violent outbursts (Rutherford et al., 2004). Developments in behavioral genetics have provided good evidence that each of these conditions is at least partially influenced by genetic factors and that there is a complex interaction between genes and environment (Plomin, 2003). It is likely that many of these conditions emerge because of genetic influences, regardless of the nature of parental intervention.

Beyond the obvious conclusion that parents should have access to genetic counseling so that they are aware of these facts, what should decision makers do about this information? Can the genetic makeup of a newborn be screened to alert parents early to a potential for problems? Other possible responses are using gene replacement and trying to genetically engineer children so that they would be without negative genetic potential. These considerations have more than a whiff of Huxley's (1932) *Brave New World,* but there is also the opportunity to provide meaningful help to these families. Soon, many of these rare disorders and their causes will be better understood, and with understanding, researchers may well discover some additional treatments. Such advances take time, however, and these students need the best of special education now.

Although genetics are involved, problems from these conditions are not inevitable. To say that Bobby has a genetic tendency toward aggressive behavior does not mean his behavior should be approached with a sense of fatalism. It does mean that special efforts may have to be made to ensure that Bobby develops prosocial skills for handling conflicts at a young age.

Biomedical Advances

Another advancement in the medical domain is the continued research into pharmaceutical products. Can drug therapy help children with attention-deficit/hyperactivity disorder or with seemingly uncontrollable behavior? A meta-analysis summarizing 115 different studies clearly indicated that behavior and academic performance of children with attention-deficit/hyperactivity disorder showed definite improvement with medication, but a combination of medication and psychosocial treatments appeared to attain the best results (Forness, Kavale, Sweeney, & Crenshaw, 1999).

A fine example of how forces outside special education and even outside the schools can shape and influence special education can be found in the continuing discussion about health care reform. Hebbeler described the chronic personnel shortages in programs for young children with disabilities:

> If health care is changed to provide access to services that many people now need but cannot afford, demand will increase. Young children with disabilities will be competing with an even larger pool of individuals requiring the services of the already undersupplied health care professions. (1994, p. 32)

The clear interaction between environment and biology noted throughout this volume means that many more combinations of biological and educational treatments will likely be found that can bring some relief to these children and their families.

Economic Competition

The degree to which education and nurturance can be provided to children with disabilities depends on a variety of factors in the larger society. Social policy determines the allocation of scarce resources to almost unlimited needs. That principle caused the federal government to break its promise in terms of the share of the costs that they would bear in disability and education legislation. PL 94-142 promised in 1975 that the federal government would pick up 40% of the costs of educating children with disabilities. The most that they have funded is 15% or less of the costs (U.S. Department of Education, 2003).

Because there is a societal competition for these scarce resources, major governmental expenditures in other areas such as Medicare or national defense puts an automatic brake on increases in education programs. In this sense, the young naturally compete for scare resources with older adults. The greater the needs of older adults in terms of health and social security, the fewer resources can be delivered to children. As was pointed out, because older adults vote in large numbers and provide campaign contributions, whereas the young cannot, it is not surprising that the majority of available funds seem to be distributed to older adults. This is true even when policy makers clearly recognize that the future of society depends on the well-being and proper upbringing of young children.

State Budgets

The states still bear the largest fiscal responsibility for education, so anything that has a major impact on state budgets inevitably influences education. One of the competing forces is clearly Medicaid funds. Medicaid is considered an entitlement; that is, everyone who needs the funds is expected to receive them regardless of the condition of the budget. Because the demands of Medicaid are increasing sharply, states may have to limit their expenditures for education, such as special education funds, despite good intentions (Ladenheimer, 2002). The Congressional Budget Office estimated that state budgets related to Medicaid will increase by 9% per year. In 2001, more than two thirds of the states were reporting shortfalls in Medicaid budgets.

Many states have a further restriction. They must, according to their state constitutions, balance their budget every year. If the revenues coming into the state to pay for state responsibilities are level or declining and the demands for Medicaid or other entitlements are increasing, the state can spend only a limited amount on general and special education.

The solution to this issue lies in either increasing revenue (and politicians have a dread of raising taxes) or cutting other state expenditures. State lotteries are increasingly popular because the lottery appears to be one way of raising money for state expenditures without increasing citizens' tax bills, a politically unacceptable option in many states. Three states' methods of raising funds for special education were declared unconstitutional, and some serious discussions about how to pay for educational expenses need to be conducted.

National Security

One of the most profound recent changes resulted from the terrorist attacks in the United States on September 11, 2001. The attacks changed the national attitude and priorities and even eroded citizens' confidence in America's secure place in the world. The demand for greater domestic security creates budget issues that tend to take away resources from education and focus on short-term goals of survival, as opposed to the long-term goals of educating the young and making sure that all children receive a free appropriate public education. The war in Iraq and increased military presence in Afghanistan and other foreign nations have the additional effect of shutting down educational investments.

Early Child Care

The prekindergarten movement aims to encourage the start of educational programming for children at the age of 3 or younger. The movement is based, in part, on the need for working parents to place their children in a secure setting, but it is also supported by research on early brain function, which suggests the need for nurturing early intellectual development (Clifford & Gallagher, 2001). PL 99-457 provided the opportunity for infants and toddlers with disabilities to have early training and therapeutic experiences. Head Start began even earlier to provide opportunities for children living in poverty to gain some of the developmental foundations of language and social development so that they are prepared to begin kindergarten (Zigler & Styfco, 1994).

International Influences

Some of the influences on education and special education actually occur beyond the boundaries of the United States. In 1998, the Office of Economic and Cultural Development (OECD) undertook to study the early childhood education and care policies in 10 European countries, plus Australia and the United States. An international team of early childhood specialists visited various early childhood programs in the 12 countries and interviewed many specialists in the early child care community. The OECD (2001) reported their conclusions.

The early childhood planning problems these countries face had many similarities. For example, all were concerned about the low wages and high turnover of personnel in the programs. They all struggled with the establishment and maintenance of high-quality programs. They sought support mechanisms for service programs with the belief that programs "need to be supported by a quality infrastructure for planning, monitoring, support, training, research and development" (p. 95).

Table 10.1 reports some of the major policy lessons learned from the OECD study team's experience and observations. The emphasis on an integrated approach to policy development and a strong partnership with the education system should strike home in the United States, where such goals are still to be achieved. The OECD report mentioned that particular attention should be given to children in need of special support and underlined the need for high-quality support services and infrastructure. How these desirable goals will be financed remained a matter of concern for the decision makers in each of the countries. Also, the OECD report recommended a number of supports for education: public investments in the infrastructure and appropriate personnel preparation, systematic attention to evaluation and to data collection, and continued research and evaluation. In short, the OECD report argued for the same support system components as are in this volume for children with disabilities.

Some tend to discount European practices because the political, cultural, and economic contexts are so different, but the report is a strong statement about what is needed for high-quality education of young children. The OECD recom-

Table 10.1. Policy lessons from international study of early childhood

A systematic and integrated approach to policy development and implementation

A strong and equal partnership with the education system

A universal approach to access, with particular attention to children in need of special support

Substantial public investment in services and the infrastructure

A participatory approach to high-quality improvement and assurance

Appropriate training and working conditions for staff in all forms of provision

Systematic attention to monitoring and data collection

A stable framework and long-term agenda for research and evaluation

Source: Office of Economic and Cultural Development (2001).

mendations also resemble closely policy recommendations for prekindergarten and child care programs in the United States (Clifford & Gallagher, 2001).

FORCES WITHIN EDUCATION

Although society clearly affects public school programs for children with special needs, forces or initiatives within the broad boundaries of education can also influence children with special needs. Education initiatives have spawned a number of alternative education approaches, such as charter schools, educational vouchers, magnet schools, and even homeschooling. In addition, there have been arguments about standards set by content specialists. Children with special needs are rarely directly involved in such arguments, although they are affected by the outcome of these disputes.

Alternative Education Settings

One major value that has entered the discussion of how to educate young children is *privatization,* giving greater power to an individual citizen to decide the type and kind of education that his or her child should receive. This argument holds that the public schools are a monopoly with heavy bureaucratic overtones that educates children in the manner that anonymous education experts determine with little or no input from those who might disagree with them.

Educational Vouchers

One of the options that have become available for parents in some communities is the parental voucher, which allows parents of a child with disabilities to choose a school for their child and to use the voucher as payment. Several trial voucher programs have been used in Milwaukee, Wisconsin; Cleveland, Ohio; and Florida. In Cleveland, children with special needs are entitled to the regular voucher plus an additional amount to take care of the special costs of their program (McGroarty, 2001).

In Milwaukee, children with special needs get the same voucher as other students, and a few students take advantage of the special option of choosing a private school for their education. Few results are available regarding the impact of these schools on children with disabilities. Florida adopted a pilot program for children with special needs that is available to any student across the state, known as the McKay scholarship program for students with disabilities. Students are eligible for vouchers if they demonstrate failure to improve in their public school.

The arguments for and against educational vouchers for all children carry over in the special education field. Supporters maintain that vouchers provide a choice for parents, particularly when schools are not doing well. They assert that the voucher programs resemble the post-World War II program of the G.I. Bill, one of the most popular of government programs, which gave returning veterans their choice of higher education institutions to attend with a voucher or its equivalent.

However, opponents of voucher programs point out that it is not clear how welcome children with special needs are in many private schools. Private schools participating in voucher programs are prohibited from rejecting applications from children with special needs. This does not necessarily mean that children with special needs are welcome in these schools or that the schools have personnel who are capable of providing an effective education for them. Perhaps the most serious complaint against vouchers is that they threaten to transform public schools into isolated, second-best options for students with limited financial support and students who are difficult to educate, including those with disabilities (Watson, 2002).

The issue of public support for religious schools also is involved because the vast majority of vouchers in Cleveland go to Catholic schools, and opponents contend that this is a disguised subsidy for those schools. The U.S. Supreme Court ruled that the Cleveland school program was constitutional (Greene, Howell, & Peterson, 1998), but the issue continues to be controversial.

Not enough is known about the educational outcomes of students using these vouchers to form a judgment about whether vouchers represent a viable option for the parents of children with disabilities. One of the difficulties in assessing the results of voucher programs is that such assessment has become a part of an ideological war between supporters of the public school and supporters of private school initiatives, and each group publishes results to support its position.

Charter Schools

Another educational alternative available in many communities is *charter schools* (Finn, Mauno, & Vanourek, 2000). Charter schools are free from many of the regulations followed by public schools and are able to try out new ideas and new methods in the hopes of improving the educational services to children with and without disabilities (Brouillette, 2002). Current charter school laws prohibit the discrimination of individuals on the basis of disability, race, or creed. Enrollment must be open and tuition free. But whether a particular charter school will have the facilities, finances, and staff to cope with children with special needs is an open question because charter schools are often underfunded for their tasks. Charter schools represent a laboratory for programs that might become a part of public school programs if only good data about their impact on students and families are gathered.

Homeschooling

More and more parents appear to be choosing *homeschooling* for their children. Some reports estimate the number of children in homeschooling at 2,000,000 (Bauman, 2001). This number of children reflects the number of parents who believe that public schools are not doing an adequate job for their children. This option was first used by parents who were disturbed that their children were not receiving religious instruction or were being taught things antithetical to their religion (e.g., evolution) in the public schools. Accordingly, students from such families were allowed to stay home from school and be taught by their parents and now by the Internet. As long as they are able to pass the examinations that public school students pass, they are able to continue in this mode. Homeschooling is also used by parents who simply believe they can provide more focused and appropriate instruction to their children in the home.

This homeschooling approach is increasingly being used by parents like Gretchen's who despair that their gifted students cannot get an adequate education in the public schools (Gallagher, 2002). In response to the claim that such children are denied the social interaction and physical education programs available to other students, parents have formed informal clubs and groups to promote social interaction among students who are being homeschooled. Whether other children with special needs (e.g., Arnie, Les, Bobby, Cathy) could profit from homeschooling is doubtful unless it involves high-quality tutoring. Also, the needs of the children with disabilities for social contact and the development of social skills makes homeschooling a questionable proposition. As is the case with the other alternative options, decision makers lack clear evidence about the impact of homeschooling efforts on students with special needs and on public schools.

Magnet Schools

Another option for students with special needs is *magnet schools,* which have a special focus, such as art or mathematics. Students wanting to take advantage of the special theme or interest apply for entrance to these schools. In many ways, magnet schools resemble the charter schools that they antedate by some years. Magnet schools are not available in all school districts. Again, parents of gifted students like Gretchen can be particularly interested in magnet schools because these programs give students a special emphasis in content fields that such students crave in their education (Gallagher, 2002). Pipho summed up the alternative approaches to education:

> So far, the growth of charter schools, open enrollment, and provisions for home schooling has been slow, but steady. There does not appear to be any move to stop or slow this growth, and a safe prediction is that these new structures are here to stay. (2000, p. 16)

Values and Ethical Judgment

There has been a renewal of professional interest in the role played by values in decision making and in the development of character in students. Two consequent interests are whether ethical values can be taught and the role of teachers' own ethical judgments and values in educational goals. Professionals are particularly interested in the values of teachers and caregivers of children with special needs.

Lying just below the surface of many decisions about children with disabilities are the values and ethical theories of the decision maker. Every person has a value system that helps him or her when that person faces difficult decisions. Sometimes a person is not even aware of his or her internal systems. Argyris and Schon (1974) described unarticulated personal values as *values in use.* These values are revealed in the consistency and patterns of an individual's decision making, even if not named or verbalized by the person him- or herself. If, for example, every new initiative is rejected by an individual as "too costly," colleagues can deduce that the cost of policies is a high value for that person. Another example of *values in use* is making decisions that always support public schools in any controversy, revealing a high value placed on the public school system.

Table 10.2 reveals some of the major competing ethical theories (Howe & Miramontes, 1991). Ethical theories can be categorized as one of two types: principle based and virtue based. Principle-based theories typically identify some principle and then apply it to determine what is the morally right choice in a given situation. Ms. Thompson, Bobby's teacher, faces a significant problem. Bobby has gone on a rampage again, hitting other children and destroying some classroom drawings. Ms. Thompson now faces a decision as to whether she recommends suspension for Bobby or tries some other methods to control his behavior.

If Ms. Thompson supports the *utilitarian* view, which follows the principle goal of the greatest good for the greatest number, then she opts for suspension because Bobby is clearly a distraction and disruptive force in the classroom affecting some of the other students. But if she holds to the principle of *nonconsequentialism*, she may well believe that justice and Bobby's right to an education trump the utilitarian view. The current disability legislation seems nonconsequentialist because it limits the school's ability to suspend Bobby except in extreme circumstances. Bobby clearly cannot be educated at home or in the neighborhood, and he has a right to a free appropriate public education.

Virtue-based theories identify the characteristics of an ethically virtuous person and then use those characteristics to decide what is the morally right choice

Table 10.2. Ethical theory and social policy

Ethical theory	Description
Principle-based	
Utilitarian	The greatest good for the greatest number. Actions should be judged according to their consequences.
Nonconsequentialism	Utilitarianism should be modified by values, such as justice, rights, and duties, which can trump the value of utility.
Virtue-based	
The caring person	The rightness of an action would be that decided on by the wisest person in the community. Abstract ethical principles should not override the welfare of an individual in a caring relationship.
Communtarianism	The shared values of the community should be the foundation of ethical deliberation.

From Howe, K., & Miramontes, O. (1992). *The ethics of special education.* New York: Teacher's College Press; adapted by permission.

in a given situation by asking how that ethically virtuous person would behave. Perhaps Ms. Thompson subscribes to one of the virtue-based ethical theories and shapes her action by what the most ethical and caring person she knows would do. Ms. Brown is a senior teacher with 25 years of experience who might suggest convening a meeting with the parents before taking any drastic action. If Ms. Brown is her model, Ms. Thompson will act on the basis of what she thinks Ms. Brown would do.

Finally, Ms. Thompson might respond to the *communitarian* view. She knows that many community members have been trying to reduce violence in schools and would be astonished at the treatment given to Bobby so far. It is easy to see how disagreements occur about how to handle a particular situation because so many different value systems are alive in the school and the community.

Certainly, the *utilitarian* view of the greatest good for the greatest number is bad news for children with disabilities because that principle isolates children with disabilities and others who did not fit the acceptable mold of performance or behavior. The *communitarian* view is different from one community to another because values and points of view vary in different parts of the country. The shared values of some communities at one time supported racial discrimination as an important value. How does one balance the needs and standards of the many with the value of justice in specific cases in the nonconsequential point of view? Although ethical viewpoints may provide general guidelines for decision making, they obviously do not help to avoid some agonizing issues raised by children with special needs. Perhaps the caring person approach by Noddings (1984) and others is a way out, depending on who is picked as the "caring person."

Standards Movement

Another professional initiative that has had major impact on exceptional children is the standards movement (McDonnell et al., 1997). This movement originated from concern over whether the students in American schools were being given a rigorous enough program of study. Several international studies compared the performance of American students with students from other countries and found that the performance of American students did not compare well against students from other nations (U.S. Department of Education, 1997). When the math curriculum of American schools was compared with the curricula in Japan, France, and Belgium, it was found to feature extensive repetition and review, with little intensity of coverage (Schmidt et al., 1997). These findings confirmed other data coming from the results of the National Assessment of Educational Progress examinations, which also revealed the limited performance of American students, with only a few students reaching the top level of achievement (Berliner & Biddle, 1995). Consequently, there has been considerable public support for establishing higher standards in the content fields that students should be required to meet.

As Wiggins (1981) once said, "The trick is to have standards without standardization." Many of the general educators creating standards appear to have little understanding of the distribution of individual differences in any given age range. Others hope that these higher standards might positively influence another problem that American general education faces: the achievement gap. The reasoning was that the higher standards could be used to pull up the performance of students in minority groups, improve schools in poor socioeconomic areas, and reduce the achievement gap between rich schools and poor schools (Ravitch, 1995).

Who should set such standards? One answer to that question is to identify distinguished scholars in each of the content fields and ask them to set the standards. The National Council of Teachers of Mathematics (1989) established voluntary national standards in mathematics and updated them in 2000. The American Association for the Advancement of Science (1989) began the development of voluntary national science standards set by the National Academy of Sciences (National Research Council, 1996). Few, if any, of these scholars had any extensive contact with children with special needs.

An interesting consequence of a group of historians setting up voluntary national history standards was that the United States Senate, in a vote of 99 to 1, passed a resolution condemning these standards, which some saw as being too critical of the United States (Lewis, 1995). Not everyone was willing to hand over the responsibility of determining educational standards to content area specialists. Sizer (1992) asked whether subject matter specialists, neither elected nor representative of the interests of all citizens and who operate at a distance from most local communities, should decide what students should or could learn.

Even if there were unanimous agreement as to what the phrase "high standards" translates into at a practical school level, decision makers would still have to determine whether it is right and appropriate to apply the standards to all exceptional students. This is a particularly pertinent observation in view of the lack of representation of special educators in the creation of standards. McDonnell and colleagues pointed out that

> It appears that special education has not played a major role in the development of either state content standards or specific curriculum frameworks in most

states. Rather, special education involvement has generally been limited to a review of standards and curriculum documents prepared by other educators.
(1997, p. 35)

It has not been easy to implement these standards for other reasons as well.
Once one goes from the general concept of higher standards to defining what
"higher standards" actually means, there have arisen very special controversies.
How does the general mandate to meet proscribed standards fit in with the IEP
that is supposed to characterize the special education philosophy to plan for
each child according to his or her special and individual needs?

The Goals 2000: Educate America Act (PL 103-227) legislation enacted
by the Congress in 1994 attempted to codify a set of national education goals
and standards by encouraging states to adopt high content standards and performance standards for their schools. The Goals 2000 legislation stated that

- All children can learn and achieve high standards and must realize their
  potential if the United States is to prosper.

- All students are entitled to participate in a broad and challenging curriculum
  and to have access to resources sufficient to address other educational needs.

But does "all children" really mean *all* in this instance? Although the legislation specifically includes children with disabilities, there is reason to wonder
how thoroughly such children were considered in the discussions of the bill or
of the standards. If such standards mean a different and more complex set of
testing of higher-level thinking in mathematics, science, and social studies,
then how will that affect Les, with his learning disabilities; or Arnie, with his
autism; or Cathy, with her physical disabilities and mild mental retardation?
Are all of these children expected to master a rigorous secondary school curriculum before they are allowed to receive their high school diploma? And what
about earlier levels of school (e.g., middle schools) that have become deeply involved with the concepts of accountability as well? Are people in the accountability movement really paying attention to children with special needs?

Accountability

Educators are involved in many different efforts at accountability to demonstrate that they can accomplish the goals and standards that they set for themselves. This is done largely through testing to demonstrate student mastery of
essential content and skills in many different subject fields. This movement
has been given momentum through government actions to bring accountability to federally supported programs to discover whether the money that has
been spent has resulted in expected or positive results.

The Government Performance Results Act of 1993 (PL 103-62) was established to obtain some findings on the relative effectiveness of government programs and to either support those programs doing well or reduce or eliminate those that seemed to have no positive effect. The Program Assessment Rating Tool (PART; U.S. Department of Energy, 2004) followed up on the earlier act by laying out specific questions to be posed to a wide range of government programs and to assess the degree to which these questions can be answered.

Two examples of PART accountability can be seen in the personnel preparation segment and preschool grants program of IDEA 2004. The Department of Education stated that persistent shortages of qualified personnel in special education have been identified since IDEA's first enactment of 1975 but that the program lacks quantifiable long-term measures and that no independent evaluations of this program exist. The OSEP personnel preparation program does not regularly collect timely and credible performance information. OSEP was directed to develop performance measures and goals that appropriately reflect the impact of the federal government's investment in increasing the supply and quality of special education personnel. Therefore, the PART program judgment is "results not demonstrated."

The preschool grants program of the IDEA legislation was also reviewed with a similar summary view of "results not demonstrated." In this instance, it stated that the program has no long-term performance goals or annual performance data. This program was originally considered to be an incentive for states to initiate programs for preschool children, which have now been established. This program will be reviewed with attempts made to develop long-term performance goals and improve collaboration with other federal programs. Similar analyses have been done for many of the Department of Education programs.

No Child Left Behind

Another major piece of federal legislation has established a new series of standards and accountability to be met. The focus is on students who are not performing well, but it does not directly recognize the special needs of children with disabilities or children who may be gifted. There are provisions for alternative methods of assessment for students with disabilities when the child has serious impairments. Every state must administer annual statewide assessments in reading and mathematics for grades 3–8. States are required to set a minimum performance threshold and then raise that threshold every 3 years. The effect on children with disabilities depends on what happens to students or schools who do not meet the threshold.

All teachers must be highly qualified, meaning that they will be certified or licensed by a state and must demonstrate a high level of competence in the subjects that they teach. That would seem to mean that teachers should have special education certification if they are directly teaching or supervising children with special needs, but they may have to meet content area standards as well. It is probable that states will not come close to meeting the teacher standards, given the major teaching shortages already existing, even with the proposed combining of the Eisenhower professional development programs with class size reduction programs. Obviously, such standards will cause major shifts in emphasis in schools across the country. How these fit into the IEP procedures and the demands for standards remains to be seen once administrative decision makers discover these conflicts.

Gatekeepers of Knowledge

The rapidly expanding technology related to information dissemination has captured the attention of the public and educators alike (see Chapter 8). Education professionals are so fascinated with the Internet and computer technologies that they have had little time to think about the broader meanings and implications of the technology movement itself. The collection and dissemination of information to others, particularly to the next generation, has long been seen as a source of power and authority. As long as the clerics in their monasteries in the Middle Ages were the only source of information, they were extremely important to the community and country in which they operated (Cahill, 1995).

With the emergence of printing, a new source of status was born: teachers and professors. They have largely controlled the flow of information to the younger generation. They wrote the curricula and decided what information should be shared and what should not. In the case of Gretchen, the gifted student, they could open new vistas for her intelligence or they could well deny her access to library readings beyond her grade level, even when her intellect could easily comprehend the material.

When professors' lectures and textbooks were the primary source of information of students in higher education, professors acted as gatekeepers of knowledge. A professor's assignments and tests controlled and shaped the flow of information around his or her own particular topic or classroom. Even though the adult world has many more sources for information, the teachers and professors have remained the major gatekeepers to knowledge for the young.

Education professionals are in the beginning stages of realizing how thoroughly the new information technology has changed that situation (see Chapter 8). Now, all that students have to have is a computer and access to the Internet, and they can gain information from a variety of sources without the approval or assent of the teacher or professor. The increase in homeschooling in recent years is one indicator that parents no longer feel obliged to have their child attend school in order to learn necessary information. They can set up their own sources of information through the computer and the Internet that range over a broader range of subjects than any teacher could match.

The downside of this information access is, of course, that users can no longer rely on educators, scientists, or experts to screen information for accuracy or objectivity. Wild-eyed conspiracy theories jostle for attention with hard-won historical facts. Musical quality sometimes gives way to musical volume. As yet, information sharing on the Internet is subject to no one's standards.

Nor have educators solved the problem of how children with disabilities can have easy access to this information bonanza. There have been many ingenious forms of access technology, such as UDL, which requires alternative presentation of materials to a common curriculum goal. UDL is sometimes very expensive and requires some time before children with disabilities can master the necessary skills to engage the information technology where the knowledge exists (see Chapter 8). The technology gap exists between students without disabilities and students with disabilities, and it will take all possible ingenuity to keep it from getting larger. The UDL approach is well accepted in principle but has yet to be fully implemented.

DECISIONS AHEAD

What decisions will special educators make in the future to confront the variety of other forces presented here? What new forces from outside special education will they face? Predicting the forces that will affect a society in the future is perilous business. Unanticipated events will emerge and change society in an unpredictable fashion. There may be a new war, for example, or new medical discoveries to prolong life, or catastrophic weather changes. These will require adjustments not yet contemplated. Some trends can be reasonably anticipated and planned for.

Common Standards and Individual Plans

Some decisions regarding older children with disabilities are going to have to be made around the issues of accountability and the No Child Left Behind legislation. Although some common standards, such as the mastery of basic reading skills and simple arithmetic, seem reasonable standards for almost everyone, the situation changes whenever educators consider children with special needs in middle and secondary school.

Arnie's IEP goals may not include mastery of history or science curricula of the secondary school. Instead, he may be asked to spend time attacking the central issues of his autism, communication skills, and social skills. Must Arnie take the high-stakes tests required of other students? Will all students be required to pass those exams? At what point in the K–12 program are the schools, educators, or political decision makers willing to give up the "one-size-fits-all" examinations and recognize the specific needs, goals, and objectives of individual children?

Future Technology

One reasonable assumption that can be made about the future is that the technological revolution that has already transformed libraries, communications systems, and classrooms has not ended. There will be more assistive technology designed to improve communications with children with disabilities and more instructional technology likely to create major curricular challenges for such children. Can innovators hold to the principles of UDL so that new technologies have built in special provisions for children with disabilities to share in the benefits of that technology? How will policy makers modify the training of specialists in the field of education to take into account the expectation that they will be able to help their students master the technological skills sufficient to benefit them in their lessons? These changes are coming so fast that postsecondary educators need to be ready to change their own educational delivery systems, which often seem so slow to modify in response to new events.

Medical Advances

The initial completion of the remarkable Human Genome Project, as well as many other medical advances, raises many different possibilities for those interested in children with special needs. With human chromosomes under inspection and noxious genes under suspicion, will certain disabilities diminish in frequency or severity? Will the number of children with Down syndrome or fragile X syndrome be reduced through gene replacement or other genetic manipulations? Can researchers identify the positive gene structure for children like Gretchen and thus pass along some of the extraordinary talents that such children possess?

As one physician said, the practice of medicine has reached the point where the question "Can we do this?" has been replaced with the question "Should we do this?" Should doctors tag individuals with defective genes so that they cannot pass them along? Will special education expand or diminish in size and influence through such advances? The time to think about such matters is now because discoveries and new procedures will not allow us much time for contemplation. The question "Should we do everything to human beings that we know how to do to human beings?" cries out for an answer from special educators and all citizens.

The intention of this chapter is to identify specifically major forces within and outside the field of special education that have had a role in shaping the current special education programs and that will likely influence special education planning and action. Education is not a self-contained field in which decision makers can determine their own future without reference to the rest of education or, indeed, the rest of society. The final chapter is an attempt to bring together many of the forces in this and other chapters and to present three alternative futures for special education.

CHAPTER 11

Some Alternative Futures for Special Education

W hat does the future hold for special education and for children who are different and who defy the easy application of the general education curriculum? The five children who we have been following—Arnie, who has autism; Bobby, who has behavior disturbance; Cathy, who has cerebral palsy; Gretchen, who is gifted; and Les, who has learning disabilities—have each had a difficult time adapting to settings and tasks that did not have their needs in mind. But we have seen in the first 10 chapters determined efforts by special educators and general educators to help these students cope and to build support systems that create a more feasible learning environment.

The first 10 chapters explore the educational status of exceptional children today and describe many of the educational and social forces that have shaped the current special education programs. The first three chapters cover decision making in the determination of eligibility for special programs and the nature of the special education programs for Arnie, Bobby, Cathy, Gretchen, and Les. Chapters 4–8 outline the necessary support system components that undergird the programs: personnel preparation, research and evaluation, finance, comprehensive planning, and technology. Chapter 9 explores the special issues of educating gifted students, and Chapter 10 puts forth the effect of outside forces that impinge on the special and general education enterprise.

The question is where to go from here. It is time for thoughtful consideration of major alternatives to the current special education enterprise that, if agreed on, can provide the basis for future planning and action. (The term *enterprise* is used instead of *system* because there are few systems properties in education.) Being forced to respond to events, inside and outside of education, without a clear vision of a high-quality program leads to intensely garbled results. Chapter 1 introduces the *engines of change,* those forces that can influence and modify the present in some systematic fashion.

- *Legislation* to mandate and specify the nature of change

- *Court decisions* to make sure educational decisions are equitable and fair to the individual

- *Administrative rules* to put the operational flesh on the bones of legislation

- *Professional initiatives* to use research and good clinical practice to find better ways to achieve goals and perhaps to influence and shape the other three engines of change

If decision makers want to make a major effort at changing the present to a better future, then they will have to use these four engines with efficiency and purpose.

The goal established for all children with special needs is preparation for a productive and useful life. They should become as self-sufficient as possible, while maintaining the ability to interact with other individuals and groups in a constructive manner. They should be prepared to take their place in society through vocational preparation and should enjoy their recreational pursuits. The alternative plans presented here are designed primarily for children with high-incidence disabilities (e.g., mild mental retardation, learning disabilities, mild emotional problems).

This final chapter describes and critiques three alternative futures from the many that might be conceived to meet the special needs of exceptional children. These futures are based on the material in previous chapters and seem to be the most plausible. As the chapter weighs each of these alternatives, it also indicates how each might affect the five students—Arnie, Bobby, Cathy, Gretchen, and Les—and the professionals who work with them. Sometimes large policy moves in the general education field have been made with little consideration given to the exceptional children who will be affected.

The three major models discussed here are

1. *The special education status quo:* Continuing current special education policies that are reactive to events outside and inside education as they occur but have little future or long-range perspective

2. *General Education Initiative (GEI):* Making a deliberate effort to bring special education back under the general education administration as one component in the larger education enterprise, not as a separate entity operating independently of the general administration

3. *Multidisciplinary support system (MSS):* Designing a special services unit that brings together multidisciplinary services in an attempt to serve all children and play a leadership role in the educational establishment

One of the key elements for each of the models is how the model plans to interact with families who have played such an important role in special education, in raising their children with special needs, and in providing the "parent power" necessary to influence public decision makers.

The three separate models that this chapter presents are not designed as blueprints for action but rather as a general guide for plans and actions that have to be taken at the state and local levels. Indeed, it would be folly to suggest that a single model could be activated for rural Montana, urban Atlanta, suburban Chicago, and all of South Carolina. Each of these diverse geographic areas has to design a special education program that fits the very different needs of the area. What these three models do provide is a template that could be modified as necessary to meet the diversity of the American society. The attempts to implement No Child Left Behind have already demonstrated the difficulties of implementing a single, rather inflexible model in diverse communities across the country. Families and schools have rushed to present waivers or exceptions to this legislation in order to meet distinct community needs.

But no comprehensive plan can ignore the additional important subpopulations of children with special needs. Two subpopulations require special attention, regardless of what future or model is chosen. The first is children with low-incidence moderate or severe disabilities, who pose a special instructional challenge wherever they are. How will they adapt to the particular administrative arrangement that is being chosen? The second subpopulation is the growing group of children identified at the preschool age level as having disabilities or as being at risk for disabilities. Although special educators have paid attention for some time to young children with disabilities, general educators have approached the preschool area gingerly, partly because of unknown costs or administrative problems that might be posed by such a move.

In order to meet the main goal of preparation for a productive life, schools must provide each child with a *free appropriate public education,* and families should receive support to help the child develop. There is little argument about the necessity of a free appropriate public education or its value of equity, but the manner by which these necessary services are delivered and to what extent the parents should be involved remains under discussion. For example, IDEA 2004 established a trial program for 3-year IEPs to reduce personnel time and paperwork (CEC, 2004). The IEP process seems to work well with many individuals, but an individual teacher may be involved in the development of 20 or more IEPs, which is a major burden on the teacher's time (Gallagher & Desimone, 1995). Reduction of unnecessary paperwork has been a legislative goal.

The decision matrix in Figure 11.1 provides the three major options: 1) the special education status quo, 2) the general education initiative, and 3) the MSS. The chapter discusses the advantages and disadvantages of each option. It explains my entries and judgments in the decision matrix.

Options	Criteria for choice					
	Cost	Personnel needs	Children's outcomes	Public acceptance	Family involvement	Special education policy influence
Special education status quo	Substantial	Always shortages	Modest	Mixed, still supportive	Mixed	Considerable
Regular education initiative	Fewer costs	Reduced shortages	Uncertain	Uncertain	Less involvement	Much less
Multidisciplinary support system	Increased costs	Shortages at first	Uncertain	Approve, but with cost concerns	Likely supportive	Strong

Figure 11.1. Special education reform decision matrix. (*Note:* Ratings here are provided by the author based on research reviews, program reports, and personal experience.)

OPTION 1: SPECIAL EDUCATION STATUS QUO

One of the three alternatives is the *special education status quo* because what currently exists is always one of the choices in a planning model (Fullan, 1993). A number of common phrases reflect this position. "Don't make things worse" is a common argument for the status quo, as is "If it ain't broke, don't fix it." I feel that there are substantial reasons for considering the two major alternatives presented here. A variety of individuals or organizations have pointed out that the status quo special education programs have not served many children with disabilities well. Skrtic (1991) showed that the rhetoric of special education has not often matched the actual service delivery on site.

Complex organizational components, such as special education, have not been developed according to one grand master plan and incorporated into American education. Special education policy is formed by a series of separate decisions that have been made, more or less, independently and that now consist of the special education enterprise. At the policy and administrative levels, a history of decisions with little unified context, aim, or philosophy shape the current special education enterprise.

Does the current special education enterprise continue to meet the needs of the children and families that it was designed to serve? The changing political and social forces and the wide range of decision makers (from parents to administrators to political leaders) who have continued to create the current enterprise deserve respect and admiration for their efforts in a noble cause. But, as times change, so should organizations if they wish to improve their operation and services.

Modifying a large enterprise or organization requires major shifts in philosophy and power. The existing enterprise is likely to swallow up any small attempts at readjustment and continue much as it had been (Fullan, 1993). The 40-year effort in special education is a noble experiment from which many useful results have emerged. It casts a spotlight on many children who were ignored and rejected by the educational establishment, and it has shown ways to help these students survive and prosper in an educational world that was not designed for them.

The diversity with which special education services are provided in this country makes describing the status quo a difficult task. The current mode is inclusion of children with high-incidence disabilities in the general classroom, but many school systems still use pullout programs and one-to-one remediation activities. Most school systems have a director of special education who administers the current service system and oversees the personnel in that department. The services needed for children with low-incidence and severe disabilities have been incorporated into the total service program, though the degree of separation necessary in the educational environment in order to take into account these differences (e.g., separate travel training for children with visual disabilities, social skills training for children with autism) is under dispute.

Within special education may be found special education teachers, speech-language pathologists, school psychologists, occupational therapists, and a variety of other specialists. The IEP plays a major role in the operation of the special education program for individual students, and there has been a strong emphasis on finding children who are eligible for special education services. Compliance with federal and state regulations demands much effort on the part of the staff to meet accountability requirements.

Although mandatory participation of parents in the IEP conferences and implementation is part of the status quo, the role parents actually play shows considerable variance from one community to another. The more a parent differs from school personnel in social class, race, or income level, the more difficult it appears to be to incorporate the parent into the special education program (Harry, 1994). Parent training centers and other institutional assistance have provided help in this regard.

The special education legislation has encouraged an interest in early childhood, and some important initiatives have been taken for infants and toddlers from birth to age 3 and for children ages 3 and 4 with disabilities. Research institutes in early childhood have been established (e.g., The Beach Center at the University of Kansas and the Early Childhood Research Center at the University of North Carolina), and personnel preparation programs have begun to focus on early childhood, with encouragement from OSEP in the U.S. Department of Education.

Arguments for the Special Education Status Quo

Familiarity

One strong argument for the status quo is familiarity. Educators who have lived with the current special education enterprise are accustomed to it and, at least, know where they stand. Politicians and other decision makers are used to dealing with the current program, and its presence in the budget and in school system structures is familiar to them.

A considerable support infrastructure has been established behind the current service delivery system. For example, through its large personnel preparation program, OSEP allocates more than $80 million per year to institutions of higher education and state departments of education to aid in the continued production of special educators. A modest research program, a multitude of technical assistance (TA) units and demonstration programs, plus state special education programs of considerable magnitude and financial support have also been developed. One concern is what would happen to the support system if major changes were made. All of these support features could be at some risk if major program shifts are introduced.

Public Support

One great advantage to the status quo option lies in the public view of the clientele itself. Children with disabilities are the most vulnerable citizens. Any politician or decision maker proposing to take away existing resources, or even to change the shape of these resources, runs the risk of appearing to be an insensitive bully, ignoring the long-cherished American principle of helping those in need.

The American public has been supportive of the families of children with disabilities and willing to help them, to some degree. Particularly important is the concept that parents raising children with disabilities are not at fault for the particular problems they face but are merely confronted by a combination of circumstances that could happen to any parent. Of course, it has not always been this way. Parents have sometimes been blamed for their children's problems, but there is now substantial empathy for these parents and a willingness to help them.

Adequate Success

Given the benefits that students with disabilities receive under the status quo, some may ask, "Why tinker with success?" This approach has brought services to countless numbers of children with disabilities who did not have them previously, and it has built an important infrastructure of services that serve a broad age range of children from early childhood to adulthood.

As is true with the special education status quo, there are major variations of services for gifted students like Gretchen. She may have pull-out classes that are more challenging an hour per day, advanced placement courses or honors courses in secondary education, or perhaps nothing beyond the general class activities that are boring her (see Chapter 9). As is true with Gretchen's classmates with disabilities, whether the special experiences are intense enough or long enough to make a difference is a serious question.

Arguments Against the Special Education Status Quo

Given these tangible advantages for the status quo, what then are the arguments that would cause decision makers to consider alternatives? The number of these arguments is growing, and the arguments are increasing in intensity.

Changing View of the Causes of Disability

There has been a disjunction between the original basis for categorizing children with disabilities and current knowledge of the causes of many of these high-incidence disabilities (e.g., mild mental retardation). Educators once thought of these disabilities as being a property of the child, who would be expected to be in special education settings for his or her entire school career. Evidence now exists of a substantial interaction between genetics and environment, influencing the development of many children with disabilities (Plomin & McGuffin, 2003).

Les, Bobby, and Cathy are all children whose disabilities appear to be partly caused or influenced by environmental conditions, but if environment plays a role in the emergence of these disability categories, then diagnoses cannot be considered permanent! Special education professionals can possibly increase or decrease the prevalence of disability by changing the environment itself. Considering the impact of environment, the categories and classifications of disability become fluid and nonpermanent. This malleability is a statement of optimism, but the interaction of genetics and environment is less easy to address on a policy level.

There is the additional problem that a medical diagnosis does not lead naturally to education treatment. The World Health Organization (2004) has stimulated an international effort to codify conditions and develop an international classification of functioning, disability, and health. The purpose of this initiative is to standardize classification across countries and also to focus on functioning rather than the physical diagnosis as the key to effective action for children.

Grumbling over Costs

The heavy cost of special education, now estimated at more than $50 billion per year, has gained the attention of decision makers and administrators (see Chapter 7). Educational administrators who have some other potential uses in mind for scarce resources cast covetous glances at special education funds. The expansion of disability categories and the increasing number of children in these categories mean that program costs will continue to go up. Wildavsky (1979) commented that once a public program such as special education is established three things inevitably happen:

1.   The number of people eligible for these services increases.

2.   The number of services provided by the program increases.

3.   Therefore, the cost of the program must certainly increase.

There is little evidence that special education contradicts these principles. This issue over increasing costs is complicated by the perceived shortage of solid data indicating program success, except for early childhood intervention, which appears positive (Guralnick, 1997).

Shortage of Strong Program Success Stories

Have these expenditures been used to good effect? Is there evidence that the costs are paying off in results? Special education costs increase at a rate of more than 50% of the rate of cost increases for general education. A multitude of case studies indicate successful outcomes for individual children (see Chapter 5), but although program success has been demonstrated, the amount of that success has not always been impressive. The problems concerning the need for special instruction are recognized for children with disabilities, but the current atmosphere of accountability dictates that researchers need to show positive student outcomes if they expect expenditures to continue at the current level or to increase. Finn, Rotherham, and Hokanson (2001) leveled a strong comprehensive critique on the status quo by calling for greater accountability, more local flexibility, and a stronger emphasis on early intervention.

Tension Between General and Special Education

General education and special education have often been seen as two separate and parallel programs. Children were either in one program or the other. With the emergence of inclusion as a powerful drive to change, many children with disabilities are in the general classroom, and general education teachers are responsible for their primary instruction. Certainly, one of the advantages of preinclusion special education, in the view of some general education teachers, was the removal of troublesome children like Bobby, difficult learners like Les, or children with unusual behavior like Arnie from their classrooms. If these children are now to be educated in the general classroom, then special education loses one of its advantages from the perspective of some general education teachers.

Chronic Personnel Shortages

The continued yearly shortages of well-trained special education personnel raises the question of whether the special education enterprise, as it is now structured, could ever meet its personnel goals. Are educators going to be forced to rethink programs to reach a more affordable and accessible set of program goals? No Child Left Behind requires that qualified personnel be available for all children by 2005–2006. This clearly cannot be done for children with special needs under the current personnel preparation system. So what now?

Special education is now a huge bureaucracy with perennial personnel shortages, increasing costs, and limited data justifying the enterprise itself (Hallahan & Kauffman, 2000). As has been the case with other large enterprises, its purposes and energies may have been diverted somewhat toward maintaining itself, rather than for the original purposes for which it was established. The reluctance to abandon the resource room model, despite limited evidence of its efficacy, may well reflect the need to preserve jobs more than a result of careful analyses.

Increasing Disability Categories

The multitude of diagnostic categories is confusing to outsiders and to special educators themselves. New categories keep appearing as additions to the existing classifications. By all odds, the most troubling of current categories of high-incidence disabilities is *learning disabilities*. Although this diagnosis was originally meant to be applied to a small number of children with striking intra-individual differences (Kirk, 1963), it has now become, through successive transformations, the largest of all subpopulations in special education. Often, it seems to include almost all children who are having difficulty learning. States have limited the number of children with learning disabilities who can be counted for reimbursement purposes because decision makers have become alarmed at the growth of the category and associated costs.

How useful is such a category as learning disabilities? One analogy would be if physicians had identified a category of "children with high fevers." How much would this help the physician toward diagnosis and treatment? The existing category of learning disabilities blurs the line between special education and general education and calls for major reconceptualization and different means of educating (Swanson et al., 2003). The status quo should not even be considered an option in the case of children with learning disabilities. No matter what other policies are considered, educators and decision makers must think of a new plan.

One remedial approach that seems to have promise is early intervention with an emphasis on reading skills. Torgesen (2000) reported five different early intervention studies that increased the mastery of reading problems by more than 50% in samples of children from disadvantaged backgrounds. Still there remained about 5% of the children who did not respond and who may make up the core of the learning disability population.

In summary, increasing knowledge of the potential malleability of many children with disabilities—together with the increasing costs, chronic personnel shortages, and the lack of program accountability—have led to a consideration of alternative models that might achieve the goal of a free appropriate public education with less administrative hassles and costs and with better student outcomes. Table 11.1 summarizes the benefits and drawbacks of the status quo. The argument for familiarity is a powerful one. Parents, unfamiliar with what might be possible, are grateful for the gains they see in their children. However, shortages of personnel, rising costs, and lack of dramatic improvement cause many to seek another delivery system.

Impact on Five Children

What are some of the expectations for the five students this volume has followed if the status quo is maintained? Under the status quo, Arnie receives some assistance from special educators to help him with social skills problems and communication limitations due to his autism. Under the status quo, Bobby receives some professional attention (e.g., individual counseling, consultation among general education personnel and behavior specialists) because of his behavior and emotional problems (Rutherford et al., 2004). He also gets some remedial education because of his academic problems. The issue is whether the intensity of treatment is sufficient to make a difference. Cathy continues to get remedial attention for her academic problems and perhaps some physical therapy for her cerebral palsy in a pull-out program. She may be able to continue some reasonable progress because her problems are not as severe as Arnie's or Bobby's.

For Gretchen, the general education program has little to offer. Depending on her school, she may become involved in an advanced curriculum or an

Table 11.1. Future of special education—Option I: Special education status quo

Benefits	Drawbacks
Public decision makers and the general public have provided impressive support for special education.	Costs increase as number of eligible students increase.
Professionals, general education teachers, and special education personnel are familiar with its design and operation.	Chronic shortages of qualified personnel seem to have no end.
Infrastructure (personnel preparation, research, technical assistance) is partially present to support the service delivery of special education.	Shortage of systematic program evaluation is chronic.
Parental support for the special program is provided.	Tensions between general education and special education continue as they battle for resources and status.
It has brought special services to many children in need of them.	

advanced placement program, which could challenge her and draw her away from her boredom with school. Gretchen may also be able to participate in a pull-out program for an hour per day with other gifted students to receive intellectual stimulation from a specially trained teacher. Whether that is enough to make a difference in her attitude and performance is a big question. Acceleration remains an often-overlooked possibility (see Colangelo et al., 2004).

Finally, Les receives some help for his dyslexia from some specially trained teachers. As with the other students, this is done in a pull-out model, with tutorial help measured in a few hours per week. Some help can be expected for each of the students, but whether it will be enough to undo their academic problems or meet their other needs is a question mark. Just how appropriate is their free appropriate public education?

OPTION 2: GENERAL EDUCATION INITIATIVE

The General Education Initiative (GEI) advocates that the programs and resources now devoted to exceptional children be folded back into general education, with the possible exception of services for children with sensory impairments or severe disabilities, who clearly need teachers trained in alternative means of communication. Children with severe emotional disturbance or learning problems (low-incidence disabilities) receive services in a similar fashion, with specially trained personnel. In following this initiative,

• The money spent at the federal level through state grants supporting special education programs would be provided to general education through block grants, and this would allow, among other things, for the establishment of smaller class sizes.

• Research and development money allotted to OSEP would instead be added to and committed to studies of learning and teaching in the general education classroom. This move has already been made in IDEA 2004, transferring the research authority from OSEP to the Institute for Education Sciences (CEC, 2004). Similarly, major centers of research now supported under OSEP might be incorporated in the program within general education.

• Personnel preparation money committed to prospective teachers of children with special needs would be redirected to general education. Elementary and secondary teachers would be prepared in methods of coping with children with special needs, instead of expecting special education experts to provide needed services for the children. This would also encourage teacher education programs in higher education to incorporate teaching skills for children with special needs in their programs instead of ignoring them, as has been done generally over the last few decades, with the rationale that special education training is taking care of that problem.

- Major investments made in TA centers and regional resource centers will be redirected to regional service centers in the states that will employ specialists to aid general educators with educating children with special needs.

- Similar changes would be made at the local and state levels, disbanding an increasingly complex and administratively awkward special education establishment that sometimes operates separately from the general education establishment. This would not mean firing thousands of special education personnel but reassigning them to the expanded general education program. They would report to the principal rather than to the special education director.

- Such devices as the IEP, which requires such expense of time and personnel, would be reserved for individual children with unusual problems requiring personal clinical attention.

It is likely that under the GEI the services for preschool children with disabilities would be incorporated into the growing prekindergarten initiatives now underway. Infants and toddlers would be unlikely to receive any attention from education sources for some time to come because of financial barriers and uncertainty about the role of educators with very young children.

In the GEI, the general education enterprise is responsible for providing the basic educational experience for children with special needs with added help from specialists to aid the general education teacher. A major change that characterizes the GEI is organization, with special education personnel placed in an auxiliary and helping role to general education administrators and teachers. In this model, it is not necessary, for example, to have a director of special education in the school administration. State departments of education would possibly move special education under the division of elementary and secondary education, and a similar organizational change would be expected at the federal level. The elevation of special education organizationally would be seen as a mistake that should be remediated so that the schools would have a simpler organization pattern and function.

In order to provide the services that children with special needs should be provided with a free appropriate public education, educators and other professionals would offer as much support to children and their families as necessary. How such help would or could be provided, particularly with students with low-incidence, moderate, and severe disabilities (e.g., vision and auditory problems, autism), would remain an administrative issue. It would be possible to establish a much smaller special education services unit to provide programs for these children, but the unit would still be housed under the elementary and secondary education program.

The GEI incorporates earlier concepts from the Regular Education Initiative. (*Note:* Whereas the term *regular education* used to be widely used, the term *general education* is now preferred language.) In the 1980s, Wang, Reynolds, and Walberg (1987) began the movement, which stressed the importance of bringing children with disabilities, particularly mild disabilities, back into the educational mainstream. The Regular Education Initiative met with limited success primarily because it never was a "regular education initiative" but rather a special education initiative for general educators, who appeared to have little enthusiasm for the move.

The Regular Education Initiative was a rather natural extension of the concept of least restrictive environment that the student with disabilities should be educated in an environment no further from general education than absolutely necessary to achieve special educational goals. It has now been taken to mean that the general education setting is the proper one and that any deviation from that setting has to require extensive explanation by those proposing such a shift.

The Regular Education Initiative recognized some of the gains that had been made through the establishment of separate laws and regulations for children with special needs but called for the reformulation of the effort to help children with special needs within general education. The movement was associated with the development of inclusion as a key educational philosophy and strategy (Stainback & Stainback, 1996). With the movement toward integrating children with special needs in the general classroom, why, they asked, should we maintain a separate administrative establishment of special education apart from general education?

One of the important aspects of GEI is the establishment of standards that have to be met. Although this interest has been most often attributed to the requirements of No Child Left Behind and the testing requirements for local schools, there has been a movement to raise the level of acceptable student performance in content-based subject areas (e.g., math, science, history; see Chapter 3).

Because inclusion has brought many children with disabilities back to the general classroom, these students were now expected to meet the same standards as their classmates. Although this has created opportunities to have a more rigorous curriculum than might be promised by the IEPs of the status quo, it has also raised the possibilities of failure, of confronting the student with a challenge too difficult for his or her abilities. For Cathy, still a marginal student, this may be the final straw to her academic respectability, unless she gets some tutoring and other help. The same can be said of Les, whose dyslexia prevents him from performing at grade level. Unless he gets special remedial work, he will likely not meet the standard.

The situation for Arnie is even more serious because his autism creates communication problems that interfere with attempted special instruction. The provision of appropriate special instruction within the framework of the general education classroom remains a challenge for those supporting this model.

Arguments for the General Education Initiative

Reintegration

The major argument for the GEI model is that it would bring into the general education classroom students who had previously been separated. Students with mild disabilities should have the ability to socialize with their age peers and deserve the chance to perform to the standards set for general education, instead of some special program of indeterminate character and results.

Although the special education program has taught educators much about the special needs of children with disabilities, it has now become a huge bureaucracy within education. The separate research and personnel preparation programs in special education have led to the unanticipated consequences of discouraging the general education research and personnel preparation programs from taking responsibility for children with special needs and have resulted in some major conceptual gaps between special education and general education.

Reduction of Unnecessary Testing

One of the disadvantages of the current special education program is the extensive assessment that has to be done to determine a child's eligibility for special education services. This use of testing for classification purposes tends to exhaust the existing short supply of school psychologists who otherwise could be doing much more productive work in helping the general education staff cope with children with special needs. Assessment in this model would be done for specific instructional purposes.

The development of an IEP for every child with disabilities is also an extreme usage of personnel time. Each IEP session may include the general education teacher, the special education teacher, the principal, and a number of other support personnel. Although it may be useful in special circumstances to insist on an IEP meeting for a particular child with disabilities, it is a poor use of scarce personnel resources when used for every child with a disability. Again,

IDEA 2004 established a pilot program of having an IEP for 3 years unless a particular difficulty arises.

Standardized Discipline

By setting up different disciplinary guidelines and rules for children with disabilities and children without disabilities, the special education program has received serious criticism. When two students are in an altercation, school administrators may have to explain to parents that these students may be treated differently because of the special education laws and regulations. The "stay put" regulations that keep a child with disabilities in the general classroom even after committing offenses against teachers and other students is a morale problem for the teaching staff. This provision has since been modified. Alternative education settings are now proposed in IDEA 2004 for those students who are a threat to others (CEC, 2004). These differential responses to behavioral outbursts would disappear in the GEI.

Technology Access

The relatively generous allotment of advanced technology or materials in the special education programs may not be accessed to the benefit of all students. Even when the materials and equipment are not being used by children with disabilities, they still cannot be utilized by other students under current administrative rules.

Cost Savings

No small advantage of this model would be the apparent savings of resources currently in short supply. Schools would not need to hire as many special education personnel, and keeping the children within the general classroom is an additional saving because the major costs in education are due to the teacher–child ratio. Special education tends to reduce that ratio with individualized or small-group work. It may be true that costs of not serving students in need of intensive services would add expense to other segments of the society over time, as additional treatments may be needed in adulthood (e.g., vocational rehabilitation, social work, prisons), but those expenses would not add to short-term education costs.

It *appears* that children with disabilities—once shunned and discriminated against in school—now might even have an unequal advantage over other students with regards to some of the rules, materials, and educational equipment available, and it would be the goal of the GEI to equalize these situations.

Arguments Against the General Education Initiative

Regression to the Earlier Model

The GEI model basically proposes reestablishing the educational system as it was prior to the advent of special education. The inability of that earlier system to cope with the needs of children with disabilities was what stirred educators and parents in the first place to propose special education as a way to ensure that these children have their needs met. Before the courts mandated a free appropriate public education, many children with disabilities were removed from the educational system or were allowed to flow through the system with no account taken of their special needs.

What makes anyone think that things would be any different now than they were in the past under a new blanket of general education? Would there likely be a center for evaluation of children with special needs under a new research system, or would there be special training for teachers to cope with children with autism under the general education enterprise? Would TA be available to help groups organize effective service programs for children with disabilities? The special education infrastructure would likely be folded under general education and lose some of its identity.

Reduced Power and Influence

The special education administrative organization that would be disbanded in this option has had the responsibility of keeping the needs of children with special needs in front of educational leaders of the school systems and state departments of education. Special education leaders generally have been included in the small group of decision makers who create policy for a school system or at the state department of education level because of the organizational structure of special education. The presence of special education leadership made it likely that someone representing these children and their families was "in the room" when important decisions were made about the allocation of scarce resources.

Under the GEI, what is the likelihood that such special interests would be attended to by the decision-making education bodies, school boards, or state department of education? Would there be anyone "in the room" to argue for the needs of children with disabilities? Congress actually had to mandate the establishment of a federal Bureau of Education for the Handicapped (under PL 88-164), now OSEP, before the administration of the then U.S. Office of Education would agree to an organizational way of protecting the needs of children with disabilities. Would the GEI reinstitute the same practice of administratively ignoring the special needs of these children?

Reduced Parental Influence

It is difficult to see how the return to the general education model would be of great help to the parents of children with special needs. Parents have played a minimal role in the education of their children in many school systems. Many systems have not been aggressive in seeking parental interaction, particularly at the program level. Although the existence of the IEP would still require parental interaction for those students for whom such a program was required, a major shift in current policies would be required to encourage extended parental participation as part of the general education program.

Table 11.2 summarizes the major benefits and drawbacks of the GEI, showing the results of a changed organizational pattern being proposed. One clear advantage is a simpler organizational system and some realistic expectations of reduced costs and paperwork burdens. Schools would be more able to meet accountability requirements. However, the GEI seems to be a retreat to the educational enterprise of the past in which children with special needs received little attention and the impressive special education infrastructure (e.g., personnel preparation, research, technical assistance) would be disbanded.

Table 11.2. Future of special education—Option II: General Education Initiative

Benefits	Drawbacks
All services would be under one educational leadership instead of sharing authority.	Major legislative and/or organizational structures would have to be enacted to bring this alternative about.
Children with special needs would now presumably interact and socialize with their peer group.	Special education would have little voice in educational policy.
Costs would be lessened because special educators would now be consultants to general education teachers and could serve more children.	It is just proposing the system that was in place prior to the advent of special education.
Personnel needs would be reduced because the service delivery patterns would be changed and specialists would be itinerant.	Children with special needs might be lost in the larger needs of general education. Parents could be even less involved than is now true.
It would reduce the need for individualized education programs and other burdensome paperwork.	Research centers, personnel preparation, and technical assistance for children with special needs would be reduced and changed.
Schools would more easily meet their accountability requirements.	Professional groups linked to special education would view this change as damaging to them and their clients.

Impact on Five Children

What are some predictable fates for Arnie, Bobby, Gretchen, Cathy, and Les under this reintegration model? Although these outcomes are less certain when compared with the status quo, some conjecture is possible. Some special education help would probably be available for a teacher in a GEI classroom, but "How much?" would be a question in financially threatened systems.

Arnie would likely be a troubled and troublesome child in a GEI classroom, even with some special help for the general education teacher. His poor social skills, lack of communication abilities, and stereotypic motor movements would make his integration or inclusion in the classroom a difficult one. His parents might well be pushed to seek a private school where he could receive the intensive care that he requires.

Bobby also would be a challenge for the general education teacher, even with specialized counseling or help. He might well be considered for suspension or expulsion at some future time, if he were not under the protection of the provisions of IDEA 2004. The general education teacher would likely be unacquainted with ABA or other special techniques for controlling behavioral outbursts and would likely use more traditional discipline methods that have failed Bobby in the past.

Cathy would probably get along reasonably well in a GEI classroom. Her social skills would help her. Other students could be encouraged to provide help so that her lack of mobility and motor coordination would not be a crucial problem. If she has a teacher who can adapt her style to a student who is a grade or two below expectations, Cathy may well adapt satisfactorily.

Les would fall farther and farther behind his classmates because he takes more time to do assignments and needs some special remedial lessons. Again, it would be crucial how much special support personnel would be available and whether they can devote sufficient time to Les.

To Gretchen, a GEI classroom would just be another opportunity to be bored. Unless her teacher has great empathy for a student who is two or three grades in advance of the other students and can provide extra assignments or tiered assignments, she is likely to remain disappointed in the lack of challenges in school, operating like a six-cylinder car running on four cylinders.

As noted previously, the Regular Education Initiative consisted of reducing special education resource rooms and reintegrating children with disabilities into the general classroom. It gained considerable momentum from the fact that one of its proponents was Madeleine Will, who was an Assistant Secretary of Education in the U.S. Department of Education in the 1980s (Will, 1986).

The Regular Education Initiative was not able to sustain itself for a number of reasons. One was that it appeared coincident with a demand for the raising of educational standards and more rigorous curriculum for the schools, which made such integration more difficult. The support services needed to make it a success were underestimated, and also it never was a "regular education" initiative. It was a plan devised by some special educators to be implemented by general education and was resisted strongly by many general educators. (Hocutt & McKinney, 1995).

Skrtic (1991) provided some additional support for change and strongly criticized the bureaucratic nature of special education. Skrtic claimed that special education was actually preventing general education from reforming itself by passing the problems of their students off to another group, special educators. Lipsky and Gartner (1995) presented another strong review and critique of special education and advocated for inclusion as a desirable program alternative, as well as being morally justified. They stressed the importance of appropriate teacher preparation for the new roles that they would have to perform. The likelihood that Arnie, Bobbie, Cathy, Les, and Gretchen would profit from such changes would depend on the quality of the support services provided. What has been needed is a strong and viable model to follow.

Schoolwide Applications Model

A model reported by Sailor and Roger (2005), the schoolwide applications model (SAM), pays special attention to children with disabilities and the philosophy of inclusion. The emphasis here is on planning on how to organize the school environment so that it is receptive to children with disabilities. They contended that past failures of inclusion are the result of trying to make the necessary adaptations at the classroom level, a model that does not have the flexibility of a schoolwide approach. The solution is the SAM program, in which resources are available to all students and education of students who have special needs is planned for on a schoolwide rather than a classroom basis. "All students in SAM schools are members of age-appropriate, grade level classrooms, and they attend all non-classroom functions with their classmates" (p. 507). In the establishment of open boundaries for families with family resources centers, the whole program is still under the leadership of general educators and contains elements of both the GEI and the MSS.

A variety of structural elements are necessary for the SAM program, including a site leadership team, consisting of 8–12 members, that evaluates progress and sets priories, goals, and objectives for each school term. A school-centered planning group sets up the measurement strategies designed to discover measurable progress from SAM. In this model, district leadership teams and district resources teams allocate resources to programs as needed or as resources are available. The support of the district is essential to the SAM approach. Overall, this is a strategy to incorporate children with disabilities within the general education framework.

OPTION 3: MULTIDISCIPLINARY SUPPORT SYSTEM

The current special education status quo (Option 1) has grown substantially as one additional category or classification after another is added (e.g., learning disabilities, autism, attention-deficit/hyperactivity disorder). What is the nature of the service delivery system that might be constructed to meet the diverse needs of these various groups of children?

Description of the Multidisciplinary Support System

Any attempt to build an alternative service system should first establish criteria to guide the designers and implementers. Two generations of experience with the existing special education enterprise should help to emphasize some of those criteria.

The MSS should ensure that services are delivered to all those students who need them. If students need social, mental health, or remedial services as revealed by screening and assessment procedures, they should receive them regardless of any label that is, or is not, applied to them. This means that a student should receive counseling when needed, whether or not he or she has been identified as having emotional or behavioral disturbances. Examples of this approach are now in place in current programs for preschool children with special needs. Such programs now use *developmental delay* as the distinguishing characteristic that triggers special services. This is a treatment-oriented approach that ignores classification in favor of assessing where the child is developmentally and providing appropriate stimuli for effective development.

The MSS should incorporate the current special education services plus related services (e.g., school psychology, speech pathology, health, social work). The MSS would be primarily focused on instructional goals and responsibilities and in blending special services with the general education services (in planning and instruction) provided by the school system. Many of the services would be provided in collaboration with general education teachers. This would be an extension of the current related services. The family help and support features would be a responsibility of the MSS.

For rural communities or low population areas the MSS can be organized to serve a regional area instead of a single school system. This would be similar to the Board of Cooperative Education Services in New York State. Iowa and Texas have similar support centers designed to serve an area rather than a school system.

The MSS should maintain the legal obligation to provide free and appropriate services to all children with disabilities. The local school system should develop a 5-year plan that clearly states how it plans to provide services for children with special needs who are within their responsibility, together with documentation of the actual provision of services and outcomes. Such a plan should be easily accessible to parents and interested citizens. The changed service system should not be an excuse for not delivering on the promise to provide a free appropriate public education for all children.

The MSS should have an assessment component that conducts diagnoses for instructional purposes and provides evidence of progress. Much of the energies of school psychologists have gone toward certifying the eligibility of children for special services. These energies should be transferred to improving the instructional and assessment programs. Two special responsibilities of the MSS would be evaluating the student outcome dimensions of the program and creating differentiated curricula and adaptations for children with special needs.

The MSS should have an administrative leader with responsibilities for overseeing the MSS program. This person should also serve on the top decision-making team of the school system and report directly to the superintendent. This would establish the importance of the MSS unit within the system and ensure that the plans for children with special needs will be adequately monitored and accounted for. Parallel changes at the state and federal levels of administrative organization to provide a voice for children with special needs in these circles should also be considered.

The MSS should have a separate and identifiable budget apart from that of general education. The expenses of the MSS should be kept apart and not commingled with the overall general education budget. It would be too easy, otherwise, for stressed administrators to appropriate the money they need for the general education program from MSS. Because the majority of any education budget is personnel, this would also tend to keep the MSS accountable by identifying those personnel specifically assigned to the MSS and seeing to it that they have the proper credentials.

The MSS would be financed on a block grant approach from the state and federal resources at approximately 25% of the previous year's general education budget, more in impoverished districts (i.e., with 50% or more children participating in the free or reduced-price lunch program). This fiscal approach would allow for maximum flexibility on the part of local schools to meet their idiosyncratic needs while still providing a comprehensive plan that serves all children. Such percentages would be modified with experience. The money should come from local and state sources and should be supplemented by federal dollars from a variety of funding streams already existing to fund support system elements such as personnel preparation, leadership training, TA, and program evaluation. The purpose of such consolidation would be to make more efficient the application of multidisciplinary services to meet the needs of individuals or groups of students that may have many kinds of special needs, not just federally or state-defined disabilities.

At the local level, a range of services could be provided, from consultation to the teacher in the general education classroom, to the conduct of resource room programs, to special groups of students receiving intensive tutorial services when they are in serious academic trouble. This MSS department would attempt to respond to the concerns of other students that general education teachers and administrators also worry about besides children with identified disabilities.

Children with disabilities need a variety of related services not often provided by the public school (e.g., mental health services, health services, social work), and they often have interactive problems of behavior, physical health, and mental health that hinder their school progress. Related services are intended to address the individual needs of students with disabilities in order that they may benefit from their educational programs. Thirteen of such services are noted in IDEA 2004, including audiology, occupational therapy, physical therapy, special transportation, and parent counseling. Most of these special services would be incorporated into the MSS organizational design.

Public schools, as major organizations in most communities, are likely to assume more future responsibilities in the social and health areas and incorporate these various services as part of their overall responsibilities. The public schools may become a year-round community center of services. Although it might be administratively tempting to return to a simplified system as suggested in Option 2, the history of the growth of organizations and professions suggests that the school organization will become more complex over time rather than less. Increased complexity would be required as educators gain more knowledge about the children and families that they serve. The picture of a general education teacher with limited knowledge and skills trying to cope with students like Arnie, Les, and Cathy, in addition to providing a stimulating educational experience for the remainder of her class, is not a pretty one. How best to support this teacher, personally and organizationally, is the challenge.

One alternative is to establish a MSS that would house the various professional specialties needed to provide collaborative support for the general education enterprise. Some distinguishing features of this new support system are 1) less emphasis on diagnosis and classification, 2) greater emphasis on family and community factors, 3) a multidisciplinary team operation with general education, 4) less emphasis on IEPs, and 5) more emphasis on early education and treatment.

Children in need of early intervention and children with moderate and severe disabilities would be well served by the MSS model. With many disciplines involved, the odds of finding children with problems earlier in the developmental sequence would be much better. Also, the commitment to working with the family would be more established because the family is a major part of early remediation and treatment in the preschool years.

For children with more severe disabilities, the MSS model would also have many benefits. Rarely do such disabilities affect only one aspect of the developmental sequence. Instead, severe disabilities present a multitude of problems that may need the consideration of a number of different helping disciplines.

Arnie, for example, has many different problems connected with his autism. He needs communication skills help from a speech-language pathologist, behavior modification from a school psychologist, medical help for his hyperactivity, and special education help from a qualified specialist in autistic behavior. Such a combination of talents is more easily assembled within a specific organization such as the MSS, rather than trying to bring personnel in from many different parts of the community.

The costs of the MSS would be substantial, but funding does not have to come strictly from the existing education budget. Many existing social service, mental health, and health funds can be blended into such an organization. The gain in efficiency and effectiveness would be substantial and would save money and resources in the long run. Nevertheless, money has to be appropriated in the short run, so it is important to realize that such funds do not need to be generated from scratch—widely separated funds are already available through other agencies.

Early Intervention

There is a current segment of the special education community that comes closest to the MSS system—early education or early intervention with children with special needs. Early childhood programs take a multidisciplinary approach to problems, with professionals from many disciplines participating, a strong emphasis on family, and a lesser emphasis on traditional diagnostic procedures such as testing. The social service units of the community are more involved with early childhood programs than with traditional school programs, and a greater emphasis is made to establish contacts with family and community resources. Perhaps early childhood programs are the base from which a new service system can evolve.

Referral

A teacher referral would result in an interview with a staff member from the MSS to determine the degree of the problem and start the process of designing specific assessment and program adaptations for general education placement of the referred child. One striking difference from the current special education operation is that there would be no classification work to determine if the student were eligible for services. Any testing that would be done would be educationally diagnostic in nature to determine the particular educational and social needs of the child by the assessment section of the MSS.

IEPs would be instituted only for specific children who have an unusual problem or pattern of development that would necessitate individualization of programs. The current concern with the use of IEPs is that they must be done routinely for every child who is eligible under IDEA 2004, resulting in excessive paper work and poor use of personnel resources.

One of the clear concerns that would arise in the change from current special education practices to the MSS model is that some children with disabilities could be shortchanged or ignored under the new program. A 5-year plan, designed to state how children with special needs would be served, should be constructed to counteract this concern. Mediation services would be accessible to parents with special concerns. The current infrastructure of research and development, program evaluation, personnel preparation, TA, and data systems for children with special needs at the federal or state level would be maintained with the following changes.

Research and development would focus on the design and testing of differentiated and adapted curricula (through universal design for learning [UDL]) for children with special learning needs. State and federal efforts in research and development would include the periodic program evaluation of multidisciplinary services operations. Unless there is some degree of monitoring and evaluating for child progress, these services could become routine and fall back into bureaucratic procedures.

Personnel Preparation

The changing roles of service personnel in the MSS (e.g., focusing on interdisciplinary planning and treatment) would require comparable changes in personnel preparation programs. Support for personnel preparation programs in higher education or state departments of education from federal government sources would require a multidisciplinary approach in staffing and match the current needs for such cross-discipline services in the field. This, in turn, means that personnel preparation programs for children with special needs would be multidepartmental in institutions of higher education. Accreditation organizations, such as NCATE, and professional organizations, such as CEC, would need to take these changes in higher education programming into account in their standards for personnel preparation programs.

TA to individual districts could be provided on a regional center basis within each state. E-mail queries could be responded to, short-term training carried out, and communication provided on special issues of concern to local districts. Teams of special personnel would work in conjunction with general education teachers, on request, to plan curriculum or remedial work for individuals or small groups. If UDL is a serious goal, special education must help to effectively adapt the general curriculum for children with special needs.

The director of the MSS would be expected to be a part of the leadership group in the district and would be able to be in the room with other school leadership when key policies are made. The importance of this leadership role of representing children who need help cannot be overemphasized because the children who are the direct clients of the special service systems are often those who have been left out or ignored in district policies and in the allocation of resources.

Arguments for the Multidisciplinary Support System

Ability to Reach All Students

The MSS model can reach *all* children who need help, not just those who are declared eligible. One of the larger frustrations of the current special education enterprise is that it freezes out children whom professional staff members know need help because these children cannot reach a level of eligibility for current special services. Also, materials and equipment designated for special education are often not accessible to other students. This model would make such resources available to all served by the special services system but would still provide special equipment (e.g., Braillewriters) for children with special needs.

The MSS eliminates some of the nonproductive elements of the current special education operation. The excessive time spent on classification and eligibility can be reduced in this model. This time and personnel can be applied to making functional behavior assessment, charting the strengths and weaknesses of specific children, and increasing adaptive strategies.

Retained Influence

The MSS would retain a presence in policy and decision-making circles for children with special needs. The history of general education has generally indicated a limited commitment to children with special needs with the scarce resources available. Legislation and court decisions have had to be invoked in the past to get the attention of general education leaders. It is important, therefore, that children with special needs have representation in the decision making at the highest policy levels at the local, state, and federal levels.

The MSS can be used to staff a variety of delivery system components from inclusion to a continuum of services. The use of multidisciplinary teams for either consultation or the provision of direct services means that the MSS can have flexibility in adapting to whatever service delivery model the particular school system adopts as most desirable for their needs. In inclusion, the MSS can provide a team to work with the general education teacher. In a continuum of services model, the MSS can provide direct services for special subgroups (e.g., preschool children with autism).

Support Infrastructure

The MSS could maintain infrastructure elements of personnel preparation, research, TA, and other supports. Some of special education's most important contributions are its efforts with major research and demonstration centers supported by OSEP. Personnel preparation funds allow many higher education institutions to become involved in teacher preparation for children with special needs. TA provides systematic help for service deliverers. All of these support features should be continued in the MSS and their roles expanded to help students in general education.

Accountability

The MSS model has built in accountability procedures for systematic monitoring of service programs. The requirement of a 5-year plan with specific goal and measurable objectives provides the basis for accountability for children with special needs for the delivery systems that have clearly been needed. This monitoring would focus on student attainment rather than the presence of administrative procedures.

Parental Interaction

The MSS would have more promise in bringing parents into the special education programming. First, there would be social workers and psychologists who have been trained to bring families into the program and additional personnel beyond the classroom level to ensure parental interaction, particularly for students who needed special help. Again, the help would be given as needed without asking children to prove that they were eligible to receive help.

Arguments Against the Multidisciplinary Support System

Legislative Changes

Such a major policy shift would require changes in key legislation. There would have to be many changes in authorizing legislation that would follow from the MSS model. Eligibility for services would have to be expanded beyond customary classification, and the regulations regarding IEPs would have to be modified from the current insistence of a yearly IEP for every child identified as having a disability. Oversight and monitoring responsibilities from Congress and state legislatures would have to be changed, with predictable conflicts with legislators and administrators who have been used to exercising authority and power over these programs.

Reaction of Professionals and Parents

Professional associations and parent advocacy groups that would be affected by such a change are likely to react with suspicion and concern about major changes in practice proposed in the new model. They would have to be convinced that the status of their clients and their organizations would not suffer as a result of these changes and that the budgets would not be harmed.

Blending of Funding Streams

The process of blending of funding streams as required by the MSS would be awkward and contentious. Blending money from special education, mental health, and other funding sources would require agency agreements and some additional accounting to ensure that no child loses as a result. This requirement to blend funding streams could face major political barriers and consequences in funding from state legislatures and from Congress.

Coordination

The MSS model maintains parallel systems of general and special services in the education organization. A major problem with the status quo is that general education and special education have drawn apart from one another and now operate as separate systems. What is there about this new model that would not result in a similar undesirable separation? It would take major joint planning efforts to create a cohesive, integrated system. A series of task forces at the state level with joint membership could be utilized to integrate goals and purposes.

The MSS may create a larger bureaucracy. Some teachers give the problem of too much paperwork as the reason for their leaving the teaching profession because it results in too little time for the students. The MSS would not lend itself to a more nimble bureaucracy and could increase that problem.

Expenses of the Multidisciplinary Support System

The MSS would seem to satisfy the need for a comprehensive system of services in modern school systems. The cost figures would increase for a short time, but such a system would have the promise of saving money in the long run by reducing the heavy costs involved in not catching a variety of problems earlier in the child's tenure in the school system. A small amount of impact on young children with disabilities could have large long-term repercussions. For example, identifying and treating children at risk for serious emotional and behavior problems could have enormous benefits for everyone. The costs of incarceration are estimated at more than $50,000 per inmate per year by the Bureau of Federal Prisons. Any program that saves 1% of adolescent students from being jailed saves large sums of money for society.

The comparison of current costs with prospective future cost savings in a cost–benefit model does not often comfort decision makers because the current costs must be met now, whereas future savings are someone else's department and may be assigned to someone else's credit. If special services budgets are merely what are left over from the available funds after general education's needs are met, then there will predictably be a shortfall for the special services unit.

One possible solution is to index the special services funds with the general education funds so that changes in the special education budget are proportional. A budget of $50 million for general education would result in a $12.5-million budget (i.e., 25%) for special services. If the city council or other funding agency decides to cut the education budget, then both general education and special services would be cut proportionately. This would make the costs predictable so that the special services unit would not be differentially shortchanged during budget shortages or cutbacks.

We should not underestimate the challenge of integrating the special service system with the general education enterprise. The use of teams or task forces of personnel from both sections on curriculum development, assessment, and professional preparations should help in this regard. Similarly, comprehensive planning can be carried out including leaders from both dimensions of general education and the MSS.

Pilot Studies

It would be unrealistic, to say the least, to expect that any set of major changes, such as those suggested in the MSS, would be easily adopted by major political entities at the local, state, or federal levels. Even if the basic arguments are accepted, the issues of how one gets from here to there and who will accept the risks are still under question.

One possible approach is to identify four or five states that would be willing to try out the MSS for a 5-year period. The federal government would have to agree to give a waiver on existing rules and regulations in order for such a change to take place and would provide supplementary funds to allow the state to initiate such organizational changes that need to be made. Each state would agree to put into place the various planning and interagency agreements necessary to bring the wide variety of interests together in a multidisciplinary effort to provide effective services to children who are in need of them. There are governors who would be willing to embark on such an adventure in their state if given reasonable assurances against unanticipated consequences of major change.

There is some truth in the old adage that "things have to get worse before they can get better." If people are largely accepting of the status quo, then it is hard to get them to try major shifts in their work and relationships. Table 11.3 lists the benefits and drawbacks of the MSS approach. The thesis of the MSS approach is that major forces will negatively affect on the status quo soon and should cause decision makers to consider major shifts in their professional and political lives.

Impact on Five Children

The fate of the five children under this third alternative depends in large measure how successfully the general education and the specialized systems are integrated. The presence of the social services and mental health personnel in the schools should lead to more multidisciplinary planning and programming for

Table 11.3. Future of special education—Option III: Multidisciplinary support system

Benefits	Drawbacks
It would integrate health, social, and educational services into a multidisciplinary system for all students.	It would require major changes in legislation and existing rules. A reorganization of legislative oversight and organizational structure would be required.
It would reach all children in need of special services, not just eligible children.	Professional associations, advocates, and parents would be concerned about the impact of such a change.
Special education would retain a position of influence in educational decision making for special education and other auxiliary services.	It would require the change of many existing funding streams at federal and state levels (e.g., mental health, school health, child care).
It would maintain the existing infrastructure elements (research, personnel preparation, technical assistance).	It could possibly create a larger bureaucracy and separation from general education.
It would allow for a diversity of educational adaptations to meet local needs.	Initial costs would increase at a considerable level.

students. Presumably, this would be aided by more extensive in-service training by the MSS staff to benefit general education personnel. The costs of MSS programs need to be carefully monitored and the various streams of funds supporting professional services brought together in some type of economy of scale (e.g., less duplication of effort and personnel in scattered agencies than in a central service system).

Arnie would be identified much earlier in a system that screens young children with special needs. He would likely receive more tutorial instruction and would have speech specialists available to aid his communication problems at a young age. Arnie would be one of those students who would still have an IEP because his needs require a comprehensive program involving many specialists in speech, language, social skills, and remedial academic problems.

Bobby should profit from the increased accessibility of professional help in the mental health field, which would be closer physically than has been true in the general education program. Even so, he will be no easy child to work with, and much attention and help should also be given to his mother and her special needs as a one-parent family trying to cope with an aggressive and angry child.

Cathy would have easier access to special personnel to help with her health needs and motor development and special remedial personnel to work with her academic problems. This assumes that sufficient personnel are available to cope with her problems.

Les would have a larger contingent of multidisciplinary remedial personnel available, and his family could profit from some counseling as well. Some medical help for attention problems could be provided. The year-round programming would be especially useful to Les.

Gretchen's problems would not change appreciably, unless some special program is designed for advanced students that challenges them to do better than either the status quo or general education program could do. Some curriculum experts could produce more challenging programs for students like Gretchen under the UDL philosophy.

Again, the effectiveness of the MSS depends on the level of support provided by the school system, the state, and the federal government. Some attempts need to be made to support the MSS as funded at a consistent proportion of the general education program (by indexing) and not waver about depending on local financial conditions.

Table 11.4 provides a brief summary of the differences between the three models of special education designed primarily for children with high-incidence disabilities. The status quo option currently leans toward the general education model with its emphasis on inclusion and special education consultation.

Table 11.4. Summary of program contrasts for children with high-incidence disabilities

Policy decisions	Status quo	General Education Initiative	Multidisciplinary support system
Who is served?	Broad spectrum— heavy emphasis on children with learning disabilities	All children with special needs within general education	All who would need special help
Where are students served?	A mix of pull-out and inclusion settings	Most likely the general classroom (inclusion)	A variety of settings fitting least restrictive environment for individuals
Who is the server?	Certified teachers and aides	General education teachers with expert consultants	A multidisciplinary team fitting each individual case
Who is primarily responsible for students?	Special educators	General education teachers	Variable depending on the case
Will support services be available?	Mixed—some available in most places	Probably fewer services for budget reasons	Should be extensive and multidisciplinary
What linkages are there with other programs?	Limited contact with other disciplines, except in preschool	Limited contact with other disciplines	Extensive use of other disciplines in community center concept
What are the costs?	High costs with yearly increases	Likely lower costs with fewer special personnel	Likely higher costs but with blended funding across disciplines and agencies
Who handles administration?	Joint responsibility with general and special education	General education, with help from special education	Special services unit, with help from general education

The GEI places the prime responsibility for administering the program to general education, whereas the MSS advocates a multidisciplinary staff and a leader from that staff to administer the services.

The GEI would clearly be the least expensive of the options, at least for the present. Whether the outcomes of the program justified the economies made or whether a more elaborate support system would, in the long run, be more economical by producing better student outcomes is something to be tested empirically. Better student outcomes means more students with special needs graduating from a secondary education program and going on to advanced vocational education or higher education. In the end, it means a good community adjustment with a high degree of self-sufficiency. The interest in bringing a stronger multidisciplinary presence in the program seems to justify some trial runs with the MSS model.

OTHER OPTIONS

This presentation of a multidisciplinary model is, of course, not the only expression of educational reform in this direction. Two attempts to achieve similar results are briefly noted here.

The Comer Process

One of the earliest attempts at multidisciplinary programming was designed by James Comer and became known as the Yale University School Development Program (2004). In 1968, Comer brought social workers, psychologists, special education teachers, and a child psychiatrist to two public schools. He believed that healthy child development was necessary for students to be effective in an academic setting. Out of these early efforts, an operating system emerged for school organization that included a school planning and management team, which designed a comprehensive school program and set academic, social, and community goals; a student and staff support team, which connected all of the school's student services including principal and staff as well as counselors, social workers, and so forth; and a parent team, which involved parents in activities that supported the school's social and academic programs (Comer, 2005).

The guiding principles of the Comer approach are consensus, collaboration, and no-fault placing. Emphasis is placed on personnel preparation for implementation of the program, and a field guide is produced that creates a mindset, common language, and expected behavior. Improved academic performance is reported as a result of a full implementation of the Comer process in *Transforming School Leadership and Management to Support Student Learning and Development* (Yale University School Development Program, 2004).

Full-Service Community Schools

Dryfoos and Maguire (2002) reported on attempts to integrate health, family support, youth development, and other community services to support student learning. A number of states (e.g., California, New Jersey) and cities (e.g., Boston, St. Paul) have begun programs. Year-long planning seems necessary to organize a full-service community school, and this includes, as a key member, a community school coordinator with an understanding of community agencies as well as the public school.

After-school programs are seen as a good entry point to the establishment of a multiple set of services designed to aid the goal of providing almost any human service in a school building. Schools might move on, for example, to establishing family service centers. The governance of the school–community partnership effort is diverse, depending on community factors and conditions. Efforts at accountability are considered essential and are presented, in part, through the Coalition for Community Studies, who are carrying out a Linkage to Learning study to determine the most effective components of these programs.

Dryfoos and Maguire were frank about the additional costs required by these partnerships, estimating about an additional $250,000 per 1,000 students, but they also pointed out that this is still less than already spent on Title I of PL 90-247.

POSSIBLE CHANGES IN THE LARGER COMMUNITY

One of the prominent responses to many suggestions for educational change or reform is that "It is an interesting idea but we have no money." Such a statement by a responsible person in American society at the beginning of the 21st century is ridiculous on its face. When we total up what we spend on personal transportation, on recreation, on any variety of luxuries, it is quite clear that there is money. What the person means, of course, by such a statement is that there just is no money for your ideas of improving education. Generations of public policy persons have "talked the talk" on education and how precious it is to the prospering of the American society. They need to "walk the walk"— pay the bill for quality education or else stop making speeches about how important it is to educate the next generation of Americans.

Some further assumptions about the near future of the larger community can be made during this time. One assumption is that the schools will increasingly become community or neighborhood centers with many services for children and adults being integrated with the traditional school program. The schools will be open year round, with education being provided in blocks of time separated by short periods of vacation times (2–3 week intervals). The anachronistic summer break will go the way of the typewriter and the slide rule.

All such predictions, of course, do not consider the introduction of an unexpected development that changes the factors influencing education. Still, past and current trends must be used as a basis for planning, and then decision makers must adapt to the unexpected. The most likely *wild card* in evidence today is that of educational technology. As noted in Chapter 8, the new technology is in the process of changing the traditional roles of teachers and professors as exclusive guardians and dispensers of knowledge. Who can predict the effect this change will have on the education enterprise itself, much less what impact it will have on children with special needs?

GETTING FROM HERE TO THERE

The theme of the present chapter is what future special education operations should look like; however, once decision makers settle on an acceptable future model, they still face the prospect of how to get from here to there. The engines of change would then have to be called on to move the policies from here to there, once they have settled on where "there" is. The MSS, the most extensive of the three options, would require a lot of work.

Legislation would be needed to amend current education laws and allow for a much more flexible, yet accountable, system. The administrative rules would need to be changed so that the rules for program components, such as the IEP, could be modified to reflect the notion that only children with special individual problems would be provided with such assistance. Meanwhile, multidisciplinary team meetings for planning and coordination with general education would be codified in rules and regulations. Court decisions might even be sought to lay the groundwork for changes in certification of specialists and to ensure parents that free appropriate public education was indeed being practiced in the school systems. Finally, a giant push would be required from the professional community to create and conduct the pilot programs and the changed protocols that would be necessary for a changed program. Key professional organizations that see the need for the new programs and have the consistent membership and priorities to see a multiyear process through to its conclusion must spearhead a strong and coordinated effort.

Although the three models differ substantially from one another, it is not necessary to think of having to choose one model totally over another. Major components can be selected from Option 2 that could be added to Option 3, for example. The purpose of presenting them as a whole is to provide an opportunity for discussion of the various models, their components, and their advantages and disadvantages. Because it will take a long period of time before any new model of special services is established and well accepted, a long-range goal (the desired model) should be kept in mind and worked toward. As long as the goal is kept in sight, modest gains toward that goal can be accepted and tolerated.

If one of these two alternative models is accepted as a goal, then there would inevitably be a long period of transition, measured in years, from the status quo to the new model and a multitude of decisions needed to bring such change about. Experimental or pilot programs would need to be designed to illustrate the impact of the changes, new multidisciplinary personnel preparation programs would need to be designed and funded, and these new efforts would need to be carefully monitored for unexpected consequences or side effects on children like Arnie, Bobby, Les, Cathy, and Gretchen.

LAST THOUGHTS

In this rapidly moving culture, it is safe to say that the future is not going to be like the past in special education or in other dimensions of society. If current trends continue in special education, more multidisciplinary cooperation and more team play and consultation is more likely than an increase in the work of the individual general educator or special education teacher. The further development of a support infrastructure can be anticipated, which appears to be necessary for high-quality education of children with special needs. This infrastructure building should occur even if the American economy dips.

Special education has had a remarkable half century of innovation and change and has transformed the shape and contour of American education. Its goals fit well with key American values such as individualization and helping those who need special help. It has used the engines of change extensively: new legislation, landmark court cases, extensive administrative rule making, and many diverse professional initiatives. It has built an impressive infrastructure of personnel preparation, research centers, and TA programs that have been models for all of education. Yet, it is often in the implementation of ideas that many good intentions fall short.

A rich body of experience suggests that some of the first ideas and assumptions about exceptional children and special education were not quite correct and that educators now have access to many new methods and skills that that were unknown in the 1960s. Also, the surrounding culture, inside and outside education, has been transformed by conflict, discovery, and reassessment, together with hope for the future.

Many factors combine to make public decisions and public policy. Research findings, by themselves, can be cancelled out by biases and attitudes of the general public and by those of the decision makers. Nevertheless, research findings and evaluation data should play an increasingly important role in future decision making as one essential part of any future program designs. As comprehensive planning becomes more a part of long-range decision making at the federal and state levels, one criterion for future action should be evidence for a new course of action provided by the proponents of such a course. At the very least, the new course of action should include serious attempts to collect information on the outcomes of the proposed actions.

The message of this volume is that education professionals and decision makers need to seek ambitious goals for children with special needs and to promote programs to find new ways of reaching those goals. Their first need is to think about what they want the future special education enterprise to become and then to work toward it. The alternatives suggested here are clearly only three of many possible ones. The main task is not necessarily to marry the future to major alternatives but to use them to think in a future-oriented way. If this volume has stimulated such thoughts, then my own goals will have been achieved.

References

Ali v. Wayne-Westland School District, 19IDELR 511 (E.D. Mich. 1992).

American Association for the Advancement of Science. (1989). *National science standards.* Washington, DC: Author.

Americans with Disabilities Act (ADA) of 1990, PL 101-336, 42 U.S.C. §§ 12101 *et seq.*

Argyris, C., & Schon, D. (1974). *Theory in practice: Increasing professional effectiveness.* San Francisco: Jossey-Bass.

Assistive Technology Act of 2004, PL 108-364, 118 Stat. 1707.

Attwood, T. (1998). *Asperger's syndrome: A guide for parents and professionals.* Philadelphia: Jessica Kingsley.

Bailey, D.B. (1991). Issues and perspectives on family assessment. *Infants and Young Children, 4*(1), 26–34.

Bailey, D., Farel, A., O'Donnell, K., Simeonsson, R., & Miller, C. (1986). Preparing infant interventionists: Interdepartmental training in special education and maternal child health. *Journal of the Division for Early Childhood, 11,* 67–77.

Bailey, D., & Wolery, M. (2002). Early childhood special education research. *Journal of Early Intervention, 25*(2), 88–89.

Baker, B., & Friedman-Nimz, R. (2001). *State policies and equal opportunity: The example of gifted education.* Lawrence: University of Kansas, Department of Teaching and Leadership.

Barnett, W. (1991). Long-term effects of early childhood programs on cognitive and school outcomes. *The Future of Children: Long Term Outcomes of Early Childhood Programs, 5,* 25–50.

Barnett, W.S., & Masse, L. (2003). Funding issues for early childhood education. In D. Cryer and R.M. Clifford (Eds.), *Early childhood education and care in the USA* (pp. 137–165). Baltimore: Paul H. Brookes Publishing Co.

Bateman, B. (1965). An educational view of a diagnostic approach to learning disorders. In J. Hellmuth (Ed.), *Learning disorders* (Vol. 1, pp. 219–239). Seattle: Special Child Reflection.

Bauman, K. (2001). *Homeschooling in the United States: Trends and characteristics.* Washington, DC: U.S. Census Bureau.

Benbow, C., & Lubinski, D. (1996). *Intellectual talent: Psychometric and social issues.* Baltimore: Johns Hopkins University Press.

Berliner, D. (2002). Educational research: The hardest science of all. *Educational Researcher, 31,* 18–20.

Berliner, D., & Biddle, B. (1995). *The manufactured crisis.* Reading, MA: Addison-Wesley.

Berman, S., Davis, P., Koufman-Frederick, A., & Union, D. (2001). The rising costs of special education in Massachusetts: Causes and effects. In C. Finn, A. Robinson, & C.

Holkanson (Eds.), *Rethinking special education for a new century.* Washington, DC: Thomas B. Fordham Foundation.

Berman, S., & Union, D. (2003, March). The misdiagnosis of special education costs: District practices have no bearing, but medical and social factors accelerate spending. *School Administration,* 1–3.

Bettelheim, B. (1967). *The empty fortress: Infantile autism and the battle of the self.* New York: The Free Press.

Bettelheim, B. (1974). *A home for the heart.* New York: Alfred A. Knopf.

Blackhurst, A., & Edyburn, D. (2000). A brief history of special education technology. *Special Education Technology Practice, 2*(1), 21–36.

Brantlinger, E., Jimenez, R., Klingner, J., Pugash, M., & Richardson, V. (2005). Qualitative studies in special education. *Exceptional Children, 71*(2), 195–207.

Board of Education, Sacramento Unified School District v. Holland, 786 F. Supp. 874 (E.D. Cal. 1994).

Bolick, C.M., & Cooper, J.M. (2003). *An educator's guide to technology tools.* Boston: Houghton Mifflin.

Boswell, J. (1988). *The kindness of strangers: The abandonment of children in Western Europe from late antiquity to the Renaissance.* New York: Pantheon Books.

Branstad, T. (2002). *A new era: Revitalizing special education for children and their families.* Washington, DC: President's Commission on Excellence in Special Education.

Bronfenbrenner, U. (1989). Ecological systems theory. *Annals of Child Development, 6,* 187–249.

Brouillette, L. (2002). *Charter schools.* Mahwah, NJ: Lawrence Erlbaum Associates.

Brown v. Board of Education, 347 U.S. 483 (1954).

Bruder, M., Lippman, C., & Bologna, T. (1994). Personnel preparation in early intervention: Building capacity for program expansion within institutions of higher education. *Journal of Early Intervention, 18,* 103–110.

Buck v. Bell, 274 U.S. 200 (1927).

Byrnes, M. (2004). Alternative assessment FAQs (and answers). *Teaching Exceptional Children, 36,* 58–63.

Cahill, T. (1995). *How the Irish saved civilization.* New York: Doubleday.

Caldarella, P., & Merrell, K. (1997). Common dimensions of social skills of children and adolescents: A taxonomy of positive social behaviors. *School Psychology Review, 26,* 265–279.

Callahan, C., Tomlinson, C., & Pizzat, P. (Eds.). (1993). *Contexts for promise: Noteworthy practices and innovations in the identification of gifted students.* Charlottesville: University of Virginia.

Campbell, F.A., & Ramey, C.T. (1994). Effects of early intervention on intellectual and academic achievement: A follow-up study of children from low-income families. *Child Development, 65*(2), 684–698.

Campbell, F.A., & Ramey, C.T. (1995). Cognitive and school outcomes for high-risk African American students at middle adolescence: Positive effects of early intervention. *American Educational Research Journal, 32,* 734–772.

Campbell County School District v. State, 907 F.2d 1238 (1995).

Carlson, E., Schroll, K., & Klein, S. (2001). *OSEP briefing on study of personnel needs in special education.* Washington, DC: WESTAT Corp.

Casto, G. (1987). Plasticity and the handicapped child: A review of efficacy research. In J.J. Gallagher & C.T. Ramey (Eds.), *The malleability of children* (pp. 103–114). Baltimore: Paul H. Brookes Publishing Co.

Cawley, J., Hayden, S., Cade, E., & Baker-Kroczynski, S. (2002). Including students with disabilities into the general education science classroom. *Exceptional Children, 68*(4), 423–436.

Cawley, J., Paramar, T., Foley, T., Salmon, S., & Roy, S. (2001). Arithmetic performance of students: Implications for standards and programming. *Exceptional Children, 67*(3), 311–328.

Ceci, S., & Laker, J. (1986). A day at the races: The study of IQ, expertise, and cognitive complexity. *Journal of Experimental Psychology, 115,* 225–266.

Center for Advanced Technology in Education (CATE). (2000). *Computer based study strategies: Empowering students with technology.* Eugene: University of Oregon.

Center for Talented Youth. (2001). CTY Talent Search, 2001: Seventh and eighth grades in Talent Search Report. Baltimore: Johns Hopkins University, Center for Talented Youth.

Chalfant, J. (1989). Learning disabilities: Public issues and promising approaches. *American Psychologist, 44,* 392–398.

Chambers, J., Parrish, T., & Harr, J. (2002). *What are we spending on special education services in the United States, 1999–2000?* Palo Alto, CA: Center for Special Education Finance.

Children's Health Act of 2000, PL 106-310, 114 Stat. 1101.

Churton, M. (2002). The utilization of distance learning and technology for teaching children with disabilities. In J. Paul, C. Lavely, A. Cranston-Gingras, & E. Tayles (Eds.), *Rethinking professional issues in special education* (pp. 251–266). Westport, CT: Ablex Publishing.

Clarke, S., & Campbell, F. (1998). Can intervention early prevent crime later? The Abecedarian project compared with other programs. *Early Childhood Research Quarterly, 13,* 319–343.

Clifford, R.M., & Gallagher, J.J. (2001). *First in America special report: Designing a high quality pre-kindergarten program.* Chapel Hill: North Carolina Education Research Council.

Cochran, P.S. (with Appert, C.L.) (2005). *Clinical computing competency for speech-language pathologists.* Baltimore: Paul H. Brookes Publishing Co.

Colangelo, N., Assouline, S., & Gross, M. (2004). *A nation deceived: How schools hold back America's brightest students.* Iowa City: Iowa State University.

Colangelo, N., & Davis, G. (Eds.). (2003). *Handbook of gifted education* (3rd ed.). Boston: Allyn & Bacon.

Comer, J. (2005). The rewards of parent participation. *Educational Leadership, 62*(6), 38–42.

Cook, K. (1977). Exchange and power in networks of interorganizational relations. *Sociological Quarterly, 18,* 62–82.

Council for Exceptional Children. (2000). *What every special educator must know* (4th ed). Alexandria, VA: Author.

Council for Exceptional Children. (2003). *Professional standards.* Retrieved November 30, 2005, from http://www.cec.sped.org/ps/perf_based_stds/standards.html

Council for Exceptional Children. (2004). *CEC comments on the proposed IDEA regulations.* Retrieved November 30, 2005, from http://www.cec.sped.org/pdfs/IDEARegs_022805.pdf

Culp, R., Little, V., Letts, D., & Lawrence, H. (1991). Maltreated children's self-concept: Effects of a comprehensive treatment program. *American Journal of Orthopsychiatry, 61,* 114–121.

Darling-Hammond, L., & McLaughlin, M. (1999). Investing in teaching as a learning profession: Policy problems and prospects. In L. Darling-Hammond & G. Sykes (Eds.), *Teaching as the learning profession* (pp. 183–232). San Francisco: Jossey-Bass.

Deno, S. (1985). Curriculum-based measurement: The emerging alternative. *Exceptional Children, 52*(3), 219–232.

DeRolph v. State, 78 Ohio St.3d 193 (1997).

Donovan, S., & Cross, C. (Eds.). (2002). *Minority students in special and gifted education.* Washington, DC: National Academies Press.

Dryfoos, J., & Maguire, S. (2002). *Inside full service community schools.* Thousand Oaks, CA: Corwin Press.

Dunn, L.M. (1968). Special education for the mildly retarded: Is much of it justifiable? *Exceptional Children, 35,* 5–22.

Dunst, C., Trivette, C., & Cutspec, P. (2002). Toward an operational definition of evidence-based practices. *Centerscope, 1,* 1–10.

Early, D., & Winton, P. (2001). Preparing the workforce: Early childhood teacher preparation at 2- and 4-year institutions of higher education. *Early Childhood Research Quarterly, 16,* 285–306.

Economic Opportunity Act of 1964, PL 88-452, 42 U.S.C. §§ 2701 *et seq.*

Edgar, E. (1997). Service delivery options in special education: Building consensus. In J. Paul, M. Churton, W. Morse, A. Duchnowski, B. Epanchin, P. Osnes, et al. (Eds.), *Special education practice: Applying the knowledge, affirming the values, and creating the future* (pp. 75–90). Pacific Grove, CA: Brooks/Cole Publishing.

Edman, I. (Ed.). (1928). *The works of Plato.* New York: Simon & Schuster.

Education Commission of the States. (2002). *Appropriate inclusion of students with disabilities in state accountability systems.* Denver: Author.

Education for All Handicapped Children Act of 1975, PL 94-142, 20 U.S.C. §§ 1400 *et seq.*

Education of Mentally Retarded Children Act of 1958, PL 85-926, 72 Stat. 1777.

Education of the Handicapped Act Amendments of 1968, PL 89-750, 80 Stat. 1191.

Education of the Handicapped Act Amendments of 1986, PL 99-457, 20 U.S.C. §§ 1400 *et seq.*

Edyburn, D. (2000). Assistive technology and students with mild disabilities. *Focus on Exceptional Children, 32*(8), 2–24.

Elder, G. (1998). The life course as developmental theory. *Child Development, 69,* 1–12.

Elementary and Secondary Education Act Amendments of 1967, PL 90-247, 81 Stat. 783.

Etscheidt, S., & Bartlett, L. (1999). The IDEA amendments: A four-step approach for determining supplementary aids and services. *Exceptional Children, 65*(2), 163–174.

Farran, D.C. (2001). Critical periods and early intervention. In D.B. Bailey, J.T. Bruer, F.J. Symons, & J.W. Lichtman (Eds.), *Critical thinking about critical periods* (pp. 233–266). Baltimore: Paul H. Brookes Publishing Co.

Fermin v. San Mateo-Foster City School District, No. C99-3376 S1, 2000 U.S. Dist. LEXIS 11328 (N.D. Cal. 2000).

Feuer, M., Towne, L., & Shavelson, R. (2002). Scientific culture and educational research. *Educational Researcher, 31,* 4–14.

Finn, C., Mauno, B., & Vanourek, G. (2000). *Charter schools in action.* Princeton, NJ: Princeton University Press.

Finn, C., Rotherham, A., & Hokanson, C. (2001). *Rethinking special education for a new century.* Washington, DC: Thomas B. Fordham Foundation.

Flannery, D., Vazsonyi, A., Liau, A., Guo, S., Powell, K., Atha, H., et al. (2003). Initial behavior outcomes for the PeaceBuilders universal school-based violence prevention program. *Developmental Psychology, 39,* 292–308.

Fombonne, E. (1999). Epidemiological surveys of autism: A review. *Psychological Medicine, 29,* 769–786.

Ford, D., & Harris, J.J., III. (1999). *Multicultural gifted education.* New York: Columbia University, Teachers College.

Fordham, S., & Ogbu, J. (1986). African-American student school success: Coping with the burden of "acting white." *The Urban Review, 18,* 176–206.

Forness, S., Kavale, K., Sweeney, D., & Crenshaw, T. (1999). The future of research and practice in behavioral disorders: Psychopharmacology and its school implications. *Behavior Disorders, 24*(4), 305–318.

Fuchs, D., Fuchs, L.S., McMaster, K.N., & Al Otaiba, S. (2003). Identifying children at risk for reading failure: Curriculum-based measurement and the dual-discrepancy approach. In H.L. Swanson, K.R. Harris, & S. Graham (Eds.), *Handbook of learning disabilities* (pp. 431–449). New York: Guilford Press.

Fuchs, D., Fuchs, L.S., Thompson, A., Svenson, E., Yen, L., Al Otaiba, S., et al. (2001). Peer-assisted learning strategies in reading: Extensions for kindergarten, first grade, and high school. *Remedial and Special Education, 22*(1), 15–21.

Fuchs, D., Mock, D., Morgan, P.L., & Young, C.L. (2003). Responsiveness-to-intervention: Definitions, evidence, and implications for the learning disabilities construct. *Learning Disabilities Research and Practice, 18,* 157–171.

Fuchs, L., & Fuchs, D. (2003). Curriculum-based measurement: A best practice guide. *NASP Communique, 32*(2), 1–4.

Fuchs, L.S., Fuchs, D., & Speece, D. (2002). Treatment validity as a unifying construct for identifying learning disabilities. *Learning Disability Quarterly, 25,* 33–46.

Fullan, M. (1993). *Change forces.* New York: Palmer Press.

Fullan, M. (2001). *The new meaning of educational change* (3rd ed.). New York: Teachers College Press.

Gallagher, J. (1994a). Policy designed for diversity: New initiatives for children with disabilities. In D.M. Bryant & M.A. Graham (Eds.), *Implementing early intervention* (pp. 336–350). New York: Guilford Press.

Gallagher, J.J. (1994b). The pull of societal forces on special education. *Journal of Special Education, 27,* 521–530.

Gallagher, J. (1999). Knowledge versus policy in special education. In R. Gallimore, L. Bernheimer, D. MacMillian, D. Spence, & S. Vaughn (Eds.), *Developmental perspectives in children with high incidence disabilities* (pp. 245–260). Mahwah, NJ: Lawrence Erlbaum Associates.

Gallagher, J. (2000a). The beginnings of federal help for young children with disabilities. *Topics in Early Childhood Special Education, 20,* 3–6.

Gallagher, J. (2000b). Unthinkable thoughts. *Gifted Child Quarterly, 44,* 5–12.

Gallagher, J.J. (2002). *Society's role in educating gifted students: The role of public policy.* Storrs, CT: National Research Center on the Gifted and Talented.

Gallagher, J. (2003, March 8). *Accountability.* Address given at College of William & Mary conference, Williamsburg, VA.

Gallagher, J. (2005, May 25). National security and educational excellence. *Education Week, 40,* 32–33.

Gallagher, J., & Bray, W. (2002). *Report on survey of personnel preparation.* Chapel Hill: University of North Carolina at Chapel Hill, FPG Child Development Institute.

Gallagher, J., Clayton, J., & Heinemeier, S. (2001). *Education for four year olds: State initiatives.* Chapel Hill: University of North Carolina at Chapel Hill, National Center for Early Development and Learning.

Gallagher, J., & Clifford, R. (2000). The missing support infrastructure in early childhood. *Early Childhood Research and Practice, 2,* 1–24.

Gallagher, J., Clifford, R., & Maxwell, K. (2004). Getting from here to there. *Early Childhood Research and Practice, 6*(1), 1–15.

Gallagher, J., & Desimone, L. (1995). Lessons learned from the implementation of the IEP: Applications to the IFSP. *Topics in Early Childhood Special Education, 15,* 353–378.

Gallagher, J., & Gallagher, S. (1994). *Teaching the gifted child* (4th ed.). Boston: Allyn & Bacon.

Gallagher, J., Harradine, C., & Coleman, M. (1997). Challenge or boredom: Gifted students. *Roeper Review, 19,* 257–275.

Gallagher, J.J., & Ramey, C.T. (Eds.). (1987). *The malleability of children.* Baltimore: Paul H. Brookes Publishing Co.

Gallagher, J.J., Trohanis, P.L., & Clifford, R.M. (Eds.). (1989). *Policy implementation and PL 99-457: Planning for young children with special needs.* Baltimore: Paul H. Brookes Publishing Co.

Gallagher, T.M. (1991). Language and social skills: Implications for clinical assessment and intervention with school-age children. In T.M. Gallagher (Ed.), *Pragmatics of language: Clinical practice issues* (pp. 11–42). San Diego: Singular Publishing Group.

Garber, H. (1988). *The Milwaukee project: Prevention of mental retardation in children at risk.* Washington, DC: American Association on Mental Retardation.

Gardner, D. (Ed.). (1983). *A nation at risk.* Washington, DC: U.S. Commission on Excellence in Education.

Gersten, R., Fuchs, L., Compton, D., Coyne, M., Greenwood, C., & Innocent, U. (2005). Quality indicators for group experimental and quasi-experimental research in special education. *Exceptional Children, 71*(2), 149–164.

Goals 2000: Educate America Act of 1994, PL 103-227, 20 U.S.C. §§ 5801 *et seq.*

Goldstein, H., Wickstrom, S., Hoyson, M., Jamieson, B., & Odom, S. (1988). Effects of script training on social and communicative interactions. *Education and Treatment of Children, 11,* 97–177.

Gottfredson, D. (1997). School based crime prevention. In L. Sherman, D. Gottfredson, D. Mackenzie, J. Eck, P. Ruters, & S. Bushway (Eds.), *Preventing crime: What works, what doesn't, what's promising: A report to the United States Congress* (pp. 1–74). Washington, DC: U.S. Department of Justice.

Government Performance Results Act of 1993, PL 103-62, 107 Stat. 285.

Grabe, M., & Grabe, C. (2001). *Integrating the Internet for meaningful learning.* Boston: Houghton Mifflin.

Graham, S., & Harris, K. (2003). Students with learning disabilities and the process of writing: A metaanalysis of SRCD studies. In H. Swanson, K. Horns, & S. Graliau (Eds.), *Handbook of learning disabilities* (pp. 323–344). New York: Guilford Press.

Greene, J., Howell, W., & Peterson, P. (1998). Lessons from the Cleveland scholarship program. In P. Peterson & B. Hassel (Eds.), *Learning from school choice.* Washington, DC: The Brookings Institution.

Greer v. Rome City School District, 18 Individuals with Disabilities, Education Law Report 412 (11th Cir. 1991).

Gresham, F. (1998). Social skills training: Should we raze, remodel, or rebuild? *Behavioral Disorders, 24,* 19–25.

Gresham, F., MacMillan, D., Beebe-Frankenberger, M., & Bocian, K. (2000). Treatment integrity in learning disabilities intervention research: Do we really know how treatments are implemented? *Learning Disabilities Research and Practice, 15*(4), 198–205.

Gresham, F., Sugai, G., & Horner, R. (2001). Interpreting outcomes of social skills training for students with high-incidence disabilities. *Exceptional Children, 67*(3), 331–344.

Guralnick, M.J. (1992). A hierarchical model for understanding children's peer-related social competence. In S.L. Odom, S.R. McConnell, & M.A. McEvoy (Eds.), *Social competence of young children with disabilities: Issues and strategies for intervention* (pp. 37–64). Baltimore: Paul H. Brookes Publishing Co.

Guralnick, M.J. (Ed.). (1997). *The effectiveness of early intervention.* Baltimore: Paul H. Brookes Publishing Co.

Guralnick, M. (1999). The nature and meaning of social integration for young children with mild developmental delays in inclusive settings. *Journal of Early Intervention, 22,* 70–86.

Guralnick, M.J. (2001). An agenda for change in early childhood inclusion. In M.J. Guralnick (Ed.), *Early childhood inclusion: Focus on change* (pp. 531–541). Baltimore: Paul H. Brookes Publishing Co.

Guralnick, M.J., & Bennett, F.C. (Eds.). (1987). *The effectiveness of early intervention for at risk and handicapped children.* San Diego: Academic Press.

Guralnick, M.J., & Neville, B. (1997). Designing early intervention programs to promote children's social competence. In M.J. Guralnick (Ed.), *The effectiveness of early intervention* (pp. 579–610). Baltimore: Paul H. Brookes Publishing Co.

Hallahan, D.P., & Kauffman, J.M. (2000). *Exceptional learners: Introduction to special education* (8th ed.). Boston: Allyn & Bacon.

Handicapped Children's Early Education Act of 1968, PL 90-538, 20 U.S.C. §§ 621 *et seq.*

Harbin, G. (1988). Implementation of PL 99-457 state technical assistance needs. *Topics in Early Childhood Special Education, 8,* 24–36.

Harms, T., & Clifford, R. (1990). *Early Childhood Environmental Rating Scale.* New York: Teachers College Press.

Harry, B. (1994). *The disproportionate representation of minority students in special education: Theories and recommendations.* Alexandria, VA: National Association of State Directors of Special Education.

Harry, B. (1997). Applications and misapplications of ecological principles in working with families from diverse cultural backgrounds. In J. Paul, M. Churton, W. Morse, A. Duchnowski, B. Epanchin, P. Osnes, et al. (Eds.), *Special education practice: Applying the knowledge, affirming the values, and creating the future* (pp. 156–170). Pacific Grove, CA: Brooks/Cole Publishing.

Hart, B., & Risley, T.R. (1995). *Meaningful differences in the everyday experience of young American children.* Baltimore: Paul H. Brookes Publishing Co.

Haskins, R., & Gallagher, J. (1981). *Models for analysis of social policy: An introduction* (pp. 68–74). Norwood, NJ: Ablex.

Hasselbring, T. (1997). The future of special education and the role of technology. In J. Paul, M. Churton, W. Morse, A. Duchnowski, B. Epanchin, P. Osnes, et al. (Eds.), *Spe-*

cial education practice: Applying the knowledge, affirming the values, and creating the future (pp. 118–135). Pacific Grove, CA: Brooks/Cole Publishing.

Hawley, W., & Valli, L. (1999). The essentials of effective professional development: A new consensus. In L. Darling-Hammond & G. Sykes (Eds.), *Teaching as the learning profession* (pp. 139–145). San Francisco: Jossey-Bass.

Hebbeler, K. (1993). *Data systems in early intervention.* Chapel Hill, NC: Carolina Policy Studies Program. (ERIC Document Reproduction Service No. ED354689)

Hebbeler, K. (1994). *Shortages in professions working with young children with disabilities and their families.* Chapel Hill, NC: National Early Childhood Technical Assistance System.

Helburn, S.W. (1995). *Cost, quality, and child outcomes in child care centers: Technical report of the Cost, Quality, and Child Outcome Study Team.* Denver: University of Colorado at Denver. (ERIC Document Reproduction Service No. ED386297)

Heller, K.A., Holtzman, W.H., & Messick, S. (Eds.). (1982). *Placing children in special education: A strategy for equity.* Washington, DC: National Academies Press.

Hendrick Hudson School District v. Rowley, 458 U.S. 176 (1982).

Hernnstein, R., & Murray, C. (1994). *The bell curve.* New York: The Free Press.

Heward, W., & Orlansky, M. (1994). *Exceptional children* (4th ed.). Columbus, OH: Merrill Publishing Co.

Hickson, L., Blackman, L.S., & Reis, E.M. (1995). *Mental retardation: Foundations of educational programming.* Boston: Allyn & Bacon.

Higgins, K., Boone, R., & Williams, D. (1999). *Educational software for students with disabilities: The importance of formative evaluation.* Paper presented at the American Educational Research Association Annual Conference, Montreal, Canada.

Higgins, K., Boone, R., & Williams, D. (2000). Evaluating educational software for special education. *Intervention in School and Clinic, 36,* 109–115.

Hines, R. (2001). *Inclusion in middle schools.* Champaign-Urbana: University of Illinois, Clearinghouse on Early Education and Parenting.

Hitchcock, C., Meyer, A., Rose, D., & Jackson, R. (2002, November/December). Providing new access to the general curriculum: Universal design for learning. *Teaching Exceptional Children, 35*(2), 8–17.

Hitchcock, C., & Stahl, S. (2003). Assistive technology, universal design, universal design for learning: Improved learning opportunities. *Journal of Special Education Technology, 18,* 45–52.

Hobson v. Hansen (District of Columbia), 265 F. Supp. 902 (1967).

Hocutt, A., & McKinney, D. (1995). Moving beyond the Regular Education Initiative: Natural reform in special education. In J. Paul, H. Rosselli, & D. Evans (Eds.), *Integrating school restructuring and special education reform.* Fort Worth, TX: Harcourt Brace College.

Hoff, D. (2005, May 5). NCLB focuses on data tools. *Education Week, 24,* 12–16.

Honig v. Doe, 484 U.S. 305, 108 S. Ct. 592, 98 L. Ed. 2d 686 (1988).

Horner, R., Carr, E., Halle, J., McGee, G., Odom, S., & Wolery, M. (2005). The use of single-subject research to identify evidence-based practice in special education. *Exceptional Children, 71*(2), 165–180.

House, E., Glass, G., McLean, L., & Walker, D. (1978). No simple answer: Critique of the follow-through evaluation. *Harvard Educational Review, 48*(2), 128–160.

Houston Independent School District v. Bobby R., 200 F.3d 341 (5th Cir. 2000).

Howe, K., & Miramontes, O. (1991). A framework for ethical deliberations in special education. *Journal of Special Education, 25,* 7–24.

Howe, K., & Miramontes, O. (1992). *The ethics of special education*. New York: Teacher's College Press.

Hurst, M.D. (2005, May 5). Schools eye future costs. *Education Week, 24,* 34–37.

Huxley, A. (1932). *Brave new world*. London: Harper Perennial Modern Classics.

Hyatt, K., & Howell, K. (2003). Curriculum-based measurement of students with emotional and behavioral disorders. In R.B. Rutherford, Jr., M.M. Quinn, & S.R. Mathur (Eds.), *Handbook of research in emotional and behavioral disorders* (pp. 181–198). New York: Guilford Press.

Individuals with Disabilities Education Act Amendments of 1997, PL 105-17, 20 U.S.C. §§ 1400 *et seq.*

Individuals with Disabilities Education Act (IDEA) of 1990, PL 101-476, 20 U.S.C. §§ 1400 *et seq.*

Individuals with Disabilities Education Improvement Act of 2004, PL 108-446, 20 U.S.C. §§ 1400 *et seq.*

Infant Health and Development Program (IHDP). (1990). Enhancing the outcomes of low birth weight, premature infants. *Journal of the American Medical Association, 263,* 3035–3042.

Jacob K. Javits Gifted and Talented Students Education Act of 1988, PL 100-297, 102 Stat. 237.

Jacob-Timm, S., & Hartshorne, T.S. (1998). *Ethics and law for school psychologists* (3rd ed.). New York: John Wiley & Sons.

Jencks, C. (1972). *Inequality: A reassessment of family and schooling in America*. New York: Basic Books.

Jensen, A. (1980). *The bias of mental testing*. New York: The Free Press.

Jonathon G. v. Lower Merion School District, 955 F. Supp. 413 (E.D. Pa. 1997).

Kagan, S.L., & Cohen, N.C. (1997). *Not by chance (the Quality 2000 Initiative)*. New Haven, CT: Bush Center in Child Development and Social Policy. (ERIC Document Reproduction Service No. ED417027)

Kanner, L. (1973). *Childhood psychosis: Initial studies and new insights*. Washington, DC: Winston.

Karnes, F., & Marquardt, R. (2000). *Gifted children and legal issues: An update*. Scottsdale, AZ: Gifted Psychology Press.

Karnes, F., & Marquardt, R. (2003). Gifted education and legal issues and recent decisions. In N. Colangelo & G.T. Davis (Eds.), *Handbook of gifted education* (pp. 590–603). Boston: Allyn & Bacon.

Karnes, F., Troxclair, D., & Marquardt, R. (1997). The Office of Civil Rights and the gifted: An update. *Roeper Review, 19,* 162–163.

Kathryn G. v. Kentfield School District, 261 F. Supp. 2d 1159 (N.D. Cal. 2003).

Kauffman, J.M. (1994). Places of change: Special education's power and identity in an era of educational reform. *Journal of Learning Disabilities, 27,* 610–618.

Kavale, K., & Forness, S. (1996). Social skills deficits and learning disabilities: A meta-analysis. *Journal of Learning Disabilities, 29,* 226–237.

Kavale, K., & Forness, S. (1998). The politics of learning disabilities. *Learning Disability Quarterly, 21,* 245–273

Kavale, K.A., Mathur, S.R., & Mostert, M.P. (2004). Social skills training and teaching social behavior to students with emotional and behavioral disorders. In R.B. Rutherford, M.M. Quinn, & S.R. Mathur (Eds.), *Handbook of research in emotional and behavioral disorders* (pp. 446–461). New York: Guilford Press.

Kazdin, A.E. (2002). The state of child and adolescent psychotherapy research. *Child and Adolescent Mental Health, 7,* 53–59.

Kazdin, A.E. (2003). *Research design in clinical psychology* (4th ed.). Boston: Allyn & Bacon.

Kearney, K. (1999). Gifted children and homeschooling: Historical and contemporary perspectives. In S. Cline & K. Hegeman (Eds.), *Gifted education in the twenty-first century* (pp. 175–194). Delray Beach, FL: Winslow Press.

Kellam, S., & Anthony, J. (1998). Targeting early antecedents to prevent tobacco smoking: Findings from an epidemiologically based field trial. *American Journal of Public Health, 88,* 1490–1495.

Kelman, M. (2001). The moral foundations of special education law. In C. Finn, A. Rotherham, & C. Hokanon (Eds.), *Rethinking special education for a new century* (pp. 77–84). Washington, DC: Thomas B. Fordham Foundation.

Kendziora, K. (2004). Early intervention for emotional and behavioral disorders. In R. Rutherford, Jr., M. Quinn, & S. Mathur (Eds.), *Handbook of research in emotional and behavioral disorders* (pp. 322–351). New York: Guilford Press.

Keogh, B.K. (1994). A matrix of decision points in the measurement of learning disabilities. In G.R. Lyon (Ed.), *Frames of reference for the assessment of learning disabilities: New views on measurement issues* (pp. 15–26). Baltimore: Paul H. Brookes Publishing Co.

Kerr, M., & Nelson, C. (2002). *Addressing behavior problems* (4th ed.). Upper Saddle River, NJ: Prentice Hall.

Kirk, S. (1958). *The early education of the mentally retarded.* Urbana: University of Illinois Press.

Kirk, S. (1963). *Behavioral diagnosis and remediation of learning disabilities: Proceedings of the conference on the explorations into the problems of the perceptually handicapped.* Evanston, IL: Fund for the Perceptually Handicapped Child.

Kirk, S.A., Gallagher, J.J., & Anastasiow, N. (2003). *Educating exceptional children* (10th ed.). Boston: Houghton Mifflin.

Kirk, S.A., Gallagher, J.J., Anastasiow, N.J., & Coleman, M.R. (2006). *Educating exceptional children* (11th ed.). Boston: Houghton Mifflin.

Kirk, S.A., McCarthy, J., & Kirk, W.D. (1968). *The Illinois Test of Psycholinguistic Abilities.* Urbana: University of Illinois Press.

Kitano, M., & DiJiosia, M. (2002). Are Asian and Pacific Americans overrepresented in programs for gifted? *Roeper Review, 24*(2), 76–80.

Kober, N. (2001). *Closing the achievement gap.* Washington, DC: Center for Educational Policy.

Kolloff, P. (2003). State supported residential high schools. In N. Colaugel & G. Dovis (Eds.), *Handbook of gifted education* (3rd ed., pp. 238–246). Boston: Allyn & Bacon.

Kulik, J. (1992). *An analysis of the research on ability grouping: Historical and contemporary perspectives.* Storrs, CT: National Research Center on the Gifted and Talented.

Kulik, J.A. (2003). Grouping and tracking. In N. Colangelo, & G.A. Davis (Eds.), *Handbook of gifted education* (3rd ed.). Boston: Allyn & Bacon.

Kulik, J.A., & Kulik, C.-L.C. (1997). Ability grouping. In N. Colangelo & G.A. Davis (Eds.), *Handbook of gifted education* (2nd ed., pp. 230–242). Boston: Allyn & Bacon.

Ladd, H.F., & Hansen, J.S. (Eds.). (1999). *Making money matter: Financing America's schools.* Washington, DC: National Academies Press.

Ladenheimer, K. (2002). *Medicaid cost containment: A legislator's toolkit.* Washington, DC: National Conference of State Legislators.

LaFreniere, P., Dumas, J., Capuano, E., & Dubeau, D. (1992). The development and validation of the Preschool Socio-affective Profile. *Psychological Assessment, 4,* 442–450.

Lahm, E., & Nickels, B. (1999). What do you know? Assistive technology competencies for special educators. *Teaching Exceptional Children, 32*(1), 56–63.

Landrum, M., Callahan, C., & Shaklee, B. (Eds.). (1999). *Gifted program standards.* Washington, DC: National Association for Gifted Children.

Lane, K. (2004). Academic instruction and tutoring interventions for students with emotional and behavioral disorders. In R. Rutherford, M. Quinn, & S. Mathur (Eds.), *Handbook of research in emotional and behavior disorders.* New York: Guilford Press.

Lankford, H., & Wyckoff, J. (1995). Where has the money gone? An analysis of school district spending in New York. *Educational Evaluation and Policy Analysis, 17,* 195–218.

LaParo, K.M., Olsen, K., & Pianta, R.C. (2002). Special education eligibility: Developmental precursors over the first three years of life. *Exceptional Children, 69*(1), 55–66.

Larry P. v. Riles, No. 80-4027 (9th Cir. June 25, 1986).

Leaudro v. State, 122 NC App. I, II, 468 SE 2d 543, 550 (1996).

Lerner, J. (2000). *Learning disabilities* (8th ed.). Boston: Houghton Mifflin.

Levin, H.M. (1997). Doing what comes naturally: Full inclusion in accelerated schools. In D.K. Lipsky & A. Gartner (Eds.), *Inclusion and school reform: Transforming America's classrooms* (pp. 389–400). Baltimore: Paul H. Brookes Publishing Co.

Lewis, A.C. (1995). An overview of the standards movement. *Phi Delta Kappan, 76,* 744–750.

Lewis, R.B. (2000). *Project LITT (Literacy Instruction Through Technology): Enhancing the reading skills of students with learning disabilities through hypermedia-based children's literature. Final report.* San Diego: San Diego State University, Department of Special Education. (ERIC Document Reproduction Service No. ED438648)

Lewis, T., Lewis-Palmer, T., Newcomer, L., & Sticher, J. (2004). Applied behavior analyses and the education and treatment of students with emotional and behavior disorders. In R. Rutherford, Jr., M. Quinn, & S. Mathur (Eds.), *Handbook of research in emotional and behavior disorders* (pp. 523–545). New York: Guilford Press.

Liaupsin, C., Jolivette, K., & Scott, T. (2004). Schoolwide systems of behavior support. In R. Rutherford, Jr., M. Quinn, & S. Mathur (Eds.), *Handbook of research in emotional and behavior disorders* (pp. 487–501). New York: Guilford Press.

Lipsky, D., & Gartner, A. (1997). *Inclusion and school reform: Transforming America's classrooms.* Baltimore: Paul H. Brookes Publishing Co.

Loeding, B. (2002). The use of educational technology and assistive devices in special education. In J. Paul, C. Lavely, A. Cranston-Gingras, & E. Taylor (Eds.), *Rethinking professional issues in special education* (pp. 231–250). Westport, CT: Ablex Publishing.

Lord, C. (Ed.). (2001). *Educating children with autism.* Washington, DC: National Academy of Sciences.

Lord, C., & Risi, S. (2000). Diagnosis of autism spectrum disorders in young children. In A.M. Wetherby & B.M. Prizant (Eds.), *Communication and language intervention series: Vol. 9. Autism spectrum disorders: A transactional developmental perspective* (pp. 11–30). Baltimore: Paul H. Brookes Publishing Co.

Lovaas, O. (1993). The development of a treatment-research project for developmentally disabled and autistic children. *Journal of Applied Behavioral Analysis, 31*(5), 749–761.

Lowry, L. (1993). *The giver.* Boston: Houghton Mifflin.

Lubinski, D., & Benbow, C.P. (2000). States of excellence. *American Psychologist, 55,* 137–150.

Lupkowski-Shoplik, A., Benbow, C., Assouline, S., & Brody, L. (2003). Talent searches: Meeting the needs of academically talented youth. In N. Colangelo & G. Davis (Eds.), *Handbook of gifted education* (3rd ed., pp. 204–218). Boston: Allyn & Bacon.

MacArthur, C. (2003). What have we learned about learning disabilities from qualitative research? A review of studies. In H. Swanson, K. Harris, & S. Graham (Eds.), *Handbook of learning disabilities* (pp. 532–549). New York: Guilford Press.

MacMillan, D., & Speece, D. (1999). Utility of current diagnostic categories of research and practice. In R. Gallimore, L. Bernheimer, D. MacMillan, D. Speece, & S. Vaughn (Eds.), *Developmental perspectives in children with high incidence disabilities* (pp. 111–134). Mahwah, NJ: Lawrence Erlbaum Associates.

Margolin, L. (1996). A pedagogy of privilege. *Journal for the Education of the Gifted, 19,* 164–180.

Martin, E.W. (1989). Lessons from implementing PL 94-142. In J. Gallagher, P. Trohanis, & R. Clifford (Eds.), *Policy implementation and PL 99-457: Planning for young children with special needs* (pp. 19–32). Baltimore: Paul H. Brookes Publishing Co.

Matson, J., & Mulick, J. (Eds.). (1991). *Handbook of mental retardation* (2nd ed.). Elmsford, NY: Pergamon Press.

McCollum, J., & Yates, T. (1994). Technical assistance for meeting early intervention personnel standards: Statewide processes based on peer review. *Topics in Early Childhood Special Education, 14,* 295–310.

McConaughy, S., Kay, P., & Fitzgerald, M. (2000). How long is long enough? Outcomes for a school-based prevention program. *Exceptional Children, 67,* 21–34.

McDonnell, L., McLaughlin, M., & Morrison, P. (1997). *Educating for one and all.* Washington, DC: National Academy of Sciences.

McEllistrom, S., Roth, J., D'Agnastino, T., & Brown, C. (Eds.). (2004). *Students with disabilities and special education law.* Malvern, PA: Center for Education and Employment Law.

McGroaty, D. (2001). The little known case of America's largest school choice program. In C. Finn, A. Rotherham, & C. Hokanson (Eds.), *Rethinking special education for a new century* (pp. 289–308). Washington, DC: Thomas B. Fordham Foundation.

McLoughlin, J., & Lewis, R. (2001). *Assessing students with special needs* (5th ed.). Upper Saddle River, NJ: Prentice Hall.

Means, B. (2000). Technology in America's schools: Before and after Y2K. In R. Brandt (Ed.), *Education in a new era* (pp. 185–210). Alexandria, VA: Association for Supervision and Curriculum Development.

Miller, P., Fader, L., & Vincent, L. (2001). Preparing early childhood educators to work with children who have exceptional needs. In New Teachers for a New Century, *The future of early childhood professional preparation.* Washington, DC: U.S. Department of Education, National Institute on Early Childhood Development and Education.

Mills v. Board of Education of the District of Columbia, 348 F. Supp. 866 (1972).

Missouri v. Jenkins, No. 93-1823, 515 U.S. 70 (1995).

Mundy, P., & Stella, J. (2000). Joint attention, social orienting, and nonverbal communication in autism. In A.M. Wetherby & B.M. Prizant (Eds.), *Communication and language intervention series: Vol. 9. Autism spectrum disorders: A transactional developmental perspective* (pp. 55–78). Baltimore: Paul H. Brookes Publishing Co.

National Association for Gifted Children. (1991). *Position paper: Ability grouping.* Washington, DC: Author.

National Association of State Boards of Education. (2002, July). *Policy update: Special education funding.* Alexandria, VA: Author.

National Center for Educational Statistics. (1998). *What are we spending on special education in the U.S.?* Washington, DC: Author.

National Council on Disabilities. (2003). *School vouchers and students with disabilities.* Washington, DC: Author.

National Council of Teachers of Mathematics. (1989). *Principles and standards of school mathematics.* Reston, VA: Author.

National Council of Teachers of Mathematics. (2003). *Principles and standards of school mathematics* (3rd ed.). Reston, VA: Author.

National Institutes for Health. (2004). *President's budget request.* Washington, DC: Author.

National Institute of Health Act of 1930, PL 71-251, 46 Stat. 379.

National Research Council. (1996). *National science education standards.* Washington, DC: National Academies Press.

Neihart, M., Reis, S., Robinson, N., & Moon, S. (2002). *The social and emotional development of gifted children.* Waco, TX: Prufrock Press.

Nelson, J.R., Mathur, S.R., & Rutherford, R.B. (1999). Has public policy exceeded our knowledge base? A review of the functional behavioral assessment literature. *Behavioral Disorders, 24,* 169–179.

Nelson, N.W., Bahr, C.M., & Van Meter, A.M. (with contributions from Kinnucan-Welsch, K.) (2004). *The writing lab approach to language instruction and intervention.* Baltimore: Paul H. Brookes Publishing Co.

Neuman, S. (2003). From rhetoric to reality: The case for high-quality compensatory prekindergarten programs. *Phi Delta Kappan, 85*(4), 286–291.

No Child Left Behind Act of 2001, PL 107-110, 115 Stat. 1425.

Noddings, N. (1984). *Caring: A feminine approach to ethics and moral education.* Berkeley: University of California Press.

Nolet, V., & McLaughlin, M.J. (2000). *Accessing the general curriculum: Including students with disabilities in student-based reform.* Thousand Oaks, CA: Corwin Press.

Oakes, J. (1985). *Keeping track.* New Haven, CT: Yale University Press.

O'Connell, P. (2003). Federal involvement in gifted and talented education. In N. Colangelo & G. Davis (Eds.), *Handbook of gifted education* (3rd ed., pp. 604–608). Boston: Allyn & Bacon.

Odom, S., Brantlinger, E., Gersten, R., Horner, R., Thompson, B., & Harris, K. (2005). Research in special education: Scientific methods and evidence-based practices. *Exceptional Children, 71*(2), 137–148.

Office of Economic and Cultural Development. (2001). *Starting strong: Early childhood education and care.* Paris, France: Author.

Ogbu, J. (2003). *Black American students in an affluent suburb.* Mahwah, NJ: Lawrence Erlbaum Associates.

Olszewski-Kubilius, P. (2003). Special summer and Saturday programs for gifted students. In N. Colangelo & T.G. Davis (Eds.), *Handbook of gifted education* (3rd ed., pp. 219–228). Boston: Allyn & Bacon.

Opinion of the Justices, 624 So. 2d 107 (Ala. 1993).

Paige, S. (1999). *Syllabus content analysis as a measure of special education in teacher preparation for mathematics instruction.* Unpublished paper, State University of New York at Buffalo.

Palfrey, J., Singer, L., Walker, D., & Butler, J. (1987). Early identification of children's special needs. A study in four methopolitan communities. *Journal of Pediatrics, 111,* 651–659.

Parrette, H. (1998). Cultural issues and family-centered assistive technology decision making. In S. Judge & H. Parrette (Eds.), *Assistive technology for young children with disabilities: A guide to providing family-centered services.* Cambridge, MA: Brookline.

Parrish, T. (1997). The future of special education finance. In J. Paul, M. Churton, W. Morse, A. Duchnowski, B. Epanchin, P. Osnes, et al. (Eds.), *Special education practice: Applying the knowledge, affirming the values, and creating the future* (pp. 136–152). Pacific Grove, CA: Brooks/Cole Publishing.

Pennsylvania Association for Retarded Children v. Commonwealth of Pennsylvania, 343 F. Supp. 279 (E.D. Pa. 1972).

Pipho, C. (2000). Governing the American dream of universal public education. In R. Brandt (Ed.), *Education in a new era.* Alexandria, VA: Association for Supervision and Curriculum Development.

Pisha, B. (1993). *Rates of development of keyboarding skills in elementary school aged children with and without learning disabilities.* Unpublished doctoral dissertation, Harvard University Graduate School of Education, Cambridge, MA.

Plomin, R. (Ed.). (2003). *Behavioral genetics in the postgenomic era.* Washington, DC: American Psychological Association.

Plomin, R., & McGuffin, P. (2003). Psychopathology in the postgenomic era. *Annual Review of Psychology, 54,* 205–228.

Polsgrove, L., & Smith, S. (2004). Informed practice in teaching self-control to children with emotional and behavioral disorders. In R.B. Rutherford, M.M. Quinn, & S.R. Mathur (Eds.), *Handbook of research in emotional and behavioral disorders* (pp. 399–426). New York: Guilford Press.

President's Committee on Mental Retardation. (1970). *The sixth hour retarded child.* Washington, DC: Author.

Prince William County School Board v. Willis, 16EHLR 1109 (1989).

Public Health Service Act of 1974, PL 78-410, 58 Stat. 682.

Puckett, K. (2004). Project ACCESS: Field testing an assistive technology toolkit for students with mild disabilities. *Journal of Special Education Technology, 19,* 5–17.

Pyryt, M. (2003). Technology and the gifted. In N. Colangelo & G. Davis (Eds.), *Handbook of gifted education* (3rd ed., pp. 582–589). Boston: Allyn & Bacon.

Rainey v. Tennessee, No. A-3100 (Chavez Ct. Davidson County, Tenn. 1976).

Ramey, C., & Ramey, S. (1998). Early intervention and early experience. *American Psychologist, 53,* 109–120.

Ravaglia, R., Suppes, P., Stillinger, C., & Alper, T.M. (1995). Computer-based mathematics and physics for gifted students. *Gifted Child Quarterly, 39,* 7–13.

Ravitch, D. (1995). *National standards in American education: A citizen's guide.* Washington, DC: Brookings.

Rea, P., McLaughlin, V., & Walther-Thomas, C. (2002). Outcomes for students with learning disabilities in inclusive and pullout programs. *Exceptional Children, 68*(2), 203–222.

Rehabilitation Act of 1973, PL 93-112, 29 U.S.C. §§ 701 *et seq.*

Renzulli, J. (2005, May 25). A quiet crisis is clouding the future of R & D. *Education Week, 40,* 32–33.

Renzulli, J., & Gubbins, E. (1997, August 2). *The National Research Center on the Gifted and*

Talented: Lessons learned and promises to keep. Address at the Twelfth Biennial World Conference of the World Council for Gifted and Talented Children, Seattle.

Roncker v. Walter, 700 F.2d 1058, 1063 cert. denied, 464 U.S. 864 (6th Cir. 1983).

Rooney, R. (1994). *Implementation of interdisciplinary personnel preparation for early intervention.* Unpublished doctoral dissertation, University of North Carolina at Chapel Hill.

Rose, D. (2001, July 25). *Testimony on hearing on educational technology.* Washington, DC: Subcommittee on Labor, Health and Human Services and Education.

Ross, P. (Ed.). (1993). *National excellence: A case for developing America's talent.* Washington, DC: U.S. Department of Education.

Rutherford, R.B., Quinn, M.M., & Mathur, S.R. (Eds.). (2004). *Handbook of research in emotional and behavioral disorders.* New York: Guilford Press.

Rutter, M. (2003). Commentary: Causal processes leading to antisocial behavior. *Developmental Psychology, 39,* 372–378.

Sacramento City Unified School District, Board of Education v. Rachel H., 14 F.3d 1398 (9th Cir. 1994).

Safford, P., & Safford, E. (1996). *A history of childhood and disability.* New York: Teachers College Press.

Sailor, W., & Roger, B. (2005, March). Rethinking inclusion: Schoolwide applications. *Phi Delta Kappan, 86*(7), 503–509.

Salend, S., & Duhaney, L. (1999). The impact of students with and without disabilities and their educators. *Remedial and Special Education, 20,* 114–126.

Salisbury, C., & McGregor, G. (2002). The administrative climate and context of inclusive elementary schools. *Exceptional Children, 68*(2), 259–274.

Sameroff, A., Seifer, R., Baldwin, A., & Baldwin, C. (1993). Stability of intelligence from preschool to adolescence: The influence of social and family risk factors. *Child Development, 64,* 80–97.

Sapon-Shevin, M. (1996). Beyond gifted education: Building a shared agenda for school reform. *Journal for the Education of the Gifted, 19,* 194–214.

Sarason, S. (1996). Foreword. In P. Safford & E. Safford, *A history of childhood and disability* (p. vi). New York: Teachers College Press.

Schattman, R., & Keating, L. (2000). The Swanton School District (Franklin Northwest Supervisory Union): A second look at an inclusive school. In R.A. Villa & J.S. Thousand (Eds.), *Restructuring for caring and effective education: Piecing the puzzle together* (pp. 453–468). Baltimore: Paul H. Brookes Publishing Co.

Scheerenberger, R.C. (1987). *A history of mental retardation: A quarter century of progress.* Baltimore: Paul H. Brookes Publishing Co.

Schein, E.H. (1996). Kurt Lewin's change theory in the field and in the classroom: Notes toward a model of managed learning. *Systems Practice, 9,* 27–47.

Schmidt, W., McKnight, C., Valvarde, G., Houang, R., & Wiley, D. (1997). *The Third International Mathematics and Science Study.* Washington, DC: National Center for Educational Statistics.

Schweinhart, L., Barnes, H., Weikart, D., Barnett, W., & Epstein, A. (1993). *Significant benefits: The High/Scope Perry Preschool Study through age 27.* Ypsilanti, MI: High/Scope Press.

Scruggs, T.E., & Mastropieri, M.A. (2003). Science and social studies. In H.L. Swanson, K.R. Harris, & S. Graham (Eds.), *Handbook of learning disabilities* (pp. 364–382). New York: Guilford Press.

Sexton, P., Snyder, P., Wolfe, B., Lobman, M., Stricklen, S., & Akers, P. (1996). Early intervention inservice training strategies: Perceptions and suggestions from the field. *Exceptional Children, 62,* 485–495.

Shavelson, R.J., & Towne, L. (Eds.). (2002). *Scientific research in education.* Washington, DC: National Academies Press.

Shinn, M. (Ed.). (1998). *Advanced applications of curriculum-based measurement: Big ideas and avoiding confusion.* New York: Guilford Press.

Shonkoff, J., & Hauser-Cram, P. (1987). Early intervention for disabled infants and their families: A quantitative analysis. *Pediatrics, 80,* 650–658.

Shonkoff, J., & Meisels, S. (Eds.). (2000). *Handbook of early childhood intervention* (2nd ed.). New York: Cambridge University Press.

Shonkoff, J., & Phillips, D.A. (Eds.). (2000). *From neurons to neighborhoods.* Washington, DC: National Academies Press.

Sizer, T. (1992, January 30). A test for democracy. *New York Times,* p. 21.

Skrtic, T.M. (1991). *Behind special education: A critical analysis of professional culture and school organization.* Denver: Love Publishing.

Slaven, R., & Masse, L. (2002). Success for all and African-American and Latino students. In J. Chubb & T. Loveless (Eds.), *Bridging the achievement gap.* Washington, DC: Brookings

Smith, B. (2001). *IDEA requirements for preschoolers with disabilities.* Washington, DC: Council for Exceptional Children, Division for Early Childhood.

Social Security Act of 1935, PL 74-271, 42 U.S.C. §§ 301 *et seq.*

Soraruf v. Pinckney Community Schools, 208 F.3d 215 (6th Cir. 2000).

Sparling, J., & Lewis, I. (1984). *Partners for learning.* Lewisville, NC: Kaplan Press.

Sparrow, S., Balla, D., & Cicchetti, D. (1984). *Vineland Adaptive Behavior Scales (VABS).* Circle Pines, MN: American Guidance Service.

Speece, D.L., Case, L.P., & Molloy, D.E. (2003). Responsiveness to general education instruction as the first gate to learning disabilities identification. *Learning Disabilities Research and Practice, 18,* 147–156.

Spellings, M. (2005, May 10). Spelling announces new special education guidelines, details workable, "common sense" policy to help states implement No Child Left Behind. Retrieved October 12, 2005, from http://www.ed.gov/news/pressreleases/2005/05/05102005.html

SPeNCE. (2002). *Key findings for SPeNCE.* Washington, DC: U.S. Department of Education, Office of Special Education Programs.

Stainback, S., & Stainback, W. (1996). *Inclusion: A guide for educators.* Baltimore: Paul H. Brookes Publishing Co.

Stanley, J. (1996). In the beginning: The study of mathematically precocious youth. In C. Benbow & D. Jubiuski (Eds.), *Intellectual talent: Psychometric and social issues* (pp. 223–230). Baltimore: Johns Hopkins University Press.

Stephens, K., & Karnes, F. (2000). State definitions for the gifted and talented revisited. *Exceptional Children, 66,* 219–238.

Sternberg, R., & Gregorenko, E. (1997). *Intelligence, heredity and environment.* New York: Cambridge University Press.

Still v. DeBuono, 101 F.3d 888 (2d Cir. 1996).

Stowe, M.J., & Turnbull, H.R., III. (2001). Legal considerations of inclusion for infants and toddlers and for preschool-age children. In M.J. Guralnick (Ed.), *Early childhood inclusion: Focus on change* (pp. 69–100). Baltimore: Paul H. Brookes Publishing Co.

Strauss, A.A., & Kephart, N.C. (1955). *Psychopathology and education of the brain-injured child: Vol. 2. Progress in theory and clinic.* New York: Grune & Stratton.

Subotnik, R., & Arnold, K. (Eds.). (1994). *Beyond Terman: Comtemporary longitudinal studies of giftedness and talent.* Norwood, NJ: Ablex Publishing.

Sugai, G., Lewis-Palmer, T., & Hagan-Burke, S. (1999). Overview of the functional behavioral assessment process. *Exceptionality, 8*(3), 149–160.

Swanson, H.L., Harris, K.R., & Graham, S. (Eds.). (2003). *Handbook of learning disabilities.* New York: Guilford Press.

Tannenbaum, A. (2000). A history of giftedness in school and society. In K. Heller, F. Monks, R. Sternberg, & R. Subotnik (Eds.), *International handbook of giftedness and talent* (pp. 23–54). New York: Elsevier.

Taylor, M.D. (1976). *Roll of thunder hear my cry.* New York: Dial Press.

Teachers of the Deaf Act of 1961, PL 87-276, 75 Stat. 575.

Technology-Related Assistance for Individuals with Disabilities Act of 1988, PL 100-407, 29 U.S.C. §§ 2201 *et seq.*

Terman, L.M. (1925). *Mental and physical traits of a thousand gifted children, I.* Stanford, CA: Stanford University Press.

Terman, L.M. (1947). *The gifted child grows up, twenty-five years follow-up of a superior group: Genetic studies of genius, III.* Stanford, CA: Stanford University Press.

Terman, L.M., & Oden, M.H. (1959). *The gifted group at mid-life, thirty-five years follow-up of the superior child: Genetic studies of genius, III.* Stanford, CA: Stanford University Press.

Thernstrom, A., & Thernstrom, S. (2003). *No excuses: Closing the racial gap in learning.* New York: Simon & Schuster.

Thompson, B., Diamond, K., McWilliam, R., Snyder, P., & Snyder, S. (2005). Evaluating the quality of evidence from correlational research for evidence-based practice. *Exceptional Children, 71*(2), 186–194.

Tomlinson, C. (2002, November 6). Proficiency is not enough. *Education Week, 22*(10), 36–38.

Torgesen, J. (2000). Individual differences in response to early interventions in reading: The lingering problem of treatment resisters. *Learning Disabilities Research and Practice, 15,* 55–64.

Trohanis, P.L. (1989). An introduction to PL 99-457 and the national policy agenda for serving young children with special needs and their families. In J.J. Gallagher, P.L. Trohanis, & R.M. Clifford (Eds.), *Policy implementation and PL 99-457: Planning for young children with special needs* (pp. 1–18). Baltimore: Paul H. Brookes Publishing Co.

Trohanis, P. (2001). *Design consideration for state TA systems.* Chapel Hill, NC: National Early Childhood Technical Assistance System.

Trotter, A. (2005, May 5). Federal role seen shifting. *Education Week, 24,* 26–29.

Turnbull, R., Beegle, G., & Stowe, M. (2002). The core concepts of disability policy affecting families who have children with disabilities. *Journal of Disability Policy Studies, 12*(3), 133–143.

Turnbull, H., & Turnbull, A. (2000). *Free appropriate public education: The law and children with disabilities* (6th ed.). Denver: Love Publishing.

Turnbull, R., & Turnbull, A. (2003). Reaching the ideal. *Education Next, 3,* 32–37.

Union School District v. Smith, 15 F.3d 1519 (9th Circuit 1994).

U.S. Bureau of the Census. (2000). *National population projections: I. Summary files.* Retrieved November 20, 2001, from http://www.census.gov/population/www/projections/natsum-T3.htm

U.S. Department of Education. (1997). *Third International Mathematics and Science Study (TIMSS)*. Washington, DC: Author.

U.S. Department of Education. (2002). *Twenty-fourth annual report to congress on the implementation of the Individuals with Disabilities Education Act*. Washington, DC: Author.

U.S. Department of Education, Office of Special Education Programs. (2000). *Twenty-second annual report to Congress on the implementation of the Individuals with Disabilities Education Act*. Washington, DC: Government Printing Office.

U.S. Department of Education, Office of Special Education Programs. (2003). *Twenty-fourth annual report to Congress on the implementation of Public Law 94-142: The Education for All Handicapped Children Act*. Washington, DC: U.S. Government Printing Office.

U.S. Department of Education, Office of Special Education Programs. (2004). *About Child Find*. Retrieved November 30, 2004, from http://www.childfindidea.org/overview.htm

U.S. Department of Energy. (2003, April). *The human genome and beyond*. Washington, DC: Author.

U.S. Department of Energy, Office of Science. (2004). *Program Assessment Rating Tool (PART)*. Washington, DC: Author.

Van Tassel-Baska, J. (2003). What matters in curriculum for gifted learners: Reflections on theory, research, and practice. In N. Colangelo & G. Davis (Eds.), *Handbook of gifted education* (3rd ed.). Boston: Allyn & Bacon.

Vaughn, S., & Fuchs, L.S. (2003). Redefining learning disabilities as inadequate response to instruction: The promise and potential problems. *Learning Disabilities Research and Practice, 18,* 137–146.

Vaughn, S., Gersten, R., & Chard, D. (2000). The underlying message in LD intervention research: Findings from research syntheses. *Exceptional Children, 67,* 99–114.

Verstegen, D. (1998). *Landmark court decisions challenge state special education funding*. Palo Alto, CA: Center for Special Education Finance.

Vocational Education Act of 1963, PL 88-210, 20 U.S.C. §§ 35 *et seq.*

Volkman, F., Cohen, D., & Paul, R. (1986). An evaluation of DSM-III criteria for infantile autism. *Journal of the American Academy of Child Psychiatry, 25,* 190–197.

Vygotsky, L.S. (1978). Interaction between learning and development. In M. Cole, V. John-Steiner, S. Scribner, & E. Souberman (Eds.), *Mind in society: The development of higher psychological processes*. Cambridge, MA: Harvard University Press.

Wagner, M., & Blackorby, J. (1996). Transition from high school work or college: How special education youth fare. *The Future of Children: Special Education for Youth with Disabilities, 6*(1), 103–120.

Wahl, L. (2004). Surveying special education staff on AT awareness, use, and training. *Journal of Special Education Technology, 19*(2), 57–59.

Wang, M., Reynolds, M., & Walberg, H. (Eds.). (1987). *Handbook of special education: Research and practice: Vol. 1. Learner characteristics and adaptive education*. Oxford, United Kingdom: Pegamon Press.

Watson, J. (2002). *Education report*. Washington, DC: National Education Association.

Webster-Stratton, C. (1997). Early intervention for families of preschool children with conduct problems. In M.J. Guralnick (Ed.), *The effectiveness of early intervention* (pp. 429–453). Baltimore: Paul H. Brookes Publishing Co.

Wehmeyer, M. (1999). A functional model of self-determination: Describing development and implementing instruction. *Focus on Autism and Other Developmental Disabilities, 14*(1), 53–62.

Wehmeyer, M., Smith, S., Palmer, S., & Davies, A. (2004). Technology use by students with intellectual disabilities: An overview. *Journal of Special Education Technology,* 7–22.

Wehmeyer, M.L. (with Sands, D.J., Knowlton, H.E., & Kozleski, E.B.) (2002). *Teaching students with mental retardation: Providing access to the general curriculum.* Baltimore: Paul H. Brookes Publishing Co.

Weick, K.E., & Quinn, R.E. (1999). Organizational change and development. *Annual Review of Psychology, 50,* 361–386.

Weikart, D., & Schweinhart, L. (1997). The High/Scope Preschool Curriculum Comparison Study through age 23. *Early Childhood Research Quarterly, 12*(2), 117–143.

Werner, E., & Smith, R. (1982). *Vulnerable but invincible: A longitudinal study of resilient children and youth.* New York: McGraw-Hill.

Westberg, K., Archambault, F., Dobyns, S., & Salvin, T. (1993). The classroom practices observation study. *Journal for the Education of the Gifted, 16,* 120–146.

White, B., & Frederiksen, J. (1998). Inquiry, modeling and metacognition: Making science accessible to all students. *Cognition and Science, 16,* 90–91.

Wiggins, G. (1981). *Assessing student performance.* New York: Teachers College Press.

Wilcox, B., & Kunkel, D. (1996). Taking television seriously: Children and television policy. In E. Zigler, S. Kagan, & N. Hall (Eds.), *Children, families, and government* (pp. 333–354). New York: Cambridge University Press.

Wildavsky, A. (1979). *Analysis as art. Speaking truth to power: The art and craft of policy analysis.* Boston: Little, Brown and Company.

Will, M. (1986). Educating children with learning problems: A shared responsibility. *Exceptional Children, 52,* 411–416.

Winton, P. (2000). Early childhood intervention personnel preparation: Backward wrapping for future planning. *Topics in Early Childhood Special Education, 20*(2), 87–94.

Wolery, M., & Bailey, D. (2002). Early childhood special education research. *Journal of Early Intervention, 25,* 88–99.

Wolf, P. (2003). Sisyphean tasks. *Education Next, 3,* 23–31.

World Health Organization. (2004). *International classification of functioning, disability and health* (10th rev.). Paris: Author.

Yale University School Development Program. (2004). *Transforming school leadership and management to support student learning and development.* Thousand Oaks, CA: Corwin Press.

Yin, R. (1994). *Case study research, design, and methods.* (2nd ed.). Newbury Park, CA: Sage Publications.

Yin, R.K., & White, J.L. (1984, February). *Federal technical assistance efforts: Lessons and improvement in education for 1984 and beyond.* Washington, DC: Cosmos Corporation.

Yoshikawa, H. (1994). Prevention as cumulative protection: Effects of early family support and education on chronic delinquency and its risks. *Psychological Bulletin, 115,* 28–54.

Ysseldyke, J. (2001). Reflections on a research career: Generalizations from 25 years of research on assessment and instructional decision making. *Exceptional Children, 67,* 295–309.

Zigler, E.F., Kagan, S.L., & Hall, N.W. (1996). *Children, families and government.* New Haven, CT: Yale University Press.

Zigler, E., & Styfco, S. (1994). Head Start: Criticisms in a constructive context. *American Psychologist, 49,* 127–132.

Index

Figures and tables are indicated by *f* and *t*, respectively.